VANISHED

True stories from families of Australian missing persons

NICOLE MORRIS

Big Sky Publishing Pty Ltd
PO Box 303, Newport, NSW 2106, Australia
Phone: 1300 364 611
Fax: (61 2) 9918 2396
Email: info@bigskypublishing.com.au
Web: www.bigskypublishing.com.au

Cover design and typesetting: Think Productions

Printed and bound in Australia by Griffin Press

 A catalogue record for this
book is available from the
National Library of Australia

Title: Vanished. True stories from families of Australian missing persons
ISBN: 978-1-922896-77-3

VANISHED

True stories from families of Australian missing persons

BIG SKY PUBLISHING
www.bigskypublishing.com.au

NICOLE MORRIS

Contents

TESTIMONIALS

Vanished is written with insight and compassion. It comes from the author's long-term personal commitment to raising awareness of missing people and those who are left behind – the loved ones who continue to search for answers and understanding.

Dr Elizabeth Davies, Coordinator of Families and Friends of Missing Persons Unit (2010 – 2018)

Vanished is a gripping read that could only have been written by one as intimately acquainted with the families of the missing as Nicole Morris. It has the meticulous detail of an investigative deep dive, but never loses compassion for the loved ones left behind.

Meshel Laurie, host of Australian True Crime podcast and author

There is surely nobody more qualified to tell the stories of the families of missing people than Nicole Morris, who has dedicated much of her life to the selfless and relentless pursuit of information and answers on their behalf.
Nicole's knowledge of Australian missing persons cases is incredibly detailed and she tells their stories with sensitivity and thoughtfulness.

Kate Kyriacou, Jounalist – The Courier Mail, and True Crime author and podcaster

A deeply disturbing true-life account of the trauma for family members when a loved one goes missing. Well researched, easily readable, but profoundly upsetting.

Mark Tedeschi AM KC, Barrister-at-Law

My utmost respect and admiration to Nicole for the tireless work she does with missing persons in Australia in her own time. Nicole advocates for many families at the worst times of their lives, bringing focus and a voice to families without one.

Leonie Duroux, family member of a previously missing person

Nicole's commitment to finding the truth and advocating for families is an inspiration.

Esther Mckay, author of Crime Scene and Forensic Investigator, Mental Health Consultant at Police Federation of Australia, former NSW Police Officer and patron of the Australian Missing Person's Register

Nicole is an angel in the darkness for families of the missing. She can't perform miracles and bring them all home safe and sound but she gave us the chance for Trav to be found and brought home. So many others never get that and many years down the track they still don't. That saddens me so much. I always say we were lucky Trav was found or that would be our lives ... ambiguous loss must be demolishing.

Sue-Anne Davis, family member of a previously missing person

From a parent of a missing child, thank you to Nicole from the bottom of my heart for everthing she does for missing people. She is an amazing person.

Rachel McCloy, mother of missing Tori McCloy

FOREWORD
Faye and Mark Leveson

Nicole will embrace and engender the interest of the reader by her clever use imagery where she allows one to feel as though they are there with victims and their families through this nightmare ride.

She helps you to feel a range of emotions felt by people closely affected by ambiguous loss and crime.

When our son, Matthew, was taken from us in 2007, we put our faith in authorities, thinking they were acting in our best interests. Sadly, this is not always the case. The public need to understand that the authorities are not perfect, that the investigators are not always right, that victims and their families become second class citizens in the so called "justice" system.

On reading these carefully crafted chapters you can feel the emotion, feel the hope, feel the devastation of having that hope destroyed and understand that quite often two people, provided with the exact same set of circumstances, can form totally different views.

So often, victims of crime and people who have suffered

ambiguous loss, can lose friends. People just don't know what to say to you so they will hide or step away. This doesn't help victims or their families. The reader will come to understand this upon reading these pages.

Victims and those left behind, in order not to feel useless, will quite readily immerse themselves directly into an investigation, not the police's but their own. Quite often we had police asking us for intel as ours was more comprehensive and current than their own. You will become to understand why the individuals you will read about did just that.

In many cases the authorities merely "work on" these cases, however, the families have "lived in" these cases. You will discover the distinct difference.

We commend Nicole for creating this wonderful record and the fact that it also keeps alive the memory of those who may no longer be with us and are unable to speak for themselves.

INTRODUCTION

My friend died. There's no easy way of saying that, is there? You can't just sort of slip it into a conversation. What an awful thing to have to tell people. Greg died suddenly, from a heart attack, in 2009. He was the same age as me so it was a terrible shock. We had been friends since we were four or five – we were in kindergarten together. A 35-year friendship. His sister rang me to tell me. I hadn't talked to her in about 20 years, so I didn't understand why she was ringing me, although I had always remembered her as Greg's sweet little sister.

Poor Kathleen, to have to make that call, not just to me but to all Greg's friends, people she didn't know very well, people she hadn't seen in a long time, people she may not have known at all. Saying the same thing over and over. *My brother has died.* Reminding herself of the awful fact every time she had to repeat it. Calling people and explaining who she was, that she was Greg's sister and they may not know her, but she had something to tell them. Keeping her tone calm, trying not to break down while feeling like her world has collapsed around her.

But you can't break down; you have important news to tell this person, you have to stay strong. She was amazingly strong on the phone to me, probably from saying her heartbreaking rehearsed speech so many times. It wasn't until I said, 'Kathleen, it's so terrible for me to hear this, but this is so horrifically awful for *you* to have to make these phone calls and tell people.' And it was then that I heard the falter, the break in her voice as she said, 'Yes, it is…'

And that is why I wrote this book.

I started Australian Missing Persons Register in 2005, after realising that there needed to be an internet resource to help find the missing, and I decided to create one. Over the many years since then, I have come to know the families of the missing very well – they have become as close as family to me in many cases. I saw parallels with what Kathleen did for her brother and what siblings have to do when they have a missing brother or sister.

'My brother is missing – can you help me?' It's a question I get on average every week. Just as often the word brother is replaced with sister. Sometimes my help is needed only for a very short time, and I rejoice when those people are found the same day. But sometimes days turn into months, then years. Then decades.

Brothers and sisters are often in contact with each other daily. I have usually spoken to my sister before 9 am every day; I know what her plans are for the day, I know who she's meeting for lunch, I know what she's planning to make for dinner. Even though I live almost 1000 kilometres away, I could tell you where she's meant to be and when. If I didn't know that, and her husband didn't know, and our parents didn't know, then I would start to panic fairly quickly. When someone is missing, a brother or a sister often knows, *knows* something has happened. My sister would not go a day without being in contact with me.

When people do something 'out of character', a phrase I hear and use on a daily basis, then you just know something is wrong. When your sister fails to pick up her kids from school, when your brother doesn't turn up for footy training, when your sister decides to get in the car and drive interstate on a whim, when your brother is meant to come over for dinner but doesn't show. Those are the times when brothers and sisters start to worry, and that worry quickly turns to panic.

So, what do they do when that happens? At what point do they get the police involved? They think about calling the police, only to find their sister's car broke down and her mobile battery went flat, and she's fine, after all. And she's cranky that you embarrassed her by calling the police. But what if she's not fine? What if something actually did happen? Brothers and sisters of missing people live with guilt daily – did I do enough? Should I have gone out looking that night? I should have answered the call instead of letting it go to voicemail. Why didn't I spot the signs that he was depressed before he went missing? Why didn't I take her seriously when she mentioned suicide?

And then, like Kathleen, you have to tell people someone is missing. You have to tell their boss, their friends, their co-workers. At what point do you make those calls when someone is missing? After they have been missing a day? A week? When do you feel you have to start letting people know something has happened to that brother or sister? Do you keep paying your sister's rent? For how long? What about her car payments? Those practical jobs often fall to brothers and sisters.

The moment a brother or sister goes missing, lives are instantly changed. The people you will meet in these chapters are not the same people as they were the day before their sibling was last seen. I remember reading about one father of a missing girl; he was getting a haircut and he saw the hairdressers whispering together and looking his way, sympathetic but not knowing how to talk to him. He left in tears. Wherever you go, whatever you do, when you have a missing person in your world people start to see you as something or someone different to how you were before. They define you by what has happened to the missing one. You are now the missing girl's father, the missing man's brother. You are not just you anymore.

The stories in this book are all different, but they have common threads that seem to link them all. You'll see lots of similar patterns in each chapter. All of them have vivid dreams of their missing siblings, and sometimes they feel like the missing ones are trying to give them a message. Most of them still look for their siblings in crowds. There is a great deal of survivor guilt with many of them – did they do enough to try to find the missing one? Have they done enough in the years since to keep their missing siblings in the public eye and convince people to keep looking for them? Almost all of them have consulted psychics and mediums at some stage. And every single one of them cried when I spoke to them.

I hope this book will help these families to talk about what they've been through, and I hope it will give the community a glimpse into their worlds. I hope that if you have a missing person, this might give you some comfort in knowing you are not alone, and that others have been through exactly what you have. And I really, really hope that you, as the reader, will keep looking for the missing, and learn about who they were as people before it all changed. Before they became a face on a missing person poster.

So, to all the sisters and brothers who have had to make that same difficult phone call to people to say something awful has happened, this is for you. These are your stories.

CHAPTER ONE
Kay Docherty and Toni Cavanagh

Kay Docherty and Toni Cavanagh, both 15 years old, were last seen opposite the Warilla Grove shopping centre on Shellharbour Road, in Warilla, on the south coast of NSW, on July 27th, 1979.

Picture this: two Aussie teenage girls at the end of the 1970s; going to school, going to discos on Friday nights and weekends, hanging out with their friends, hitchhiking to the beaches. No longer kids, but not yet adults. In 1979 Kathy Lette and Gabrielle Carey wrote *Puberty Blues*, the classic but controversial novel about teenage girls set in the Sutherland Shire, just an hour away from where Kay Docherty and Toni Cavanagh lived, in Warilla, in the Illawarra region of NSW.

It was also the year Kay and Toni vanished, never to be seen or heard from again.

Warilla, at that time, was a growing coastal community made up of lots of young families, so there were always other kids in the local streets to play with. Tracey Shelton was one of those kids, went to the same school as Kay and Toni, and was close friends with Toni's older sister, Vicki. 'We all lived in Housing Commission houses,' says Tracey. 'Back then there was no stigma attached to Housing Commission. All the dads worked at the steelworks, a lot of the mothers stayed at home. We were all from middle-class families. We never went without; there was always meat and three veg, we always had a packed lunch and clean clothes, the houses were always spotlessly clean. Just normal families. We didn't know the Dochertys well, but you could tell they were a decent family.'

Kevin and Kay Docherty were twins, born five minutes apart in Wollongong Hospital. Kay was the first one out, Kevin tells me with a laugh. In 1965 the family moved to Warilla. Kay was a very happy-go-lucky kid. 'When I think of her...' Kevin starts to recall his sister as a child, but the emotion sweeps over him, and he struggles to get the words out. 'There was always a smile, and we had a great childhood. She was always more of a follower than a leader; she was quiet and did well at school, better than me,' Kevin says with a grin. The kids they were friends with as children remained their friends as teenagers. All the kids would play out in the streets until it got dark. 'Kay was scared of the dark,' says Kevin. 'Mum was really protective of us; we were allowed to play in the street just as long as she knew where we were, as long as she could see us, as long as she knew the other kids. Mostly we played near our house. Mum didn't like taking her eye off us.'

Both Kevin and Kay attended Lake Illawarra High School, in the same year as Toni Cavanagh. Mavia Cavanagh is Toni's stepmother, and she raised Toni and her sister Vicki from when they were very young. 'I married Toni's father when Toni was five and Vicki was six,' says Mavia. 'They'd been shuffled from pillar to post; they lived with lots of different people before we got married. It was really difficult. I was terribly young myself; I took the children on when I was only 20. Toni had a lot going on in her life; it would have been hard for her. There was a lot of unhappiness in the house. She and I got on really well, but she was insecure. She had it hard from the start, in the first four years of her life. I never had problems with Toni. She was never nasty to me, never said I wasn't her real mother or anything like that.'

Tracey, who was best friends with Toni's older sister, Vicki, remembers Mavia and Toni being very close. 'Anyone walking into that house would not know Mavia was her stepmother and not her real mother.' Toni was clearly deeply loved by her family, who find it extremely painful to talk about her. 'Toni was a bubbly sort of person,' says Tracey. 'She was very softly spoken but she was always cracking up laughing. She was very happy.'

Most people love their mums, but Kevin Docherty's devotion to his mum, Jean, is remarkable and beautiful. Part of that devotion is because when Kay went missing, Kevin was really all his mum had left. 'Mum and I were close. We were really, really close,' says Kevin. 'We became closer after my sister went missing. When I was fifteen and nine months I made a pact with my mum that I would never leave her. At that age, I probably didn't know what I was saying, but I'm a man of my word, and I honoured that. It's something I had to do. She was a beautiful person, and she didn't deserve all the hardship she had in her life. She tried to do everything right; everything was about her family. I needed her as much as she needed me. As I get older I realise that more. I'm proud to have been in the position that I was, being able to look after her. I left everything – my job, I was just about to be married and have kids and buy a house, but I left all of that to be with my mum.'

I spoke with another school friend of both Kay and Toni, who has asked to remain anonymous. She is eager to give me her perspective on the girls:

> *Kay had a different personality to Toni. They weren't close-close friends, but there were groups at the school of girls who were best friends, and those circles of girls always overlapped; they always had groups of girls who would mingle together. You'd quite often see large groups of girls together doing things. But Toni and Kay were in separate groups of friends. I'd known Toni longer than I'd known Kay; I went to kindy with Toni, then right the way through, and I met Kay in high school. I*

met her on the first day of grade seven and instantly liked her. She was just the sort of person that you couldn't not like. She was so kind, generous and open. She was quietly confident; she was a good student, she worked hard for her good grades and that was important to her. She was good at sports too. One of those kids who was good at everything. She was very popular, really well liked, because she had such a lovely personality. Both the twins were very well liked.

Kay and Toni were similar in a lot of ways, but had very different personality types. They were both quiet girls. Kay knew what she wanted to do in life. She had a smaller group of friends that she would confide in, and the rest of the girls she'd always be pleasant to.

Toni was very small, a very tiny girl. She was only five foot, two inches at best. She was thin and had strawberry blonde hair. I think she was the target of bullies at times. She lacked some self-confidence. I can remember an incident at one of the school dances where she had been bullied, and one of the girls actually punched her. I remember walking over and asking what was going on. Toni really didn't have the confidence to stand up to her.

However, Tracey disagrees with the idea that Toni was bullied, and thinks she could hold her own if necessary. 'Maybe that was a one-off occasion. She didn't pick fights, that's for sure, but if she and Vicki had a fight, it was on. Toni wouldn't back down. They had sisterly name-calling, pushing and shoving, slamming doors, like every other normal family. But at school, I never remember anyone ever picking on her.'

Mavia also doesn't think Toni was bullied at school, and remembers her having a lot of friends. 'She always had people in tow, and was bringing them home.'

It's important to Mavia and her family that people understand Toni was not the wild child she may have been portrayed as in the media, and they are upset that Toni is seen as the instigator of what happened that night. Mavia believes the girls planned the evening together and says it's not fair that people seem to think it's all Toni's fault. She says that Toni was no angel, but she was far from being 'bad'.

'I'd say she did get up to mischief at times, but no-one ever told me she did anything terribly bad. She wasn't totally innocent, but she was a kind and loving girl. She was very social. She was at that giggly girly stage that all teenagers get to; these days they'd all be on their phones together. You just can't put all the blame on one of them, especially at that age.'

Kay had a small circle of close friends, and being the same age she and Kevin often shared friends. 'When we went to high school, we started to get different friends than we'd had as kids,' says Kevin. 'Toni was in some of my classes at school. Some of Kay's friends were good friends of Toni's, so that's how they came to meet. But before they went missing they'd never been anywhere together, never spent any time together. Kay had never mentioned her name at home, ever. It was really bizarre, the way it all happened.'

Tracey agrees. 'There were two main groups of girls at school; Toni was in one group and Kay was in the other group, but now and then we did all sit together in one big group. There was no fighting, everyone got on. In Warilla, Thursday night shopping was a big thing so the two groups would get together then and go out. So, when Toni and Kay got together to plan their night out, that wasn't unusual. But it might have appeared unusual to their families.'

'When I found out it was Kay who was with Toni that night I was really surprised,' said the girls' school friend:

I hadn't pictured the two of them going off and doing something together that way, because they weren't best friends. It was one of those crossover friend things. Toni would have tried a few other girls first; I'm pretty sure her best friend was grounded that night and other people had things on so they couldn't go out. Toni never really did anything that was extremely dangerous, but she would take little risks here and there. She was very different to Kay in that respect. It was just a horrible choice that they both made. I've often wondered why.

And it was unusual that she wanted to go to the disco in Wollongong, because the ones we used to go to were at the Council Chambers, the Blue Light disco in Warilla and the one where the old library was – we used to go to that one regularly – and we'd been to one numerous times at the Spanish club in Warrawong. So, why she wanted to go to the one in Wollongong is beyond me. The roller disco was on every Friday night at Oak Flats.

Tracey was a couple of years older than Toni and Kay, and she and her friends were just starting to go out on their own at night. They'd head to the Police Boys Club disco, or the Blue Light disco in King Street, Warilla, but Tracey doesn't think Kay and Toni ever went to these together. Tracey remembers Mavia used to take the girls, including Toni, to a Christian disco at Oak Flats. They had to stay inside the hall and were not allowed to wander around outside. Tracey knew the Cavanaghs very well, and said Mavia and Barry were quite strict with their children, and they wouldn't have knowingly let Toni go out on her own to a disco.

'I can't remember Toni going to discos, unless they were to do with the school,' says Mavia. 'But she was always going to somebody's house, or bringing them home.'

Older sister Vicki was told she had to be home at a certain time if she went out with Tracey. 'There were rules we had to stick to,' says Tracey. 'There was no "free to come and go". My parents and Vicki's parents made the same rules, so we had to be home by 9 or 10, and as Toni was younger, it would have been earlier for her.'

Mavia is fairly sure Kay had been to her house once before, but says she was a new friend of Toni's. Unbeknownst to Kevin, Mavia says the girls actually approached her a couple of days before and said that Kay's aunt had asked Kay if she would like to go to the movies on the Friday night. Kay told Mavia she had asked her aunt if Toni could come too. 'I said yes, that's fine,' says Mavia.

Kevin was later approached by a woman he's known for years, who was at school with Kay and Toni. She was also re-interviewed by police to recall what she knew about the girls' disappearance. The woman told Kevin that the day they went missing, Toni had gone to all her friends at school, telling them there was a disco on that night in Wollongong, and asking if they wanted to go with her. All the girls told Toni no, they couldn't go with her, their parents wouldn't allow them. The woman recalled that Kay was not one of the girls Toni asked. The woman walked home from school with Toni that same afternoon, and Toni asked her to go to the disco. Again, Toni was told no. It was Friday, 27 July 1979.

The Cavanaghs were told the movies story; however, the Dochertys were told a different story. Kay told her mother that Toni asked Kay to come to her house to help her babysit her younger siblings, and said Toni's mother would be home by 9 pm. It was the first time the Dochertys had heard of Toni Cavanagh, and the very protective Jean Docherty was very reluctant to allow her daughter to go anywhere at night.

'Kay was in discussions that afternoon with Mum,' says Kevin. 'There was a bit of a debate going on. Mum was saying, "No, no, no." She said, "You don't go out at night." Then Kay started getting upset and crying, and went into her room. Mum started feeling guilty so she said to me, "Kevin, if I let her go, can you go there on your bike and pick her up at 9 o'clock?" I had band practice that night and was on my pushbike. I said, "Yeah, okay, not a problem." I can't really remember the details, but if I'd known more about it I would have said to Mum, "No, don't let her go." I remember Mum going into her room and saying to Kay, "Okay, if you want to go, you can go. Kevin's going to take you there and pick you up at 9 o'clock; make sure you don't leave the house." So, Mum just took her word for it. Today, one parent would probably ring the other parent, but in those days you didn't have to worry about that sort of thing. We didn't have Toni's mum's number; in fact, we'd not long had the phone put on.'

Despite not wanting to deceive her mother, Kevin says Kay would have 'easily' been talked into something. 'When you're that age, and you're in a group of girls, you're the quiet one, on the outside of the circle, not in the thick of things, and you have this other girl who's more outgoing and everyone likes her and listens to her, you'd think, well, if she says something I might just go with it. She wouldn't argue, she was more a follower than a leader.' Kevin thinks Kay would have admired Toni, as she was popular; she may have envied her.

Mavia Cavanagh had no idea the girls had lied to her. 'Apparently, they told Mrs Docherty that I was going out, and I wanted Kay to come and stay with Toni while she babysat my children. Then the story to me was that Kay's aunt was taking them to the movies. I believed them, and Mrs Docherty must have believed them too.'

Kay was wearing ordinary day clothes when she left to go to Toni's house, nothing fancy. She did own dressy clothes that she could have worn to a disco, but she didn't take these with her that night. 'When Kay left, I can't remember what she was wearing,' says Kevin. 'Mum did, though. Those little things really hurt me, that I can't remember all the details. But she wasn't dressed to go to a disco.' Police later stated that Kay was wearing fawn trousers, brown floral top, black boots; Toni a blue blouse, fawn jacket with hood and white jeans.

Tracey remembers the girls were just coming into an age where they wanted to be a little more grown up. 'Kay was definitely not outrageous; she was sometimes quiet, but opened up when she was around people she was comfortable with. Was Toni out there? Definitely not. But they were getting to the stage where boys were getting interesting. I remember Toni was starting to wear makeup. She had this really good compact foundation makeup; every time I went over there I'd borrow it. She was very freckly. She'd come off her skateboard or a bike and skinned her forehead, and she had this strip down the middle of her forehead where the freckles never grew back, and that's why she started to wear the makeup, because she was very freckly. Both she and Kay had that red hair and freckles and pale skin.'

The Dochertys did not drive, so Jean was relying on Kevin to transport his sister to and from the Cavanaghs. 'When I took her on my pushbike, she didn't have a bag or anything with her,' says Kevin. He dropped her off at Toni's house at about 5.45 pm and told her he'd be back to pick her up at 9 o'clock. It was the last time he'd ever see his twin sister.

Mavia recalls that day. 'The afternoon it happened, the day they went missing, Kay came over to our house, and she and Toni were in the bedroom, giggling and carrying on, as teenage girls that age do. Toni got dressed. It's hard to remember exactly what I thought was going to happen, but I was under the impression they were going from my house to the aunt's house. If they'd come to me and said, "We want to go to a dance in Wollongong, can you drive us in and pick us up?" then I would have done it. That's what I did with my younger daughter when she grew up and wanted to go out. Toni was probably thinking, Mum won't let me go, and Kay's mum's not going to let her go. So, they fibbed.' The girls left the Cavanagh house on foot, and that is the last Mavia saw of them.

At 9 o'clock Kevin rode his pushbike back to the Cavanagh home in Martin Street, Warilla. 'I really thought nothing more about it until Kay's brother turned up and said, "I've come to get Kay,"' says Mavia. 'I said, "Kay's not here, she's gone to the movies." He said, "But she's supposed to be here babysitting!" I told him she couldn't be babysitting, as my two children had gone to the Snowy Mountains that weekend with the neighbour across the street. Toni's father was in bed asleep and I'd been watching TV, waiting up for Toni to come home. I didn't have any idea they weren't going to the movies, or weren't doing what they said they were, until Kevin turned up.'

'When I got to Toni's house, her mum answered the door and told me they'd gone to the movies,' says Kevin. 'I was shocked. I said to her, "What do you mean they've gone to the movies? They weren't supposed to be going anywhere! She's not allowed out after dark!" And that was a big thing for me to say to an adult, at 15; you didn't question adults. Apparently, Toni gave her a change of clothes and they said they were going to the movies.' Kevin is under the impression that Mavia told him they'd gone to the movies with a girl who lived around the corner and that girl's mother; he doesn't remember mention of an aunt, but Mavia is certain that's what the girls told her.

'Some things are vague, but one thing I remember really clearly is standing there looking at her mum and thinking, I've got to go home and tell Mum now,' says Kevin. 'I didn't know what I should do, if I should just wait there for her or go home. I can't remember if I asked her mum what time they were due home. I probably did, but I was so shocked.'

Kevin was left feeling helpless and confused about what to do next. He decided he better go home and let his mother know that Kay was not at the Cavanaghs. He rode his pushbike home as fast as he could and broke the news that he didn't know where his sister was. 'Mum was devastated, really worried,' says Kevin. 'She was shattered, actually. That night is a bit of a blur. Mum and Dad didn't drive, and I was too young, and we didn't have the Cavanaghs' phone number, so Mum went to see some of the girls who were friends with Toni, who lived in our street. She got the phone numbers of some other girls and started calling all their mums, asking if the other girls had gone with Toni and Kay or if they were there, just trying to get some information. She was doing that for most of the night.

'She left the lights on all night. It got to about 11 or 12 o'clock at night and she just got to the stage where she knew something wasn't right, so she went to the police station. She walked there, at midnight, on her own. I don't know why I didn't go with her or where I was. I kick myself when I think of these things now, why I wasn't with her every step.' Kevin's father was at home, but had been out that evening and had come home and gone to bed. Jean was the one who dealt with Kay's disappearance. 'Any family issues were Mum's strongest point,' says Kevin. 'So, she went to the police station and told them Kay hadn't come home. The police told Mum it was too early to report her missing, and she should go home. Mum told them it was the first time Kay had ever been out at night on her own.'

But it made no difference; the police refused to look for Kay, telling Jean to come back the next day if she still hadn't come home.

Mavia continued to wait up that night, expecting Toni home any minute. 'I thought the movies probably wouldn't get out until nearly 11 pm, and as it was in town, in Warrawong, it would take them at least another 20 minutes or so, so, I wasn't really expecting them until sometime after 11 o'clock. I waited until then, then an hour or so later. Then I woke Toni's father and said she wasn't home. There was nothing much I could do until the next morning, then I started ringing around all her friends.'

Tracey Shelton vividly remembers that phone call. 'I even remember the phone being green. I can remember my father saying on the phone, "I'll get her," then coming to me, tapping me on the shoulder and saying, "Mavia Cavanagh's on the phone. Whatever you do, you tell the truth." I remember the phone call clearly. I remember every little detail because I know what I saw, and I know what happened.'

What Tracey actually saw was the girls immediately before they disappeared:

They were at the bus stop across the road from Warilla Grove shopping centre, on Shellharbour Road. I was on the opposite side, hitchhiking to Kiama. I actually spoke to the girls. It was right on dusk, closer to dark than daylight, being winter. I asked them where they were going. I told them I was going to Kiama. They said, 'We're going to Wollongong' and that the disco was on. I can't remember exactly, it was so many years ago, but I feel like they said they were going to Pump Hill disco. Everyone used to go there and hook up with their boyfriends.

I know that me and my friend got a lift before them. I think they were waiting for the bus, because when we hitchhiked, you'd come down Queen Street and you'd turn left, because there was room for the cars to stop there. If you were to hitchhike in front of the bus stop, which I had done before, that would usually be late at night as there were less cars, but because it was early when the girls went, there was lots of traffic — all the steelworks traffic and the retail workers, that was all flying past, you just couldn't stop a car in front of that bus stop. There was no parking lane. So, that tells me they were waiting for the bus, or waiting for a person they'd arranged to pick them up.

Hitchhiking was very common at this time, with almost everyone doing it. There was no thought to it being unsafe. As a retired police officer from Warilla said to me, 'Kids would rather spend the bus fare on something else.'

Tracey used to hitchhike everywhere. 'Vicki and I used to hitchhike all the time,' she says. 'We didn't try to hide that we were doing it. We eventually got boyfriends and that was a relief to our parents, as that meant we didn't have to hitchhike anymore. Tracey says that Toni had hitchhiked before, with her sister and Tracey. However, the experience terrified her.

'We used to hitchhike to Unanderra horse riding on a Saturday morning, all the time. This day Toni came with us, and she was crying. We told her to stop it, if she wanted to come horse riding with us she had to hitchhike. She cried all the way there. She did it because she had no choice, there was no bus. She was still very innocent.'

Mavia was unaware that Toni had hitchhiked before. 'A friend of Vicki's told me that all the girls hitchhiked. So, there were a lot of things going on that I didn't know about and probably a lot of other parents at that time didn't either.'

The girls' schoolfriend also confirmed hitching was very common amongst their group. 'Everybody hitchhiked then, we all did; we'd hitch to the disco at Warrawong. None of us ever had any bad experiences or close calls or anything like that; we never felt uncomfortable about it.'

The girls would both have likely been nervous, being out at night. Kevin says Kay was scared of the dark and would never have gone anywhere on her own. 'Especially Wollongong,' says Kevin, 'and she wouldn't want to do the wrong thing by Mum.'

I asked Mavia if Toni would have accepted a lift with a stranger, or if she would have been too scared. 'She was a bit scared,' she says. 'She was a scaredy-cat – her friends said that too – so it must have been somebody who came across as trustworthy, or somebody she knew. Thousands of kids have done it. Lied to their parents, gone out and done something and got away with it. But Toni and Kay were the unlucky ones to be in the wrong place at the wrong time, and whatever happened, happened. Whatever it was.'

The next morning Jean Docherty returned to the police station, by now absolutely frantic that Kay had not come home all night. She said to the officer, 'Don't just push me away, she's not a runaway.' The police did take her report about Kay being missing, but assumed she was, indeed, 'just a runaway'.

'Things fell on deaf ears with the police for many years,' says Kevin. 'They didn't expect people to go missing, in those days; they thought they'd just run away.' This assumption by police meant the girls' disappearance was not promptly investigated. Police did not even speak to anyone who had been at the discos in Wollongong the previous night to see if the girls had made it there. The same morning Mavia Cavanagh also went to the police to report Toni missing, and has a similar story about being brushed off.

Nobody had seen her and nobody knew anything. The police were more or less, 'Oh, they're probably runaways.' I remember a few days later, I had been at work all day and I went to Warilla Police Station. I said, 'Have you heard anything about Toni Cavanagh and Kay Docherty?' and he just looked at me and said, 'Oh, we'll let you know if we hear anything.' It made me feel like I was looking for a lost dog or something. When we moved into Warilla it was a new Housing Commission area, all brand new houses; all the people who moved in had little kids and all these kids grew up together, but there wasn't much for the kids to do. I think a lot of Warilla kids were getting into trouble. So, I think the police brushed off the girls going missing as 'just those Warilla kids', they'll turn up.

But I knew they hadn't just run away, because if you're going to run away, you take with you the things that you really love. Toni had a cassette tape deck and she used to play this thing all the time – there's no way in the wide world she would have gone anywhere without taking that. And clothes – she loved clothes, and she didn't take the clothes that she really liked. To just walk out empty handed… All she had with her was the money I'd given her to go out and nothing else. And she didn't come back to collect anything else. It was quite obvious to everybody that she wouldn't have done that. Not one of our family ever thought she'd run away.

Kevin recalls his mother being constantly on the phone to all of Kay's friends' mothers. Jean questioned all Kay's friends and learned about their intentions to go to a disco that night. They had talked to their friends about going to one of two discos – the under-18s disco at Wollongong's Pioneer Hall or the licensed Hoffra House in Crown Lane. Tracey says they mentioned Pump Hill. According to Kevin, police never interviewed anyone from any of these venues, and it is unclear which one they were heading to, or whether they even got there. It is also unclear whether police spoke to the bus drivers and ascertained if the girls ever boarded a bus that evening. The police response was poor, at best. Kevin does remember a Constable Dakers, who was helpful and in contact regularly with the family. That young police officer, now retired, is still just as keen to solve this case, and I recently spoke with him directly.

'I was the first constable to engage in the missing person enquiry,' says Jeff Dakers. 'We were working afternoon shift, and we went around making enquiries about these missing girls. We contacted all their friends, and we spent the whole shift trying to locate them. When we couldn't find them, it was passed on to local detectives. After that, we were left off the case. It was heart-wrenching at times, because Kay Docherty's father used to come into the police station quite frequently and enquire: "Have you found my daughter?" It's one of those things that, as a member of the police, you find very, very challenging.'

Jeff is clearly still emotional about that time; the helpless feeling of not finding the girls has never left him.

'We found out the girls were missing at school the following week,' says their school friend. 'I didn't know over the weekend.

I didn't think they'd run away, but maybe gone off to a party with someone for a few days. Not that I'd ever known Toni to do that before. The other girls had different ideas: some thought they'd run away and some were spot-on that they'd been abducted. I know the families suffered terribly, but it was all their friends too. We felt like the world was a safe place, you trusted everyone, you knew all your neighbours, you could walk the streets at night and be safe, and we had no idea the world was a bad place. In that moment it was like evil came into our neighbourhood and left a dreadful stain. We were all changed from that moment on. It had a dreadful impact on all of us.'

In the week after Kay went missing, Kevin actually didn't think the worst had happened to her. He also didn't think she'd run away. 'I just thought, okay, they've gone somewhere, and it's got to the stage where Kay's become too scared to come home. I thought they were staying low until things had blown over a little bit, because she knew she'd be in trouble. Mum and Dad thought that too, but Mum was more worried. We didn't really think she'd left Warilla as she didn't know anyone outside this area. We thought she was somewhere close.'

Kevin believed the Docherty and Cavanagh families never met nor spoke with each other, not even during the inquest more than 30 years later, but Mavia does recall she did a television interview at the Docherty home. Kevin feels that Jean probably quietly blamed Mavia for allowing the girls to go out. 'Mum was never one to speak out,' says Kevin. 'She'd hold her own, but she was a quiet sort of person. If she didn't have something good to say to someone, she probably wouldn't say anything.' Mavia feels this is very unfair, as she truly believed that the girls were being driven to the movies by Kay's aunt, and that they would be perfectly safe.

Within a couple of days, the Dochertys started their own search for Kay. They felt Sydney was the obvious place to start looking, being the closest big city. Every day Jean Docherty would be on the phone, calling whoever she could think of to try to find Kay. She phoned religious groups and even cults, and also the Salvation Army, shelters; anyone who might be able to help or point her in the right direction. She even quit her job to devote every day to searching for Kay.

'She was this timid little lady, walking the bad streets of Sydney with her friends,' says Kevin. Jean took on most of the searching herself, with her husband struggling to cope with what had happened to his daughter.

'Dad kept a lot of things to himself,' says Kevin. 'He did start drinking a bit more, but he'd never do it at home. He just had to get out; he'd go to the pub, and have a talk to his mates, I think. I probably didn't realise the effect it had on him, as we never spoke much. Deep down, losing a child has got to be the hardest thing. I think he was dealing with it the only way he knew how. It wasn't until years later that his mates would tell me, "Your dad used to be in tears at the pub." I couldn't believe it. I said, "My dad doesn't cry!" They told me he was saying he didn't do his job properly, to protect his daughter.'

Kevin was able to talk to his mum about the way he was feeling, but says he also went into his shell for a long time. Even now, he has painful memories of that time. 'I get flashbacks, and it tugs at my heartstrings. Mum never really talked to me about how *she* was feeling, as she would have felt that was burdening me; she was all about everyone else and never herself.'

'Mum and Dad's friends would come and pick them up and drive them to Sydney,' says Kevin. 'They'd walk the streets and put posters up, especially around Kings Cross.' The Cross was notorious for attracting runaways from all over Australia, and as much as they hated to think of Kay heading there, they knew it was possible. Kevin does not recall any police involvement at this stage, with his family and their friends having to search on their own.

The Cavanaghs also went to Sydney to search. 'It was a week later, when we got the letter, that Toni's father went up to Sydney,' says Mavia. 'He went to the Wayside Chapel in Kings Cross and put photos of Toni up there. He walked all over Kings Cross putting up photos. Nothing happened. Nothing came of that.' The letter she mentions is a very crucial piece of this complex puzzle. Both families received letters, purporting to be from the girls, about a week after they went missing. Despite thinking Kay was still near Warilla, Jean Docherty continued to search inner city Sydney. Her fears seemed to be realised when the letter came in the mail postmarked Darlinghurst, an inner city area of Sydney, not far from Kings Cross. It was addressed to Jean. The first letter is dated 30 July 1979, and this date is underlined – three days after the girls went missing. It reads, exactly as written:

Dear Mum + Dad, I have gone away with a few friends to Sydney I will be back in a week. I am all write so don't worry about me. Love Kay. Xxxxxxxxxxxx P.S. I Love you both very much xxxxxxx.

The misspelling of the word 'right' raises Kevin's suspicions, as Kay excelled in English and is unlikely to have made an error like this. 'The envelope's gone,' says Kevin. 'The police took it for fingerprinting and DNA and we never got it back. They don't have it anymore, and I think that also happened to one of the letters. In 2004 the detectives came and told us the truth about losing the envelope. They said they were very sorry, but over the years things have gone missing and records were not kept properly. It's unbelievable. It was like everything went against us from the word go, and it's still happening today. What did I do to deserve this?'

To my surprise, Kevin reveals there were actually two letters received, not one. Like most people, I was unaware of the second. When they received the second letter, they were even more certain Kay had not written either letter.

'The second letter said they were all right, but "the job fell through". What job? She was 15 years old! Then it said, "I love you both and we'll be home soon." Now, the writing – Mum knew straight away it wasn't Kay's writing. I knew too, by the 'e's. Kay did her 'e's a special way. This was our first contact since she went missing, so we didn't immediately check the writing or the spelling, we were just so excited that we got a letter from her, that she was still alive. As time went on we started to examine it more closely. What went through my mind was that someone else wrote it, or someone made Kay write it under duress, that she was forced to write it. It was the spelling, and the e's. When they sent it to forensics, more than 10 years later, they examined it and they came to the conclusion that it was Kay's handwriting. But then later we had another test done, and they said it *wasn't* her handwriting. Then they came and got the second letter, and they said that *was* her handwriting. They tested it for DNA and they took my DNA, more than 10 years ago. At that time, I thought I was a suspect! They took me to the police station, put a video camera on me, took my DNA. They had to send the sample to America because they didn't have the processes here to do it.'

The family never received any results from the DNA testing, as Kevin says police lost the envelope sample. On further examination of the handwriting, Kevin also thinks Kay would have written 'Mum and Dad', not just a plus sign in between the words. There is also, curiously, no mention at all in either letter of Kevin, her twin brother, who she was very close to. Nowhere in either letter does Kay say she's sorry to her parents for leaving, and by all accounts of her character, if she had actually run away, she would have been terribly sorry for what she'd done, and she would have known how frantically worried and upset her mother would be. Immediately after she received the first letter, Jean headed back to Darlinghurst, where the letter was postmarked. She found no trace of Kay. It was about a week after the first letter arrived that the second letter came, in the same handwriting as the first.

Toni's family received a similar letter, but Mavia does believe it was written by Toni. 'I believe it was her handwriting, because she always put a little heart above the "I" on Toni. It had to be someone who either really knew her closely, or it was Toni herself. But they were probably forced to write them, if they were with someone bad. I gave mine to the police, and never got it back. It said basically the same things that were in Kay's letter – "I'm in King's Cross with friends, we'll be home soon, love you, Toni." Mavia was not aware until I spoke to her that the Dochertys received two letters, and is sure her family only received one.

The girls' school friend said: 'I really wanted to believe the letters were from the girls but they didn't make a whole lot of sense to me; there was something weird about them. I agree with Kevin when he said Kay would have never misspelled words. She was very good at school. They would absolutely not have run away, Kay was devoted to her family.'

As I'm chatting to Kevin, I mention two other girls who went missing in Sydney around the same time as Kay and Toni, who also had strange letters sent to their loved ones. Marion Sandford, aged 24, went missing from Cammeray in Sydney in January 1980, five months after the girls. Her brother received a handwritten letter from Marion, reading, 'I am not at all sure when I will be home but it should be within 2 days to 1 week at the latest I suppose! Met a couple of friends. See you later, love Marion.' Her brother received the letter three days after she went missing. It's eerily similar to Kay's letter.

Linda Davie, aged 22, went missing from Sydney's North Shore in April 1980, about eight months after Kay and Toni. Linda's boyfriend received a strange letter from her, saying, 'I shall be gone for a few days, until the middle of the week, see you then, I love you lots.' Like Kay's letter, it ends with a large number of 'x' kisses. Like the girls' and Marion's letters, Linda's boyfriend received it three days after Linda disappeared. And like the girls, there's a Kings Cross connection, with Linda visiting the Cross and meeting two men the night before she went missing.

Photos of Marion and Linda's letters can be seen on their pages on my website, www.australianmissingpersonsregister. com. Kay's letter can also be viewed on the website, on her page. I have never seen a copy of Toni's.

Six months after Kay and Toni went missing, two other girls went missing together – Kerry Joel and Elaine Johnson. They were last seen in Cronulla, in southern Sydney, and like Kay and Toni, their parents searched the streets of Kings Cross, without success.

Another family to search the streets of Kings Cross was that of Tanya Farrington, aged 14, who went missing from Crows Nest, on Sydney's North Shore (not far from where Marion and Linda went missing) in March 1979 – she is thought to have been sneaking out to go to a disco, just like Toni and Kay.

Rather than reassuring her, the letters just made Jean Docherty worry even more. 'She's got something, but really there's nothing there,' says Kevin. The letters contained no information about where the girls were, what they were doing, or when they'd be home, and, of course, they never came home. As the months rolled on with no sign of his sister, Kevin found it very difficult to cope. 'I remember there was a party near our house, I think it was the end of school, 1979, and all Kay's friends were going. I wasn't going to go but Mum said I should. I remember talking to one of her friends, and I was crying. For me, to cry in front of her friends, it was a big thing. I never thought something bad had happened to her, but so many months of hoping had got to me.'

Like Kevin, Mavia Cavanagh waited for news that never came. She is understandably frustrated that there seems to be much more interest in the girls now than there was in 1979.

I get a bit cranky, because all of this is coming up now, but at the time we were bashing our heads up against a brick wall, all the time. We tried to get in touch with the papers about Kay and Toni, but they weren't interested. But when that poor girl[1] got killed and cut up in Wollongong I had newspapers ringing me, and I actually did an interview on TV, but that was months later. The police at the time didn't take Toni and Kay's case seriously, but down the track they did. The missing persons people were really good. Kevin Docherty really kept pushing it with the police and the papers, but there was nothing said in the papers about it for months and months.

Months turned into years of no leads, and not knowing. In 1996 NSW detectives, working on the Ivan Milat murders, visited Kevin. Ivan Milat is a serial killer who was convicted of the murders of seven young people between 1989 and 1992. He was sentenced to seven consecutive life sentences plus eighteen years, without parole, in a maximum security NSW prison. Milat never admitted to any of his murders, but is thought by investigators to be responsible for more murders than the seven he was convicted of. He is known to have been working in areas where young people have gone missing throughout NSW, and was known to have been working near Kiama at the time Kay and Toni went missing, about 15 minutes from Warilla. Milat travelled on Shellharbour Road both day and night at this time.

---

1   Mavia is talking about 19-year-old Kim Barry, who was murdered in 1981 by Graham Potter. Kim met Potter at a nightclub in Wollongong. He lured her back to his flat in Corrimal, killed her, dismembered her and dumped her remains below Jamberoo Mountain lookout. Potter spent 15 years in prison for her murder.

Police told Kevin that because they knew Milat had been in the exact area at the time the girls went missing, he was a person of interest in the investigation into their disappearance. Milat was interviewed by police about Kay and Toni but, like all his interviews, he refused to speak about them or admit anything. 'Sometimes Mum and I would watch TV and Ivan Milat's name would be mentioned, and her ears would always prick up,' says Kevin. 'Then another night they'd say bones had been found in a national park or something… Every time they said a body or bones had been found, or mentioned Milat, it was like another bloody burden. I had to watch Mum, as she wouldn't talk about it, but I knew I had to get her through those few minutes the story was on TV.'

Tracey tells me a truly spine-chilling story about a time when she and her friend hitchhiked between Warilla and Kiama:

We used to hitchhike between the hotels, Thursday, Friday, Saturday nights. We used to get a lift from near the Holden caryard, opposite the Oxford Hotel in Wollongong, because it was near the pub and we felt a bit safer if people at the pub could see whose car we got into. We were only 16. My friend got in the front and I got in the back of this car. It was a yellow Kingswood with a black stripe, and the guy had a khaki green tank top and a bit of a moustache. He didn't say much as we drove through Warrawong; we told him we were going to Kiama. We got to Warilla and he started going through a few back streets. We asked him where he was going, and he got back onto the main road.

We went through Shellharbour and Bomaderry, into a bushy

area. He turned off the road and put his foot down, so he was flying down Swamp Road. It takes you out the back of Jambaroo. He turned the stereo up. I asked him where he was going and he wouldn't stop, so I went smash in the back of his head. He hit the brakes, then turned around to me and said, 'You're not going anywhere until you give me a f**k.'

I jumped out of the car and bolted back to the highway. I didn't even wait for my friend, because I knew we were in trouble. I thought I'm getting out of here, I'm running. He chased me; we were miles into the bush. No lights, no nothing. My friend was running behind him. I got to the highway and waved a car down. It was a white van with two women and kids and I opened the door, and told the lady we'd been attacked.

The guy started running in the other direction, my friend caught up to me, and we both got in the van. The lady driving the van said she'd hit his car so he would have to stop and couldn't get away and I told her no! We were in the middle of nowhere. So, the guy took off back towards Wollongong. The lady in the van wanted to take us to the police but we said no, because we'd been drinking and were underage, so we asked her to drop us at Kiama.

She dropped us at a hotel, and we were there for a while when the police came. I thought we were going to get done for underage drinking. The police said to us they'd had a report that two girls had been attacked while hitchhiking and we said no, that wasn't us. If we'd admitted this, our parents would know we were at the pub. So, we denied it, and I rang my sister to take us home.

I didn't think much more about it until much later when I saw on TV about a girl being picked up by a man in Wollongong, being taken down a bush track by a man, and I thought, that's what happened to us. I contacted the police then and told them what had happened to us. That was when the backpackers were going missing, and then I saw on TV about those two nurses from Sydney.[2]

I told the police about the man's car, the yellow Kingswood with the stripe, about the man's moustache and his hair. Much later when I saw photos of Ivan Milat, he had the same car as the man who took us. I saw that Milat was working on the highway at that time, from Kiama to Sydney. That's when we started to think, has he picked Toni and Kay up? The police started looking into that. They really looked into where he was working and found he was working in Kiama and on the Wollongong bypass, exactly where we used to hitchhike.

The 1996 contact from police to Kevin came out of the blue. There had been only sporadic communication with them over the years. Kevin remembers his mother dealing with a couple of detectives before 2004, but there was never an ongoing investigation. Police had very little to go on. One theory was that the girls had arranged for someone, maybe an older boy, to pick them up that night. Mavia's parents lived at Cringila, a

2   The two nurses Tracey mentions were Debbie Balken and Gillian Jamieson, both 19. They went missing on 12 July 1980, almost exactly a year after Kay and Toni. The girls were known to frequently hitchhike. They were last seen at a hotel in Parramatta, speaking with a man who drove a white Holden and wore a wide-brimmed hat. Two hours later they called a friend and told them they were in Wollongong. They said they were 'with friends Gillian used to work with' and mentioned a 'gardener fellow' and a party. They have never been seen since. Ivan Milat was interviewed in prison and asked about the girls in 2004, but denied any involvement. At the time, he was working less than 2 kilometres away on the roads in Parramatta.

suburb of Wollongong, and Tracey tells me Toni had befriended a boy who also lived there. She spoke to him many times on the phone, until his mother rang Toni and asked her to stop calling. This boy was questioned by police more than once, and cleared from suspicion.

Kay and Toni's case has bothered Jeff Dakers for decades. After a serious car accident Jeff left NSW police and became a pastor. He started a food hub for the local area, helping struggling families in the Illawarra district. Now, as he approaches retirement, Jeff is determined to do whatever he can to finally find Kay and Toni. Jeff is convinced the girls were taken by Ivan Milat, because of a witness who came forward to Jeff to tell his account of a startling incident that happened to two other girls before Kay and Toni went missing.

I came across this witness, who was a young guy, about 12 or 13 years old at the time of the girls' disappearance. He used to live on Windang Road, and the beach and sandhills were across the road from where he lived. This kid used to play around this area. He said one afternoon he saw this man near the beach, who he believed to be Ivan Milat. The man was with two girls. The girls screamed out 'He's going to kill us!' The kid said to the girls, 'Run in different directions, he can't chase you both at the same time.'

These girls had apparently gotten away, and they went to a house on Windang Road. He told me the name of these people at the house, but this was never followed up by police at the time. This happened prior to Kay and Toni going missing. Things slip through the system.

On a different day, this kid was at a different part of the beach, this time on his pushbike. There's roads and tracks all through there. It used to be an effluent depot. The kid saw a ute reversed up onto a sand dune. The ute had a bullet hole in it. Then he saw a man come over the top of the sand dune, holding a shovel. The kid and the man made eye contact, and the kid thought, 'This doesn't look good' so he jumped on his bike and rode away. He could hear the roar of the engine as the car started up. The kid pedalled like crazy and got down to where he knew there was a hole in the cyclone fence into the golf course, so he knew the car couldn't pursue him.

He's kept that knowledge to himself, due to a lack of faith in the police. I did get a detective to come and meet this man and hear his story. He got all the information and forwarded it onto Crime Squad. Crime Squad said it didn't fit Milat's modus operandi.

A criminal's modus operandi, or 'method of operation', is their particular way of committing their crimes, as they often behave in a similar manner for each one; for example, they may only stalk young blonde women, or they may always pick up women in cars, or they may torture their victims before killing them. However, in this case, the events described by these witnesses occurred 10 years before Milat killed the victims that he partially buried in Belanglo Forest. It's very possible that his methods changed in that intervening time. The earliest known crime of Ivan Milat attacking teenage girls was in April 1971, when he abducted and raped two 18-year-old hitchhikers. These assaults happened at Marulan, in southern NSW, near

Goulburn. At the time Milat was picked up, he was driving a yellow Ford.

When I told Tracey about this new information, she tells me her sister was hitchhiking home from Wollongong one night with a friend. Her friend was dropped off first, then the man driving took Tracey's sister down the exact same road that Jeff's witness described. She managed to flee the car and hid in the scrub until the man left.

Jeff Dakers, in his role as a minister, made an application to visit Ivan Milat in prison. His application was denied. I wrote to Ivan Milat in prison, imploring him to reveal where the rest of his victims are buried. He did not reply. Milat died in prison in 2019.

Kevin Docherty was the face of Missing Persons Week on the NSW south coast for many years and has been interviewed many times by the media. 'I didn't want to do it, and Mum didn't want to do it, but every time they called I said to Mum, "This could be our last chance to get it out there." Every year it does dig those memories up again and you get some hope, but you just get let down when nothing comes of it. Years of constant up and down.'

Jean Docherty never gave up the search for Kay. She even kept buying birthday cards for Kay, more than 30 years after she went missing.

'That's what killed my mum,' says Kevin. 'It broke her heart. For her, it was 24/7. She used to say, "Do you think my daughter will ever come back? What do you think happened to her? You're her twin, do you feel anything?" And I did – the night after she went missing, I went to a really dark place in my mind, for a moment. It was like someone kicked me in the guts. I still remember when it happened. I was in bed. It only lasted for a moment, but it felt terrible. I really changed, from that moment. It had an impact.'

Looking back over the years, Kevin says he tried to live a normal life but he was always 'that kid with the missing sister'. 'I think, who was I trying to be? Why was I trying to be that? It was like I didn't get a chance to grow up and be me, and do my own things. It was always talked about, at school, and people would stop us in the street and talk about Kay. We were taught well by Mum and were never selfish people, and I don't think of it like my life was overshadowed by what happened to Kay, but I was always thinking about it, always talking about it, trying to find some information to take back to Mum. I would pick people to pieces when they started talking about it and ask them everything.

'People were always polite, they'd say, "I don't mean to bring this up" or "I don't like to talk about it but if you don't mind..." and I'd tell them that was fine, if they wanted to talk about it, it meant they were thinking about it, which meant they were showing some concern.'

After he finished school, Kevin continued playing soccer as he had done since childhood, only retiring after 41 years of playing. He says soccer was a great outlet for him. He joined a martial arts academy after leaving school, and continued to play drums in a band. He now teaches taekwondo and after 35 years reached the highest level in his sport; he is a 7th Dan Black Belt pro Taekwondo, WTF Taekwondo, and 4th Dan Bulmoodo-Meditation Korean (monk style). You can't help but think, as you look at the many photos on the Martial Arts Centre website of Kevin teaching the sport to so many children, that he'd wish his sister had learned the self-defence techniques of taekwondo.

'Unfortunately, I started three years after Kay went missing. Now when I teach, especially girls self-defence for local school sports, I don't push the issue of losing my sister, but I do push the importance of girls staying vigilant, keeping alert and trying not to put themselves in vulnerable places or situations.'

He faithfully kept his promise to his mum, made at fifteen and nine months, to never leave her, and he never did, continuing to live in the family home and eventually taking on the role of her carer as Jean's health declined.

'I didn't even go out at night,' says Kevin. 'I knew she'd worry. When I was caring for her, the last 13 years of her life, I never had a holiday, never went on the trips away with the soccer boys. I didn't want to leave her overnight.'

Kevin's father passed away in 2006, from a heart attack. Kevin is sure the stress of what happened to Kay contributed significantly to his father's health problems. He felt his own life was really on hold, with the search for Kay stretching into years, then becoming his mother's full-time carer. Jean survived two major operations, and was in intensive care for three months. Miraculously, against all the doctor's predictions, she recovered and opened her eyes. It seemed she still had some fighting to do, and she was not ready to give up looking for Kay. Kevin stayed awake for 65 hours straight by his mother's bedside, waiting for her to wake up. He kept his promise of never leaving her side.

The thought that Kay should have been there too, sharing her brother's vigil, helping to care for their mum, is a thought that Kevin has had often. 'It doesn't end,' he says emotionally. 'I was standing in the hospital room alone. Most people had families around them but I had no wife, and no sister. It was a very tough time.' Even now, he finds it very difficult to move forward. His grief over the death of his mother is still very raw, and his grief over losing his twin has never gone away, as she is still missing.

'I used to think I was a really strong person,' says Kevin. 'I thought people became who they are because of their thought processes and I didn't think I'd ever have to see a counsellor, but saw a psychologist for a while. She brought so much out of me; it's a very complicated grief.' He faced having to move out of the house he's lived in his whole life, the house his parents lived in, the house Kay walked out of for the very last time in 1979. He has so many memories attached to the house, and the thought of leaving them behind was unbearable. There's another important reason Kevin doesn't want to move. 'If Kay's still alive, there's only one place she knows. It's the only house she ever lived in. That's a big factor.'

Despite decades of inactivity, Darren Kelly and Cathy Flood (the police officers who took over Kay's case in 2004) have been fantastic, says Kevin. 'They're not just officers, they're friends. They became so close to us. Cathy had kids while she worked on the case, so she started looking at it from a mum's perspective. There were times when she was off duty that she'd come and visit Mum, or drop in and see me. If anything happened, they always let me know. They were great, they put so much work in. But this was almost 30 years later. It was down to my persistence, and Mum's, that they started looking at the case again.'

Like many families of the missing, the Dochertys were open to the idea of psychics being able to help them. 'We had psychics come down to Warilla; we had the best psychics in Australia,' says Kevin.

The detectives brought Debbie Malone down in 2009. They were really sceptical, because they don't deal with psychics at all, but I think I mentioned it to Cathy Flood, and told her Debbie had some information for me. That came from a friend of mine who had spoken to Debbie, as I'd never had anything to do with psychics before.

Debbie came down to our house with two detectives. The male detective stood in the background, pretty sceptical about it all, but the lady detective was sitting with Mum and Debbie. Suddenly, Debbie says to Mum, 'What's that smell?' The lady detective could smell it too, then Mum got a whiff of it as well. And you know what the smell was? It was Kay's perfume. None of the men in the house could smell it. The lady detective said the hairs on the back of her neck stood up, she couldn't believe what she'd just witnessed. Within seconds, the smell had gone. I watched it all happen.

Debbie held some pieces of jewellery from Kay's jewellery box, and vivid images came to her. 'I could smell the ocean, I could see sand, smell a leafy area and rotting leaves, and I could hear music,' Debbie told the *Illawarra Mercury* in 2010. 'I felt like I was there. I felt fear, stress, and anxiety, like I wanted to get away.' Debbie believes Kay and Toni were abducted by two men in their late teens or early 20s, one of whom was known to Toni. Debbie believes the girls were driven to bushland near a beach where they were killed, and buried in two separate graves. She compiled identikit photos of the men she saw in her visions and these are with police. Debbie returned to Warilla a week later with police, who had brought with them cadaver dogs, to search the area Debbie had indicated the girls were buried in. They travelled down the coast to Seven Mile Beach.

'I'd told Debbie to be careful what she said in front of Mum,' says Kevin. 'Mum didn't need to hear that sort of thing, so she just told me and the police. Mum kept getting her hopes up all the time, and she'd watched Debbie on TV and thought she was great; she really thought something was going to happen this time. There were about four detectives involved, and the dogs, and they took me with them. They searched all the bushland around there. Debbie Malone took them right into where they needed to be, said, "It's around this area". They stuck spikes in the ground and the dogs were sniffing all around.

'Then something happened – Debbie was with this senior police officer, we're talking 35 years' experience, and he just didn't want to be anywhere near Debbie. He said, "Kev, I've been a policeman all my life, I've been through this before, I don't hold out much hope with this but we're just following through with it." He barely spoke a word to Debbie, he was a hardened copper. So, anyway he's searching with Debbie and the dog handler. Next thing the dog does some strange things. Debbie said, "Something's not right here", then the cop started vomiting and retching. He walked out of there as white as a ghost and couldn't explain what had just happened to him. He said, "Something's there. Something's just overcome me; never in my life have I felt like this."

'We were all just staring at him. So, he wanted Debbie back again! After not wanting to even talk to her. He really thought something was going to come of it. I wanted something to happen. I walked past the spot and the hairs on my neck stood up. I felt a bit sick but I kept it all to myself. For me, I've got to see it to believe it. Apparently, there were other bodies found there.'

The body of Jodie Fesus was found in a shallow grave at Seven Mile Beach in 1997. Her husband was convicted of her murder, and died in prison.

Jeff Dakers believes his witness, who is an upstanding member of his community and very reliable and credible, and wants police to excavate the site. 'The sandhill area is undulating, and it's an easy dig. If you wanted to bury someone, why not in the sand dunes? He wouldn't have wanted to get caught driving along with dead people in his vehicle. That's my view of the situation. I've even been able to secure an excavator, free of charge, for the police to use, and there are no buildings on this site, it's an easy dig.'

Jeff has driven to the area himself and while there are gates blocking the tracks, he said it would be easy for police to go in and dig the area nominated by his witness. Jeff has a map of the area from 1979 and the witness has pinpointed the spot where he had his terrifying encounter with the man in the sand dunes. The witness also said there used to be a shed up the track. He had been in it before, prior to the incidents with the man he believes was Milat, and he said the floor of the shed was covered in blood. The shed was demolished some time ago.

In 2006 a woman who had gone to school with the girls

reported seeing Toni Cavanagh in Cairns, Queensland, in 1984. There were also reported sightings of the girls in Ipswich, and at a Gold Coast amusement park, but police investigated and discounted all these sightings.

In 2007 an inquest was held for the girls but returned an open finding. Coroner Chris McRobert stated there was no evidence to suggest the girls were deceased, and that they may still be alive. However, the families and police disagreed with this and the homicide investigation continued.

The reward for information about their suspected murder was not announced until 2009 – 30 years after they went missing. It's hard not to think these girls were just forgotten by all but those who loved them. That year was also when police approached Kevin about a second Coroner's inquest, but it would be a further four years until that second inquest took place.

The second Coroner's inquest into the suspected deaths of Kay Docherty and Toni Cavanagh took place in August 2013. After 34 years, it took just three hours for Deputy State Coroner Geraldine Beattie to state: 'I find that both girls are deceased, by criminal means, at an unknown location in the days after their [1979] disappearance. What I can't determine is how their deaths came about.'

The inquest finding hit Jean hard, as she faced the fact that it was believed Kay had been murdered. Kevin had been reluctant for it to go ahead, fearing it would mean his sister's case would be closed forever. 'I stood up in court during the inquest and asked, "Why are we here today? As far as I'm concerned, if you don't have evidence, or proof, or a body, then you shouldn't close this

case. Secondly, if you close this case, that's it – my mum dies."
And that's exactly what happened.' Jean Docherty passed away in
March 2014 at the age of 81.

'I had a psychic call me after she saw an article in the paper,'
says Kevin:

*She didn't know me or Mum, but she asked if she could come
to Mum's funeral. She said she'd been watching our case for a
long time and she wanted to talk to me. I said that was okay,
as long she stood in the background. I think she wanted to put
my mind at ease. At the funeral, the detectives talked to her,
after I asked them to, because it's really their job and they'd be
a better judge than me. I asked them to suss her out. They said
she was okay, so I went over to talk to her and she told me my
Mum and Kay were together and looking down on me.*

*Then she said she knows where to find the bodies. I said to her,
'Really?' But nothing more was said. I just didn't want to talk.*

*She called me a few weeks later and she reckons something
happened within minutes of their house and the girls didn't
survive; it was close to home and she knows where they're
buried.*

*I don't believe in all that stuff and I don't want to be led back
down that track where we've been disappointed year after year
after year, but I'm clutching at straws, I'll take anything. I
haven't told the police yet – I don't like wasting their time. Do
I go back to the police with this?*

*The police have already spoken to her, and they didn't follow
through with it, so I thought, is that because the case is now
closed (after the inquest) that they're not pursuing it?*

The case isn't actually closed; it's now in the hands of the Unsolved Homicide team. Kevin feels like he's bothering police by taking this sort of information to them, although he knows he should. 'They've been so good to us over the years, I don't want to burden them with anything else. I have a mate with an excavator … that was the idea … I'd take it upon myself. I think police would think it was a waste of time.'

Tracey has told me the story of another man who lived in Warilla in 1979. He's currently in prison, having been convicted of horrific crimes against his children which occurred, significantly, between 1973 and 1978. They only stopped when the children's mother moved them to another country. In 2014 he was given one of the longest sentences ever imposed in NSW – 18 years. He would be in his 90s if ever released.

It's hard to imagine the girls would have willingly gotten in a car with road worker Ivan Milat as he cruised the streets of Warilla. Milat's method was very much to charm people into his vehicle; he did not tend to force them. Milat would have been 34 at this time, and it's fair to assume the girls would have been a little wary of a strange man this age. But Toni knew the other man's children; they went to the same school, so it's not farfetched to think that had this man pulled up at the bus stop and offered the girls a lift, they may have gone with him, as he was not a stranger.

Mavia agrees. 'The police have spoken to this man in prison and he's denied it, so there's nothing more they can do. But the story does sound feasible to me.'

Tracey strongly feels the allegations need to be further investigated and is calling on NSW Police to speak further to a man who claims to have witnessed the girls being killed. This man also claims to know where the girls are buried. All the information has been given to police; although they did speak to the family involved, they have no evidence to proceed with a case against the man.

'I think it's disgusting that someone can say they know where they're buried, but police don't want to bring him to the beach to show them,' says Tracey. 'At least give him a big map so he can pinpoint the exact location. Police told me they don't want to spend any more money on the case. Just let him tell us where the bodies are! I'm sitting here with text messages and evidence, waiting for a detective to knock on my door and ask me for them. I now don't believe Ivan Milat had anything to do with it.'

Tracey was also very shaken to learn that in 1979 this man owned a very distinctive car – a yellow Kingswood with a black stripe. He also had a moustache, and she has photographs of both the man and his car. She believes it's highly likely the girls would have accepted a lift from this man, or from someone they also knew who was driving his car.

Tracey has shared her concerns with both Toni and Kay's families as well as police. Her passion and energy to uncover the truth is inspiring. Her career has been in a field that helps victims of violence, including children, and she is a credible witness who is highly respected in the community. Chillingly, the place the convicted man took his victim during the assaults, as documented in the court records during his trial, was Seven Mile Beach – the exact place nominated by Debbie Malone as where she believes Kay and Toni were killed and buried.

Kevin is aware of Tracey's and Jeff's theories, but is undecided about what he thinks has happened to his twin sister. 'I am invested in both theories until either is ruled out. For me, this is just another day at the office, which constantly keeps raising its head over the past 43 years. Which ones do I ignore and which ones do I follow up on? The one I don't follow up on could be the one. Until there's some evidence, until it's officially closed, with proof, I'll still have mixed feelings.

'On one hand I do still think I might walk down the street and see her, but on the other hand, after so many years, I think, no chance. If she knew Mum had passed away then surely she would have come back. I was looking pretty strongly for her at the funeral, I tell ya. I was looking for someone in disguise, glasses and wig, but I reckon I'd know her straightaway. It's been a long time, but people reckon I haven't changed much over the years. I'd have a feeling it was her. I've still got that hope but I see it isn't possible, it's been too long. But when you see these cases in America, those girls kept hostage for 20 or 30 years, you can't help but think it's possible.'

It's been a long few decades. It feels like a very long time ago that I last saw her. She used to try to make me laugh, she had a sense of humour. She loved the Bay City Rollers; I've still got their album, it was Kay's. Mum didn't change her room for 18 years; it all stayed intact. We did need more space in the house, and her room was sort of sitting there. The house was getting painted at the time and everything got stored in that room. We didn't really talk about it but it was shortly after that we reorganised things.

Jean and Kevin made the painful decision to pack up all Kay's belongings and her room. Kevin recalls going through Kay's things was very difficult for them, especially their mother, and it was too painful to hold onto them.

'I will never ever forget them,' says their school friend. 'I feel someone out there does know and they're protecting their father, their brother, their uncle, their friend, but they know and I want to prick that person's conscience by making sure the girls' faces are out there every year. We need answers; it's been over 40 years now.'

Toni's sister Vicki was in New Zealand with family when her sister went missing, which must have been very frightening and frustrating for her, being unable to help with the search. She says: 'We were very close. She's dearly missed. She was a homey sort of girl; she wouldn't have just left home. She was going to come to New Zealand with me, but that didn't happen. I think of her every day. I wish for closure, to be able to find her.'

Mavia says that Vicki talks about her sister a lot, and posts her memories of Toni on Facebook often, always remembering her birthdays and the anniversary of the day she went missing. She writes beautiful tributes to Toni.

Mavia shares her memories of Toni with me with great fondness.

I've got a photo that I look at often. It must have been my birthday, and she's standing behind me with her arms around me. I'm so pleased I've got this photo because I lost so many photos, giving them away when she went missing. I was handing them out to people and didn't get them back. I haven't got a lot of photos at that time of her life, and we didn't take all that many photos. I have lots of photos of her when she was little. She was easy to get on with; she and I rarely had bad words. Toni may have fibbed to me that night, but she made me feel like I was her mum.

Toni was very loved. I still dream about her. You wouldn't think after all this time, but I wake up and think, I wonder if she's trying to tell me something? I don't know whether I believe in all that, but I wonder. A cousin gave me some books to read and one of them a psychic had written, and Toni and Kay were in it. It had some gory details in it, and it absolutely broke my heart. I'm a bit that way now: do I really want to know what happened to her? I was on my own when I read it and it was just horrible. I wasn't expecting to read that.'

Mavia says Toni's disappearance had a devastating effect on her father. 'It's left a big hole in the family, having her gone,' says Mavia. 'You wish for your kids to have a nice long happy life. It's not just the immediate family that it affects but also cousins and other people who were in her life, like my mum. My mother took her on the train to Adelaide once, for a family visit – she really treated her like a granddaughter. It's such an awful thing to lose a child, and not know what happened. My son was about nine when Toni went missing, and my daughter was seven. Toni was older and had her own friends, but they were affected too. My son finds it really hard to talk about even now. My daughter can talk about it more.'

I said to Mavia that it can be hard for people to express that level of pain, as losing someone you love like this is about the worst thing that can happen to you, and she agrees:

> *I find I'm getting that way now. More so now than earlier on in my life. I find it harder and harder to talk about. It's the frustration. I wish people had been this interested back then – we might have her with us. People just didn't seem interested. Now, with social media, if someone goes missing you hear about it straightaway. I just got to the stage where I was really disillusioned with everything. I even said to someone the other day, when they were talking about this new police operation, I will go along with it, but why couldn't they have done something like this earlier? None of the men who were around then are probably still alive. I think she was taken by someone. Everybody's sort of jumped on the bandwagon about it being Milat.*

Mavia is disappointed when TV programs that feature Milat and talk about Toni and Kay being possible victims of his go to air without the producers informing the families. It's always a shock to turn on the TV and see a photo of your child or your sister, without warning.

'It's also really disappointing when they put these things to air and they don't have the facts correct,' says Mavia. 'They seem to put Toni in a bad light. It's heartbreaking to me when I see in the media that it was all Toni's fault My niece, who is about Toni's age, contacted the producers of the last TV show that was on and had a go at them about it.'

I told Mavia that what happened to Kay and Toni had nothing to do with their behaviour, and they were not to blame, and this brings her comfort. It's so important that 100 per cent of the blame goes to the person who harmed them. It doesn't matter what they were wearing, it doesn't matter if they were hitchhiking, it doesn't matter if they were out late at night – someone did something bad to them, and it was not their fault. 'That's what my friend said too,' said Mavia. 'It doesn't matter if they were the worst kids in the street, no kid deserves that. What happened was totally beyond the girls' control, and they just made some bad choices that night.'

Kevin still lives in the same house today. He has since married, and his wife has been a great support to him, especially after the death of his mum. 'If I didn't have her, I wouldn't be talking to you right now,' he says. 'I've got to stop beating myself up. I was just saying to my wife, "it's time for you and me now."' They finally got to go on their honeymoon a few years ago. Despite his grief and the struggle to stay in his lifelong home, Kevin will keep fighting to find Kay. He made a promise to his mother, as she lay dying, that he would never give up looking. He is desperate to stay in his house, telling me he feels like if he moves, he's moving further away from Kay and his mum.

His childhood memories of Kay are the happiest he has. 'We played handball and hopscotch out in the street, but I mostly remember her smile.' As Kevin and I chatted on the phone, there was an almighty crash in another room in my house. It was a pile of books toppling over, loud enough to be heard on the phone. Kevin said things like that happen to him all the time when he's talking about Kay, and even Debbie Malone was spooked by that. It's strangely comforting to think Kay might be watching over us, trying to get our attention, and urging us not give up. And we won't – Kevin won't ever stop looking, and he's doing it in memory of their mother, who loved them both so much.

The case is now with the Unsolved Homicide squad. At the time of publication there is a $100,000 reward on offer for information that helps solve their suspected murders and locates Kay and Toni.

If you have information, please call Crime Stoppers on 1800 333 000, and you can remain anonymous if you wish.

CHAPTER TWO
Jamie Herdman

Jamie Herdman was last seen on Sunday November 26th 2006.
He was 26 years old and was on a roadtrip from WA. His distinctively
painted Nissan Urvan was found abandoned, along with his belongings,
at a roadhouse at Daly Waters in the Northern Territory.

The disappearance of Jamie Herdman, from the middle of the Australian outback, is truly baffling. With the setting the subject of sensationalised horror films and wild speculation, it's easy to forget that at the heart of this story is a quiet young man making a new life for himself in Australia who needs to be found.

Jamie, Carl and their sister, Kim, were all born in the seaside town of Whakatane, New Zealand, a small farming and fishing town of about 5000 people. Their loving parents are Steve and Janene. Their grandfather, Don, spent 12 years with Whakatane District Council, as councillor, deputy mayor and then mayor, and he passed away shortly before I spoke with Carl, in June 2017. Don's death notice reads: 'Such a generous and caring man. A true leader and rock for all to lean on. He touched not only the lives of his family but impacted the wider community. Will be very dearly missed.' It is tragic that Don died not knowing what happened to his grandson. The Herdman family are well respected in Whakatane, and it was a great place for the kids to grow up.

Jamie went to school in Whakatane, but was always keen to get out and see the world. 'He was a pretty smart sort of dude; he always got reasonable grades without having to try too hard,' says brother Carl. 'He wasn't a huge fan of school. He was keen to get out and work, but he finished school and did pretty well.'

Tragically, their mother Janene passed away from pancreatic cancer in October 2001. Her death was shattering for the family. Jamie was most of the way through his first year of a chef course when Janene passed away, and he was devastated. Aged just 45, Janene only lived for six months after her cancer diagnosis, so it was a terrible shock.

'It was a tough time for any family, really,' says Carl. 'I was the youngest and still at home. Jamie had left home and was doing a chef course on the South Island of New Zealand, and really loved it. He was just out of home.' Dad Steve said of Jamie, on the *Missing Persons Unit* TV show that 'his mum had a way of understanding him'. After his mother's death, Jamie abandoned his chef course. He moved back to Whakatane and stayed with his family. While in Whakatane, Jamie turned to drugs and alcohol, perhaps to numb the pain of his grief. His family have been open about speaking about Jamie's problems in New Zealand, in the faint hope that it may possibly be connected with his disappearance.

'I think Whakatane is a small town where drugs are pretty rife,' says Carl. 'That's probably another reason why he wanted to go to Australia, to get away from that, and start with a clean slate. In Whakatane, I found out later from talking to his friends, he was using ice. It was just being in a small town, the flat he was living in ... he was doing it on weekends. I don't think it was a full addiction.' The loss of his mother had a major impact on Jamie. Carl remembers:

Jamie's quite a quiet sort of person, but that was a major pivotal point. You never quite know, if he'd stayed doing the chef course, where he would have ended up. He always wanted to travel, and that's why the chef thing was appealing as well, as he wanted to go and see the world. He was definitely an adventurer. We're a very outdoorsy family. We spent a lot of time skiing, snowboarding and stuff.

One of his dreams was to travel across the world and do all that. We'd been on a few family trips; to Colorado, London, Australia, and all the mountains in New Zealand. Some of the best times we had were skiing together. We skied at Whakapapa, on Mount Ruapehu in New Zealand. We used to go there every weekend; we belonged to a club and the whole family would go. That was where we'd both feel the happiest: cruising round the place with our friends and family. Those are good memories.

Carl moved to Australia when he was 21, and when he came home to Whakatane for a visit a year later, Jamie decided to fly back with his brother when Carl returned to Australia. Jamie had been working in a quarry in Whakatane, and was ready for a change. 'He wasn't sure how long he was coming over for, he wanted to try it out, have a look around, do some travelling, that was his idea,' says Carl. Carl had a job on the oil rigs off Western Australia, and Jamie went to stay with him in Perth.

'At the time there was plenty of work around, so he was just going to look for a job,' says Carl. 'He was just going to hang out and see where he ended up. My flatmate had a furniture removal business, so he did some work for him. He was in Perth for probably about a year, with us, then he decided he'd go up to Broome, as he had a pretty good group of friends there. There was some more furniture removal work up there for him. It sounded like a pretty good adventure. He drove from Perth to Broome over about two weeks; he had a bit of a holiday along the way. He stayed in Broome for about eight months.'

Around this time, Carl and Jamie's sister, Kim, was married in London, and her brothers flew over for the wedding. The family had a wonderful time and travelled around the UK before flying back to Perth, where Jamie stayed for a month before returning to Broome. Jamie was enjoying his new Australian life, and seemed to have turned a corner. 'He was in the best place we'd seen him in a long time,' says Carl. 'He was really positive and happy. When he moved to Australia, he wasn't interested in any sort of drugs. He was a typical 25-year-old, out drinking and partying a fair bit, but there was no drug use in Australia. He got away from it all.'

It was in Broome that Jamie bought his distinctive Nissan Urvan, with the intention of eventually travelling around Australia in it. However, the van needed quite a few mechanical repairs and Jamie was slowly getting those done before embarking on his road trip. 'He was planning to travel alone, and seemed happy to do that,' says Carl. Jamie hadn't mentioned any serious girlfriends either in New Zealand or Australia, so he had no commitments to stop him taking off whenever he liked. 'He was quite shy about that sort of stuff,' says Carl. 'He never brought anyone home to the family.'

Carl believes Jamie was aware of the potential pitfalls of solo travellers in the Australian outback, with many people each year succumbing to the heat and becoming lost. Vehicles often break down in the harsh conditions and on unreliable roads.

Jamie had spent a lot of time in the Kimberley region of WA, known for its beauty and wilderness. It's described as a cultural melting pot. 'Broome's a pretty remote place and he'd spent a lot of time there, doing fishing trips around there. I don't think he was planning to go too far off road in the outback. Just going across to Queensland and doing the coast road from there. We've got family in Roma, in the middle of Queensland, and Jamie planned to eventually head over that way and catch up with them. It was Mum's sister, so it was important to him to keep in touch with them. He'd definitely done his research, as he was planning to avoid all the wet season. He'd talked to people about where to go. He could be quite spontaneous, but he definitely had that sort of information; he'd thought about it and planned it for long enough.'

Jamie had also planned an overseas trip in the near future. His dad Steve said on *Missing Persons Unit*: 'The last time I spoke to Jamie was about four weeks prior to his disappearance, and he was talking about his plans of maybe coming to England to see us.'

'The very last time I spoke to him he said he still had a fair bit of work to do on the van, and he wasn't planning to go away in it any time soon,' says Carl. 'He was planning on going after the wet season.' The 'wet season' in outback Australia runs from about November to March, when the normally dry and dusty red centre transforms, with spectacular storms and flooding rains. It's generally not a great time to travel, as outback roads can quickly become cut off by floodwaters caused by monsoonal rainfall. So, it's unusual that Jamie made a very sudden and unexpected decision to leave Broome and start his road trip. He didn't tell anyone he was going, which was very odd behaviour for the normally responsible Jamie. 'As far as we know, he just packed up and went,' says Carl. 'Unfortunately, at that time I was working away on the oil rig, so he couldn't reach me if he'd needed to talk to me. Dad was in London, so it wouldn't have been easy to talk to either of us. But his best mate was up there in

Broome, so you'd think he would have spoken to him if anything was wrong.'

Jamie's sudden departure from Broome, without talking to any of his family or friends, is odd behaviour, and his family have no idea why Jamie would choose one of the worst times of the year to travel – late November – and in a van that had proved to be mechanically unreliable. Carl says:

He left a lot faster than he anticipated. We have no idea why. The only ideas we have are what has come out of the stories along the way. We had family friends up in Broome with him the night before, and they had no inkling that he was planning on leaving at all; Jamie didn't say anything.

Jamie had withdrawn $1000 cash the day before he started his road trip. Carl thinks he can explain this ATM withdrawal in Broome. 'Before he left, the van was getting some repairs done in Broome. I think he owed the mechanic about $800. That's maybe where that thousand dollars went.'

On 23 November 2006 Jamie left Broome, Western Australia – it was a Thursday. His journey, eventually ending in Daly Waters, was to take four days. On the TV show *Missing Persons Unit,* Jamie's case officer, Detective Sergeant Isobel Cummins, said that on the first day, Jamie travelled to the Willare Bridge Roadhouse in Western Australia, 147 kilometres from Broome, where he met his boss. Whether this was planned, or coincidence, is unknown. Isobel said Jamie told his boss that he had to leave in a hurry as his 'past had caught up with him'. Jamie told his boss that he didn't have a spare tyre with him, so his boss said he'd return to Broome, pick up a spare tyre and drive back to

Willare Bridge Roadhouse, where Jamie spent the night. Jamie left the roadhouse early the next morning, so his boss would have had to have been back there by 8 am, meaning an extremely early start from Broome.

On the second day of travelling, Jamie stopped for fuel at the BP service station in Derby, 54 kilometres from Willare Bridge Roadhouse. He stopped again at Fitzroy Crossing and went to the Coles Express, another service station, 257 kilometres further down the road. At just after 2 pm the same day, Jamie was at the Poinciana Roadhouse at Halls Creek, 290 kilometres from Fitzroy Crossing, and he also withdrew some cash at the ATM in town. Jamie drove on, to the Turkey Creek Roadhouse, 172 kilometres away. He made it to Kununurra, 214 kilometres further, and it's possible this is where Jamie stayed for the night.

On day three of the trip Jamie visited seven different businesses in Kununurra – the newsagent, Coles supermarket, Tuckerbox supermarket, the hotel, BP service station, Coles Express service station, and Kununurra Bushcamp (a surplus/camping type store). He spent money at all of these places, almost $300. It's strange he went to two different service stations and two different supermarkets, all within a few hours.

Also strange is no-one working at any of these businesses recall seeing Jamie at all that day.

I have spoken with a woman who lived in Kununurra for 40 years and now runs a Facebook group that has 1600 past and current Kununurra residents as members, and she asked them on my behalf if anyone remembers Jamie being in town that day. She specifically asked people who had worked in the businesses he visited, bearing in mind Jamie was very distinctive looking with his dreadlocks, he had a van painted with colourful Aboriginal paintings, and his disappearance would have been widely publicised in Kununurra not long after he went missing. But not a single person came forward to say they saw him that day.

Jamie continued on another 226 kilometres to Timber Creek, crossing the border into the Northern Territory. He stopped at Fogarty's Store, making a purchase at about 7.20 pm. It is believed Jamie either stayed in Timber Creek that night or kept driving, possibly as far as Katherine, a further 289 kilometres away. Carl says: 'When I look at the timeline, I'm trying to work out whether he's driving a lot to try to get somewhere, or is he holidaying and looking around a lot? The distances he was driving are not too quick, but he was still driving eight or nine hours a day. He was on his way to get somewhere. He wasn't on a cruise. I think the old van probably didn't go too much longer than a couple of hours at a time without heating up. It still doesn't make sense why he was stopping all the way along, although I know he was buying smokes and food and petrol.'

Day four saw Jamie in Pine Creek, Northern Territory at 7.50 am. This change of direction is significant – when Jamie got to the junction of the Victoria and Stuart highways at Katherine, why did he turn north instead of south, if he intended to travel to central Queensland to visit family? Jamie made a purchase in Pine Creek, then kept heading north to Adelaide River, 113 kilometres away, where he stopped at the BP service station. It was 10 am. Jamie then turned around and drove back the way he had come, arriving in Katherine and purchasing more fuel at 1.20 pm. Why did he come back?

A check of Google Street View shows that when you drive up to the intersection of the Victoria Highway (from Broome) to the Stuart Highway, there are no road signs to give directions to other towns. None. Jamie had never been there before – he would not have immediately known which direction to go in. Did he accidentally drive north instead of south? For reasons unknown, Jamie drove back to Katherine. The drive back from Adelaide River to Katherine would have taken about two hours, so there is some time unaccounted for here. Jamie stayed in Katherine township for the next hour and a half, before going to the Katherine Police Station at about 3 pm. Jamie's reasons for asking police for help are of paramount importance to the investigation.

Sergeant Steve Nalder, Duty Officer at the time Jamie attended Katherine Police Station, stated on the *Missing Persons Unit* TV show that when Jamie spoke to him, he said that he had been pursued the entire way from Broome to Katherine by four Maori bikie gang members, travelling in an older model red Ford Falcon. Jamie stated the men were currently in Katherine, he had seen them, and they were 'intent on harming him'.

Sergeant Nalder said: 'I dispatched a unit around town looking for these people. They apprehended a vehicle, but I determined quite quickly that these people were not, in fact, Maoris from New Zealand, they were Aboriginal, from Queensland.' When asked by Sergeant Cummins about Jamie's demeanour, Sergeant Nalder said, 'He came across as a normal, down-to-earth sort of person but with a slightly fantastic story.'

I spoke with Steve Nalder personally and he was very helpful in giving me a first-hand account of the conversation he had with Jamie that day. Jamie walked into Katherine Police Station, approached the front desk, and asked for help. Steve remembers feeling concerned about Jamie's state of mind:

The staff member on the counter came and saw me, and when they told me what the story was I actually did think … yeah, well, okay… I went out and spoke with him, and my opinion didn't entirely change when he told me the story, as it had a lot of holes in it. He told me that gang members had followed him from Broome. I spoke to him for quite some time, including questions about who they were, why they would come from New Zealand to get him, where he first saw them, his drive to Katherine… And there were a lot of things that weren't adding up.

Firstly, he told me they came off the plane the day he left Broome, and he saw them in Broome, and just decided to leave. But he couldn't name them. So, many coincidences would have had to have occurred. He would have had to have been at the airport, or driving past it and saw them. So, if he recognises these people, he must know their names.

The incredible timing of Jamie leaving Broome and arriving in Katherine, and these guys leaving Broome and arriving in Katherine at exactly the same time, yet three days on the road and they never see each other… If they were chasing him, I'd imagine they'd be driving hard, and they'd probably make Katherine in a day. It didn't make sense to me. Jamie spent about three days driving over, so it wasn't a fast trip. He said he didn't see them at all along the way.

He gets to Katherine, and he'd only been there a short time,
and there they are. It just didn't add up.

When Sergeant Nalder questioned Jamie about why these gang members might be chasing him, Jamie had a surprising answer. 'He said he had sex with the daughter of the president of one of the bikie gangs in Whakatane. I said it would be pretty extreme for someone to bring people to Australia just because you've had sex with their daughter. It's probably not something you're going to tell a lot of people – either that, or it never happened. I don't know.'

Carl did know about this information from police, but is also sceptical that it ever happened. 'That came out early on. The police looked into it, went all the way through all the connections, and discredited it. They just couldn't find the person. The gang member's daughter was a different age to what they were saying. We looked at it a few times and threw a few names around, but nothing seemed to make sense with that one. There was no clear path to link anyone with that. Jamie definitely never said anything to me about this happening. I don't think it was something he would have had to hide; it's not that big a deal. He might not have wanted the gangs to find out about it, but there was no reason not to tell friends and family.'

Although a beautiful place for the Herdmans to grow up, Whakatane nonetheless has had its fair share of notoriety involving infamous New Zealand gangs. Jamie specifically told the police in Katherine there were Maori gang members following him. Did something else happen in New Zealand that Jamie maybe witnessed? Something that caused the gang to want to find him? Something so significant, that years later gang members would cross the Tasman, track down Jamie in Broome, and chase him more than 1800 kilometres through the outback?

'I have run this through my head a thousand times,' says Carl. 'It would have to be something big for them to travel and hunt him down. Or was it coincidence they were in Broome and found out he was there? In Whakatane, the gangs are violent, but very rarely do you hear of murder with them involved. The Australian police contacted New Zealand police about it, and they dismissed the idea pretty quickly, saying they don't believe the gangs would have the resources, or enough motive, to track Jamie down in Australia.'

I asked Carl what he made of the report. 'That's one of those big questions, isn't it? If you follow *exactly* what he said, then obviously his past from New Zealand has caught up with him. We're still not 100 per cent sure what that is. Whether it involved money or something else, we just don't know. Maybe he saw someone who looked familiar from his past, or maybe he did see someone in Broome, which is very possible, as there's quite a lot of New Zealanders living in Broome. There's even a lot of people from Whakatane who live in Perth. It's not a very big world. Being a small town, if someone turned up in Broome, he'd probably know about it.'

Is it possible that Jamie left New Zealand owing money to someone, possibly for drugs, and that person appeared in Broome and spooked him? Carl says it's about the only theory that makes sense, so he tends to go along with it. 'With him leaving so quickly, it's possible that someone just turned up.'

But if this theory is correct, and someone from Jamie's past turned up in Broome, how did they then find Jamie in the outback? Broome to Daly Waters is more than 1800 kilometres; it's a long way to follow someone. Carl isn't a fan of speculation and wild theories. 'There are so many different avenues of this story, it's hard. We have to follow the basic facts that we actually know. It's interesting how, over time, some of the ridiculous stories that we've heard have ended up being believed as fact, after 10 years. It's hard to go back and see what was written down a few years ago. That's what we have to go off.'

Sergeant Nalder took Jamie's claims about the car following him seriously. 'If he believed it, then it was real to him. I dispatched a patrol to go and have a look around for the car, and I was extremely surprised when they said yeah, we've found it. We apprehended the vehicle and I went down there. The vehicle was as he described – an old square XD model Ford, a red one. The only difference was inside there were three or four Aboriginal males. They were from Queensland, and they'd only just got to Katherine. I recorded those people's details. It may have been that he saw that car and those people, but they didn't look like Katherine locals, there's a distinct difference in features, and I wouldn't have mistaken them for Maoris. I'm a Kiwi, like Jamie.'

The males in the car had never been in Broome, and it's unclear whether Jamie saw the men only inside their vehicle or out in the street. Carl is concerned about whether or not the car's occupants were truly investigated. 'When we asked the question about how well they'd checked them out, they couldn't answer,' says Carl. However, Sergeant Nalder assures me he spoke at length to the occupants of the car and verified their identities and reasons for being in Katherine.

Carl isn't sure that police got it right when they said they'd found the car Jamie described as being the one that was following him. He believes it's possible that police found the wrong car, and didn't take Jamie's concerns seriously enough.

'I think they took it very lightly at the time. I think if they'd followed their protocols, they should have kept him there for a lot longer, and figured out what was going on. Whether it was the guys in that car, or whether it was another car… I think the police very quickly found a car, stopped them, and asked them where they were going, then let them go. They didn't follow it up. The police said he was very calm and collected about it all, and they just told him there was no-one out there, that he was all good, and they sent him on his way. But they also said maybe he was psychotic or something – that was their excuse to cover up what they didn't do. They gave him a drink of water, and he sat in the police station for an hour while they went outside and looked, came back and said they couldn't see anyone out there. Either way, I don't think they handled it correctly.'

Sergeant Nalder says, in retrospect, he does wish he'd detained Jamie for longer at Katherine, now believing that he was having a mental health episode. However, police must follow strict rules regarding detaining any person against their will, and Jamie appeared to be calm and rational. 'With 20–20 hindsight, if he presented to me again, I'd drag him down to the hospital to get checked out in any case,' says Steve. 'We do have the power to do that, but one of the elements has to be that we have a belief that he's a danger to himself or others, and

I didn't really have that belief. I sort of regret not doing it. But I didn't believe at the time that there were sufficient grounds to take him for an assessment. It's quite a serious thing to take someone's liberty from them.'

Because police found the exact red car that Jamie had described, this suggested he was not delusional and hallucinating, or making things up. He really believed what he was saying.

The final stage of Jamie's journey raises even more unanswered questions. Jamie left the Katherine Police Station at about 4.30 pm. Steve said Jamie was not upset or agitated at any point during their conversation, even after being told the men in the car were not, in fact, following him. 'So, once we'd discounted that particular vehicle – potentially, I suppose, there could have been another vehicle – I went back and spoke to Jamie again and asked what his plans were. He told me he was driving to Darwin to fly out and meet his father overseas in England. I thought that sounded like a good plan. I gave him some advice about driving up the highway, where the mobile phone coverage was, where police stations were, and he left.'

This part of the conversation again raises more questions, because Jamie did not tell Sergeant Nalder that he had already been up the highway north to Adelaide River, just that morning. Sergeant Nalder was unaware Jamie had been to Pine Creek and Adelaide River until I told him during our interview, and was very surprised. 'So, he already knew which way Darwin was? That was the advice I gave him, that there was mobile phone coverage and a police station at Pine Creek, and another police station and mobile phone coverage at Adelaide River. I think he hung around Katherine for a little bit, as he made an ATM transaction. He told me he'd just driven in to town before I saw him.'

We now know that Jamie had at least been through Katherine early that morning, if not spent the night there, in order to travel north up the Stuart Highway, before returning to Katherine at about lunchtime. He made one transaction at Katherine via Eftpos, at the United petrol station at 1.20 pm, before he went to the police station at 3 pm. And instead of heading north to Darwin, as he'd just told the sergeant he was intending to do, after leaving Katherine, Jamie instead immediately drove south, to Mataranka and ultimately to Daly Waters. If Jamie had his passport and money for a plane ticket, and directions to Darwin, and told police he was going to Darwin, why didn't he go to Darwin? He instead headed south from Katherine.

Darwin is only a little over three hours' drive from Katherine. From where Jamie drove to at Adelaide River that morning, it was only another hour or so away. Why didn't he keep going? From Katherine, he instead headed south, and made a purchase at the Mataranka Roadhouse, just over an hour's drive, at 6.30 pm. A woman working there thought she remembered Jamie buying a pie, but wasn't sure. We know his van ended up in Daly Waters, parked near the roadhouse. Why did Jamie abandon the van here? As the males in the red car who police spoke to in Katherine had come from Queensland and driven up the Stuart Highway from the junction of the road at Tennant Creek, it's almost certain this same car didn't come from Broome, and nor did it then follow Jamie back south the same day, as Katherine was their destination. It's very unlikely Jamie saw the car again in the Daly Waters area, so that isn't what spooked him into disappearing here.

'What I believe, personally, is that he's had a psychotic episode,' says Steve Nalder. 'The sort of behaviour's probably not unusual; it's disorganised and fits with what I was thinking. He's gone south and, unfortunately, he's probably walked into the bush, potentially in the belief that he was being chased, and he's not come out again. Hopefully, at some point in the future, he will be found, and that will give the family some closure.' If this is what has happened, Sergeant Nalder is not surprised that Jamie has not been found. As an experienced bush policeman who knows the Northern Territory outback well, he says, 'The country's just too big. You simply don't know where they might be. There have been cases where people have been found, only just off the road, years after their disappearance.'

Steve feels it's possible that if Jamie was picked up on the road south out of Daly Waters, that the driver never came forward to police, for various reasons.

There's a good chance, if he was hitchhiking, either someone hasn't seen the story, or they don't want to come forward for some reason. My personal belief is he's gone into the bush at Daly Waters.

Carl isn't convinced this is the case. 'It's an easy way for them to palm it off. There was a lot of stuff done by police incorrectly or poorly, especially the missing person part of it. His story is the only one we've got, so we've gone with that, but it doesn't answer any questions. The whole story makes sense except for Katherine Police Station. There's a lot of questions from there, as that's the only sighting, all the way from Broome, apart from when he saw his boss. It gets confusing as to whether it was actually him in the van and making the transactions, and what really happened.'

Sergeant Nalder is not surprised about the lack of footage from CCTV of Jamie, as in 2006 there would not have been many cameras in the outback. 'Most of the small places won't have CCTV, and back then it would have been more expensive than it is now. The BP in Katherine did have CCTV. I can't recall if the United had CCTV or not. I would have thought they did.'

Jamie's family are still sceptical about why there is no proof that Jamie was the one using his ATM card along his journey and that someone may have stolen it from him. Steve Nalder does believe that anything is possible, but is sceptical that this is the case with Jamie.

Senior Constable Nathan Finn of Elliott Police Station has stated he saw Jamie hitchhiking along the Stuart Highway, near the Daly Waters Roadhouse, where his vehicle was left. He is certain it was Sunday, 26 November, during the day. However, Jamie was at the Katherine Police Station until at least 4.30 pm that afternoon, and his bank transactions show he was at Mataranka at 6.30 pm that night. He could not have arrived at Daly Waters until at least 8.30 pm.

Carl says: 'There was a transaction at Mataranka at the same time as the policeman said he saw Jamie hitchhiking at Daly Waters, an hour and a half's drive away. He couldn't have been in two places at once.' There were a couple of transactions from Jamie's account at the roadhouse at Daly Waters – there was a balance enquiry and cash withdrawal at around 9 pm, and at

10.20 pm another $100. This was the last transaction on Jamie's account. If he was at the Daly Waters roadhouse at 10.20 pm, he could not have been seen hitchhiking away from the town several hours earlier by police, at the time he was at Mataranka, more than two hours away.

According to the Daly Waters Hi Way Inn website, the service station is open until 11 pm every night. They have a pub, service station, motel, camping ground, caravan park, mechanical workshop – a bit of everything. Sergeant Nalder thinks it's possible that Jamie caught a ride out of Daly Waters. 'He may well have hitchhiked, and there was a sighting – but I've always been confused about that.'

Carl continues the story:

The owners of the Daly Waters roadhouse saw that his van had sat there for a while, so they called local police, who contacted Katherine Police, and they ran the number plate and found it was Jamie's. They realised he'd been in there, at Katherine station. They didn't really take it too seriously from the start, because they thought the van had broken down and he'd hitchhiked off somewhere. It wasn't taken as seriously is it probably should have been.

When police looked in Jamie's van they found it was full of fuel, with all his camping and fishing gear inside. There were no keys and the van was unlocked. Jamie's mobile phone was found inside. Police hotwired Jamie's van and drove it to the police station, about 20 minutes away. There seemed to be nothing wrong with the van; it was not out of petrol or overheating, which increases the mystery about why Jamie abandoned it.

Sergeant Nalder sighted Jamie's passport to verify his identity when he spoke with him at Katherine Police Station, but it was not in the van with Jamie's other possessions. A possible explanation for this, other than Jamie taking it with him, is that the van was left unlocked and unattended for almost two weeks before police secured and removed it. Carl says the police report states the van sat where it was for four days before police were notified about it, and the manager of the Hi Way Inn was actually instructed by police to go through the van looking for anything that may identify the owner – a clear breach of procedure.

'Any time in that first week, anything could have gone from that van. A lot of people pass through that roadhouse, lots of travellers.'

This also means Jamie may have left the keys in the van, and they were taken by someone intending to steal it, who thought better of it after police became involved.

Police found an envelope in the van with Jamie's grandparents' name and address on it in New Zealand. His grandparents were phoned to say Jamie was missing, and they, in turn, contacted Carl, still at work on the oil rig.

At the time I went along with the story they gave us, which was that they'd found his van broken down and they'd seen him hitchhiking off. They asked me if I knew where he might be heading. So, at the time I took it a bit lightly – I wish I hadn't. I was due off the rig two days later, so I just kept in touch every day with the police. I didn't know then that Jamie had made the report at Katherine Police Station. From what I could gather from police, there was no need to be too concerned. I

also didn't realise the van was parked up at a roadhouse that
had a mechanic's garage there.

If Carl had known that there was no reason for Jamie to have abandoned the van and hitchhiked, and also that he'd told police he was scared for his safety and someone was following him, he would have been far more worried about Jamie's disappearance.

When Carl came off the oil rig, he spoke with his sister in London, and they realised things were serious. Jamie had vanished. The police had found no further sightings of him. Because of everything their dad Steve had been through, losing his wife a few years before, Carl and Kim decided not to tell him about Jamie's disappearance immediately. It was not until about a week later, when Jamie had still not been found, that they knew they had to tell him, but they delayed it for as long as possible.

'We didn't want to stress him out, and he was on the other side of the world,' says Carl. 'At the time I truly believed he'd turn up in a couple of days, just down the road somewhere, and that would be the end of it. My sister and I said to each other that when we knew something, we'd give him a call, but at that point we really knew nothing, so we didn't have anything to tell him.'

When Carl and Kim told Steve that Jamie was missing, their dad was very worried and immediately started to look for flights to Australia. 'At the time we said to police, well, do we come up there?' says Carl. 'And they suggested there was not much point at that time. They'd started conducting the searches of the area and they didn't want more people up there, getting lost in the bush, and us wandering around, not knowing where we were going. They said sit tight, and they'd keep us updated. So, we went and did our police statements, and sat by the phone.'

Police started their searches about a week after Jamie's disappearance. They had been assuming Jamie had hitchhiked and would make contact with his family, but when that did not eventuate they escalated the investigation. Carl says: 'Once the police pieced things together a bit more, and realised they had the report from Katherine Police Station, they started the land and aerial searches. They had choppers and motorbikes down there for quite a few days. That's when it hit home that it was really pretty serious.'

Senior Constable Nathan Finn of Elliott Police said the ground search at Daly Waters was conducted over four days, as well as about 19 hours of helicopter searching.

Steve Herdman was to fly to Australia numerous times over the next few years in the search for Jamie. On one of his early visits, he and Carl and Carl's aunt took a trip to Darwin, and retraced Jamie's journey to Daly Waters.

We put up flyers and talked to people all along the way,' says Carl. 'That was about three weeks after he went missing. A few people did think they'd seen him getting food at the roadhouses. We found receipts in his van that showed us where he stopped along the way, so we stopped at all those places. We asked people what he was like at the time. Some people remembered, him, some didn't. Nothing major came of it. One lady in Mataranka remembered him buying a pie and a lady at Daly Waters thinks she remembers talking to him; he was getting out of the van and had a white t-shirt on.

We quickly learned it's a massive place, and from there you can go in four different directions. The next major place was Alice Springs, which is another day's drive. At Tennant Creek, about 400 kilometres south of Daly Waters, the road forks, it goes across to Queensland from there. I don't know why he'd leave the van and then continue the trip without it. There are not many cars or trucks on the highway. You can go for a fair while and not see anybody. It's not an ideal place to be out hitchhiking.

When Carl, his dad and aunt were in Darwin preparing to start the retracing journey, police told them about Jamie attending Katherine Police Station and reporting that he was being followed. 'They arranged for us to meet with those officers when we got to Katherine,' says Carl. 'We spoke to the officer on duty. It didn't sound like Jamie to go to the police station. For him to go to a police station and actually ask for help, then something serious was going on. I definitely don't think he would have gone in there for any other reason other than him genuinely thinking he needed help.'

When the family got as far as Daly Waters, finding nothing, they had no choice but to end their search and turn back. 'We went back to Darwin and spoke to the police in charge of Jamie's case. They told us there wasn't much we could do from there. We didn't know what to do after that. Dad stayed up there for a bit. I came back to Perth. We just hung around for a bit. There was nothing we could do at that time, so Dad went back to England. We were just relying on the police and what they were doing. Otherwise we would just drive around the Northern Territory bush for months on end and get nowhere. But if you follow the policeman's story, he saw him hitchhiking out of there, so you think he must have headed south and he might pop up in New South Wales or somewhere like that, or South Australia, but you go on and nothing happens.'

I asked Carl if he expected to find Jamie during this trip. 'Not really,' he answered. 'Not in that area. We were hoping to find which direction he went from there, or if something … what happened in Daly Waters. Everything leads to there and stops. When we got to Daly Waters, we felt more lost than ever. We realised how remote that area is. I always had this image of the outback as desert, but you get there and there's dense bush. That kept opening up more questions. People give you their version of the story and you're not really sure where you go from there. Every answer you get starts a whole new line of questions.'

It was an exhausting trip for the family, driving long distances every day, with nothing between the towns and roadhouses, and talking to every person they could find who may have seen Jamie. Carl describes it as a very confusing time. 'It's a strange situation. A lot of the transactions along the way, between Broome and Daly Waters, there were about 10 stops but no-one had CCTV or anything like that. Nothing to confirm any of those along the way. The whole way along, his card was used but there's no-one to confirm it was Jamie using it. It didn't add up.'

Dad Steve told the *New Zealand Herald*: 'It just seems odd that in a small country area – this is the only building within a hundred miles of the next roadhouse – you'd think people living in those sort of areas would remember everyone that came and went.'

Jamie's Eftpos card was used at the Hi Way Inn at Daly Waters twice that night, but not a single person remembers seeing him. 'When we got those statements, it opened up a lot more questions,' says Carl.

Jamie disappeared at the edge of summer, in outback Australia. Average daytime temperatures in Tennant Creek for that time of year are 36–37 degrees. The police reported that on the day he went missing the temperature was nudging 45 degrees. So, did Jamie take anything with him to help him survive the conditions, such as water or even a hat?

'We spent a lot of time in our young days in the bush, so he would have known to take the basic stuff, but most of his stuff was still in the van,' says Carl. 'It's confusing. It feels like he was going to come back to the van. Even if you're going somewhere remote, you still take your cell phone and whatever money you've got. His backpack and clothes were in the van, all his food still in the fridge. He wasn't planning on leaving the van for long.'

The *Missing Persons Unit* show interviewed a witness who believes she saw Jamie walking beside the highway. She noted that he didn't have a suitcase or backpack, or even a bottle of water, and appeared to be looking through the scrub with his head down. The man she saw then came to the Devonshire Tea House she runs in Larrimah, about 90 kilometres north of Daly Waters. But if this was Jamie she saw walking along the highway, where was his van? If he hitchhiked south from Daly Waters after he abandoned the van, how did he end up 90 kilometres north? The woman can't recall whether it was before or after his last sighting at Daly Waters that she saw Jamie.

In January 2007 Senior Detective Police Sergeant Scott Pollock suggested to the media that Jamie might have hitchhiked from Daly Waters to a remote Aboriginal community and he hadn't made contact as the community was cut off by the wet season floodwaters. In February 2007 Jamie's sister Kim flew to Australia to look for her brother. The ABC reported Kim as saying:

> As far as I know they're going back through everything, trying to pick up on I guess anything that could have been missed. Obviously following up on any new sightings or any new information that's coming through. But we've kind of come back to square one in a way, and we are hoping that if he is laying low, if he does hear of anything then by all means please get in touch with us.

In the months after Jamie disappeared police received calls from hundreds of people claiming to have seen him, but none of these were ever confirmed. Carl says:

> There were countless sightings. I can't remember how many the police said. In the first six months there were something like 150 sightings. At least once a week we'd get a different sighting; they'd send pictures. They'd just started to get a few reported sightings from other places, like Queensland and New South Wales. Every sighting gave us hope, but the more sightings that came in the less hopeful we got. Some of the pictures that came through ... you'd think, well, if this is what the sightings are like, then we're just wasting our time. The photos they were sending us were not even remotely close, and 99 per cent of them you couldn't follow up anyway because

they were no longer there. The police followed up everyone they could. They interviewed a lot of people, but there was nothing.

It seemed every time a young man with dreadlocks was spotted anywhere in Australia, the public would call police. In 2008 the media reported that a member of the public contacted police to say they thought they had spotted Jamie at a Canberra market. The *Missing Persons Unit* TV show also featured reports of several possible sightings of Jamie at a caravan park in the NSW town of Yass in 2008. Sergeant Mick Chubb is seen on the show speaking with several Yass locals, and showing them the photo of Jamie shirtless, with his van. Several of them said they felt he looked familiar, and some said they were sure they'd seen him. Carl doesn't lend much credence to the Yass sightings, believing that people have looked only as far as the dreadlocks, and have added together the sighting of an orange Kombi with the man, which is actually the vehicle another missing man from the outback was last seen in – Peter Falconio. Despite a thorough investigation in Yass by Sergeant Chubb, no evidence was found that Jamie had been there.

In the same episode, police attend an address in Caringbah, Sydney to speak to a woman who is sure she's seen Jamie at the pub. They check the pub, but not a single person recognises Jamie. In August 2008 Steve Herdman told the *New Zealand Herald* that the man in these sightings, from both Canberra and Yass, had come forward to police, and it was not Jamie. Police said the man was 'the spitting image' of Jamie. Another dead end.

Although the 'Outback Serial Killer!' headlines and *Wolf Creek* comparisons were upsetting to the family, Carl appreciated that the public were at least being made aware of Jamie's case.

> *We accepted early on that people are always going to make stories out of it, and we had the approach that any publicity was good publicity. If they kept putting it on TV with Jamie's face, then even better. One of the shows we did had a chain of events, so that was good, and the Missing Persons Unit show was sort of re-enacting and going back to check what they had.*

However, the publicity around Jamie's story didn't always have a positive result. A strange and upsetting side story to Jamie's case was revealed in 2015 when an Auckland teacher was convicted of stealing Jamie's identity and scamming banks out of more than $67,000. The teacher read about Jamie being missing on Facebook, and somehow managed to get Jamie's birth certificate from the Department of Internal Affairs in New Zealand. He then used the birth certificate to obtain a driver's licence in Jamie's name. He applied for three credit cards in Jamie's name and spent the money on gambling. My utter contempt and disgust for this act cannot adequately be described. To add to Jamie's family's stress at this time is disgraceful, but it also would have completely confused the investigation, to find that documents in Jamie's name started to appear, making it seem that Jamie was active. That is unforgiveable. Jamie's grandfather Don said taking Jamie's identity was 'not a nice thing to do'. The statement is evidence of how lovely and polite this family is.

Strange as it is, Jamie's case – of a man going missing after abandoning his vehicle in the outback – is not an isolated one.

I have several others on the Australian Missing Persons Register who are still missing, and several who have been found after going missing in similar circumstances. One in particular bears striking similarities. Twenty-eight-year-old Jason Richards went missing after embarking on a long road trip down the Stuart Highway from Darwin in the Northern Territory in 2011. His destination was Ballarat, Victoria. Searchers had a huge area of more than 3600 kilometres to start with, until Jason's dog was found, wandering and emaciated, near Glendambo in South Australia.

Jason's boat, that he had been towing behind his ute, was then found, partially burned, on a dirt road in the same area. Jason's body was eventually found more than a month later. His car was found in a dried-up creek bed on a remote station, north of the Stuart Highway between Glandambo and Pimba, and his body was found 500 metres away. An inquest, in 2013, found that Jason had taken his own life. The autopsy revealed a self-inflicted gunshot wound to his head. Traces of methamphetamine were found in Jason's liver, and the Coroner found this was likely to have been from Jason attempting to combat fatigue and stay awake on his long drive.

Jason was not a regular drug user, and was not suffering from a mental illness. He also consumed No-Doz and Mother energy drinks on the trip to help him stay awake. On the first leg of the journey, from Darwin to Coober Pedy, a distance of more than 2100 kilometres, Jason drove non-stop. It was during the next 370 kilometres of his trip that Jason experienced the psychosis that ultimately led to his death. He was seen driving erratically, weaving from one side of the road to the other. At one point he passed a truck, made an immediate U-turn and drove directly at the truck. Jason was encountered by other travellers who reported he was paranoid and agitated, and clearly under the influence of a substance that produced a glassy and wide-eyed effect in him. A third sighting was made by another truck driver, who saw Jason's vehicle drive towards him with its lights flashing continually, indicating for the truck driver to stop. The truckie did stop, and watched Jason drive his ute around a full loop of the truck before stopping. Jamie told the truck driver, 'He's in the back and he's trying to kill me!' The truckie looked in the ute but could only see Amy the dog, in her cage.

Jason's suicide was shocking and unexpected. He had everything to live for – he was a father of two, and was headed home to Ballarat for his son's third birthday. It would have taken a catastrophic event for him to abandon those plans, to let Amy, his beloved dog, loose to fend for herself, as she was pregnant, and then to take his own life.

In April 2006, a few months before Jamie went missing, 26-year-old Brett McGillivray, from Western Australia, was driving on the Stuart Highway from Alice Springs. His car was found abandoned, with the keys in the ignition, at a truck stop at Attack Creek. The car had plenty of fuel and all his possessions were inside it. No trace of him has been found. Like Jamie, Brett had been on a long road trip, leaving Perth and travelling more than 3700 kilometres through South Australia and up to the Northern Territory. Attack Creek is 335 kilometres south of Daly Waters.

Also missing at Attack Creek is Stanislav Dobias, who had a campsite there, and disappeared in 2005. Unlike the others,

Stanislav was a 60-year-old man with dementia and is believed to have become disoriented and lost on the property.

Thirty-seven-year-old Oswal Orman went missing in January 2007 from Barkly Homestead, about 200 kilometres east of Tennant Creek. He, too, abandoned his car and there were reports of him trying to hitchhike from the homestead. He is still missing.

Robbie Nivison went missing in the outback in 2007. His remains were found in 2010 in his vehicle, 60 kilometres north-west of Yulara in the Northern Territory. This list goes on: 34-year-old Brenton Stoddart went missing in late 2007. His ute was found abandoned by the side of the Stuart Highway, out of fuel and damaged, 20 kilometres south of Adelaide River. In 2010 Anthony Drummond left his workplace at Three Ways. He abandoned his car at Renner Springs, 245 kilometres from Daly Waters, and started walking north on the Stuart Highway. His body was found 26 kilometres away. The Stuart Highway claimed another victim when Dane Kowalski's body was found 95 kilometres south of Coober Pedy, South Australia, in 2015. A note near the body said he'd been bitten by a snake. Dane had been intending to drive from Melbourne to Darwin, a trip of more than 3700 kilometres. He was found about 160 kilometres from where Jason Richards' body was found four years earlier.

Andrew Johnson was last seen in 1994; his vehicle was found abandoned in the scrub 100 metres off the Stuart Highway near Elliott, 153 kilometres from Daly Waters. He is still missing. In November 2016, Richard Roe abandoned his vehicle on the Stuart Highway, 25 minutes north of Adelaide River, and disappeared. He is still missing. In 2015 Shaun Jones was last seen walking along the Stuart Highway, 30 kilometres south of Tennant Creek. He has not been seen since.

As much as the media would have you think there are crazed serial killers roaming the outback, and while the case of murdered British backpacker Peter Falconio lends weight to that, all of these missing men have their own unique stories. Around 52,000 people go missing each year in Australia, and there are 52,000 reasons why. Most are found alive within a couple of days. But there are exceptions. Is it possible that some of these missing men, including Jamie, like Jason Richards, suffered a sudden psychosis while driving vast distances alone in the never-ending outback? I'm not a psychologist but many missing persons do suffer from mental illnesses, whether long term or temporary. There is a condition known as brief psychotic disorder; symptoms include delusions, hallucinations, disorganised thinking and disorientation. These are symptoms it appears Jamie exhibited when he told police a gang of men was chasing him, trying to kill him.

I asked Sergeant Nalder if he believes driving those outback roads can play havoc with the mind, and he says, potentially, yes. 'There are long stretches of nothing, and particularly if you're travelling on your own … it's very different from, say, driving round Victoria or NSW. A lot of people seem to end up in the Territory with problems. There was a guy a few years ago who jumped off the bus in the central desert. We searched for him for two days. A few days later he got a ride out of the bush and turned up at a local roadhouse, very dehydrated, sunburnt and barefoot. He believed he was being chased.'

Sergeant Nalder's initial impression of Jamie was that he might have been using marijuana. 'I thought he'd been smoking a bit of gunja along the way and got a bit paranoid. But that was an assumption, I suppose I'm stereotyping. You can have a drug-induced psychosis. Ice in particular can trigger an episode, but also marijuana. I'm not a mental health expert, but I think that just because no-one had seen it in the past, doesn't mean it wasn't there. It may have been his first episode. I personally know people who have had psychotic episodes, and one person in particular was very young, who ran off into the bush, believing he was being chased. Fortunately, he came to his senses and made his way out. That particular person has no history of mental illness whatsoever, but had a lot to do with marijuana.'

In my experience with missing persons who are suffering from a mental illness, if someone is suffering from a psychosis, generally that person's behaviour is going to be noticed immediately by others, something Sergeant Nalder agrees with. 'Generally, you'll draw attention wherever you go, with a mental health issue. It's very difficult to keep a low profile.'

Jamie's dad Steve moved from the UK to Australia with his partner Deb to base himself in Darwin, with the sole purpose of continuing the search for his son. He has never wavered in his determination to find answers. Steve said on *Missing Persons Unit*: 'You don't have a choice, you have to be strong, you have to be focused; my focus is to find my son, and I won't change from that. Hope is the only option you have, being a father of a child that's missing. We will continue to have hope and believe that we're going to find him.'

Like his brother, Carl is a quiet and softly spoken man. He thinks about things logically, and is not prone to speculation and wild theories; he very much focuses on the facts that are known about the case, like receipts that prove Jamie's card was used in a certain place at a certain time, but not assuming it was Jamie who used the card, keeping an open mind. But the loss of his brother has cut deep.

You sort of go through a roller-coaster with the whole thing. We put a lot of faith into the police and what they were doing, but over time you get less and less contact. They move on to other things, and you're left standing there going, 'Okay, so what do we do?' You get back into your own life, then all of a sudden it hits you again, and you're up all night trying to figure things out. We've got a big family and big lot of friends, and they're all really supportive. Everyone still asks if there's anything new and how it's going, which can be quite frustrating as well because you start to feel a bit guilty that you're not doing anything. But what do you do? You don't know what to do. A lot of it's just not knowing what's available, what you can do.

It doesn't feel like more than 15 years. I was just looking at the photos the other day from the trip to London, and it doesn't feel that long ago at all. You have milestones that bring it all back again. I'm married and have two kids, and he's missing out on all that. He was very close to our sister as well. I don't believe he would have just walked away from that. He would have known he had 100 per cent support whatever he did.

Carl believes he's now a different person since Jamie went missing.

It's one of those things that never really goes away. It's always there. I'm lucky I have an understanding wife who helps me go through it all. Early on, I probably didn't explain it to her as well as I should have, but she understands most of it. For quite a few years I didn't really talk about it much; I'm quite a reserved person. I guess now I'm at a different point where nothing's happened for so long that there's nothing left to lose, and you hope now someone has a conscience and will come forward with some sort of information. There's definitely someone out there who knows something.

Despite the mystery and many unanswered questions surrounding Jamie's disappearance, Carl is certain that something sinister has happened to his brother. He doesn't think Jamie had been in any serious trouble before he left New Zealand. 'In Whakatane he was working at a quarry earning decent money, so I don't think he owed anyone a lot of money. Even if he had an addiction, he could have afforded to pay for it. I don't think it was a money thing.'

Nor does he believe Jamie had a serious mental illness. He remains mystified by Jamie's bizarre and seemingly paranoid behaviour on the day he went missing. I asked if he'd seen any signs at all that Jamie could have been suffering from a mental illness causing paranoid delusions, such as schizophrenia. Carl is certain there were no signs of this in Jamie.

The police went along that line to start with, because it was an easy explanation at the time, but before he went missing we'd spent a month together in England, then a month together at my house in Perth, and there were definitely no signs of anything like that. It would have been quite hard for him to hide that from me for two whole months together. All these different stories lead you in all different directions, but what it keeps coming back to is something happened on that night in Daly Waters. He never left Daly Waters, from what I can see.

The van was pretty easy to recognise, it had Aboriginal painting on the back and front and the big lettering across the windscreen. I think someone has harmed him, or he was taking off from somebody and got lost there, that's a possibility. You do consider all possibilities. The police did say that people do go off and start another life all the time, and tried to push that idea, but I don't think they can; even if it wasn't Dad or Kim or myself, he was really close to our grandparents as well. He wouldn't do that to them, as much as he wouldn't do it to us. And I don't think anyone could last 16 years without being curious as to what their family's up to.

I do firmly believe that something happened in Daly Waters, and somebody there knows something. Even if people know people in Broome who know something, people who were visiting. It's strange that you can drive for four days, go to ten different roadhouses and petrol stations and supermarkets, and not one person has CCTV or remembers seeing him. It was never 100 per cent confirmed. A lot of people said, 'Oh, yeah, I think I saw him', but no-one confirmed it. Within a year, everyone who was at Daly Waters at that time had gone, in all different directions. It's strange. A lot of backpackers work around there. But someone knows. It may only take one little comment that would point us in the right direction, or confirm one of our lines of theory.

Carl's measured manner belies the distress he feels about his missing brother. On Carl's 34th birthday I wished him a happy birthday on Facebook, and as I did I was thinking that he'd be well and truly wishing his big brother was around to share a beer with him on days like their birthdays. Carl misses his brother every day.

'I've definitely changed,' says Carl. 'It gives you a different perspective on the world, and how you live, your day-to-day life. After Kim's wedding, when he stayed with me in Perth for a month, it was really nice just to hang out as adults. We'd both grown up a fair bit.'

Carl has created a Facebook group about Jamie's disappearance: https://www.facebook.com/helpfindjamie/ and this gives his friends and family the opportunity to remember Jamie on days like his birthday, and he is remembered with great affection by all. His mate Tommy wrote: 'The best and most humble person I've ever met.'

Please join the page, share the photos; you can help spread the word and maybe it will find the person who knows what happened to Jamie that day. His family have been through enough – they need to know.

If you have information about what happened to Jamie Herdman, please call 1800 333 000.

CHAPTER THREE
Jason Mazurek

Jason Mazurek was last seen just outside the Wrest Point Casino
in Sandy Bay, Hobart, Tasmania in the early hours of Sunday,
15th September, 2002. He was 20 years old.

Jason Mazurek was all about family. That came through so clearly when I was talking to his sisters; his whole world revolved around his family. There were six kids in total in the Mazurek clan, and Jason was the only boy. Jodie is the eldest and Jessica is younger than Jason. Rose was 7 when Jason went missing and Emma was 16. They had an idyllic Aussie childhood. The family grew up in historic Bushy Park, about 58 kilometres from Hobart, the hop capital of Tasmania, a picturesque little town. It was a quiet, rural area and all the kids loved to go fishing and ride bikes.

Jason worked hard as he was growing up, helping out his mum. He was quiet at school and enjoyed the social aspect and the friendships he made there, which lasted into his adulthood. Jess remembers him as being very quiet, but a lovely boy who was very caring. 'I was the tomboy little sister. Growing up in a house full of girls, Jason tended to grow up to be quite comfortable around girls, and more sensitive.'

'He was the only boy out of the six of us, but instead of us mothering him, I think he mothered us,' laughs Jo. 'I was a little-big sister. If I was wearing a skirt he thought was too short, he wouldn't let me leave the house. He was very protective of me, and of all his sisters.' The extent of the sisters' loss is heartbreaking and was evident when I spoke to them. When they talk about him it's in a mixture of past and present tense, evidence of the limbo in which they live all the time.

'I was really close with my brother, we used to go fishing and stuff when we were kids,' says Jess. 'We'd go camping, and I was his little shadow.' She recalls one time she and Jason went to the Styx River to fish. 'One of us got the line caught on a log in the river so he waded out to unhook it. Next thing he turned around and he's got this big fish in his hands! It was this big rainbow trout that had been swimming past and he caught it with his bare hands. He wrapped his arms around it, it was huge! He was screaming at me to get his t-shirt, so I went running down and got it so he could wrap it in the shirt and hang onto it properly.'

Emma fondly remembers the river also, tubing with her brother. 'I was on a little baby tube and Jason was on a big tractor tube; we floated until there was no turning back, and we decided to enter the Derwent, and float to New Norfolk. Completely dangerous, although we were both great swimmers; we knew Mum would kill us if she found out! Jason kept telling me not to tell Mum! We got to a part with rapids and I became scared, so he had to carry me and the two tubes to the shore. We walked barefoot home through dry, waist-high paddocks until we reached the main road into Bushy Park. I'm pretty sure I told Mum after the fact! We were always getting up to the most crazy adventures, like skateboarding down the biggest hill behind our house in Bushy Park. Gosh, we had the best childhood, growing up with your sisters and big brother as best friends!'

Jo remembers a time when she was about six and Jason was five, and they got into big trouble. 'We chopped into an apricot tree with wooden axes that our uncle had carved for us; we had one each ... I can still see Mum chasing us round the back yard trying to catch us to give us a paddle on the bum! We didn't have the axes for long!'

Jason was a happy kid, if very shy. His shyness and reserved nature remained throughout his life. He was one of a kind, says Jo. 'He loved his friends, did everything with them, but when it came to meeting new people he was a bit reserved.'

Jess remembers wanting to protect Jason. 'I stood up for him!' she says with a laugh. 'He hated confrontation, whereas I was straight in there. I stuck up for him all the time. He'd tell me to leave it, that it was okay and I'd say, "No, Jason, it's not okay!"'

Jason had dated a few girls but was single at the time he went missing. 'He wasn't the type of person to pick up a girl and take her home,' says Jess. 'He'd never done that. He's always been in a family full of girls so he's got a bit more respect for females.' Jason had worked at casual jobs since leaving school, as a farmhand and mainly cherry picking. He would mow lawns back in Bushy Park to save up enough money to move to the city. He had decided he wanted to go into the Navy, so in 2002 he was in the process of joining, with best mate Michael also applying with him. Jason had been in a car accident when he was younger that resulted in damage to his front teeth. The navy required Jason to have some dental work; a damaged tooth had just been removed and he was to have a plate and new tooth fitted. His missing person report from police mentions he was missing a top left front tooth, but this was only temporary; he had an appointment the Monday after he went missing to have the tooth replaced. Jason had been through all his navy interviews and was all set to join; he was very excited about it.

He was staying with his sister, Jo, and her former husband, as they were in the city and close to his naval and dental appointments. He travelled back and forth between Jo's place and his mum's home in Bushy Park, almost an hour's drive north of Hobart. Jess says, 'He used to do all the gardening for Mum. We'd just randomly potter around but he'd have these ideas and he'd do these things around the garden, things that he wanted to do. I used to have to follow him out to chop the wood, though, because he was afraid of the dark.' When he stayed at Jo's house he was happy spending time with her and her husband. He didn't go out often, and when he did it was with close friends, sometimes going out rollerblading, but he was mainly just happy to kick back with a few drinks at home, sitting together and chatting.

On Saturday 14 September 2002, Jason was planning to spend his Saturday night at Wrest Point Casino in Hobart, with his sister Jessica and best mate Michael. Jason was staying at Jodie's house for the weekend so he could attend his dental appointment on the Monday. Jason had been to the casino a few times, but not regularly. He never gambled there, just usually had a few drinks. Jason and Michael spent the day watching Jess' hockey grand final, and celebrated when her team won. Jess spent some time with her team while Jason headed back to Jo's. Jess said to him: 'As soon as I'm finished I'll give you a call and meet you at the casino.'

Jo remembers that night well. 'He came home and said, "Jo, I feel like going out." I said, "Okay, but leave your bloody phone behind!" Every time he went out, he'd lose his phone, and he'd only just bought that one. So, that night I told him to leave his phone at home. He was in a really happy mood that day; he'd pop in and out the door saying, "Love you!" He'd open and shut the door, open and shut, and every time he'd open the door I'd tell him to piss off,' Jo says with a laugh. 'When he left he said,

"See ya! I won't thump the door when I come in!" That's the last time I saw him.'

After her hockey win celebrations Jess headed to the casino, where she found Jason and Michael upstairs in Regine's nightclub, and they had a few drinks together. Jason was in a very positive frame of mind that night, and Jess told me a beautiful story that captures Jason's character perfectly. Jason was on the dance floor and saw a girl in a wheelchair, off to the side. 'He didn't want anyone to miss out on anything, so he went over and asked the girl, who was sitting in the corner in her wheelchair, if she'd like to dance. That's the kind of person that he was. He's lovely,' says Jess proudly.

After the hockey game and celebrations lasting much of the day, Jess wasn't really up to partying all night. At around 2 am they decided to call it a night. 'It was a bit boring actually, so we decided to head home,' says Jess. 'I met up with Jason down in the foyer of the casino. Michael wasn't with him. I asked Jason if he wanted to get a taxi home and he said, "Yeah, no problem". I asked him how much money he had on him, and I worked out how much money I had on me, and then I went to find Michael. We had plenty of money for a taxi home, we were just trying to work out how to split it. I asked Jason if he had a coat-ticket number, he said no. I asked him where Michael was and he said he wasn't sure. I was pretty sure I'd last seen Michael upstairs in Regines, so I said to Jason, 'You wait here and I'll go and grab Michael from upstairs and we'll head off.' So, I went upstairs, grabbed Michael – it was probably less than 10 minutes – then I came back down, and he was gone.' Jess never saw her brother again. It was 2 am, Sunday 15 September 2002.

When Jess and Michael got back to the foyer there was no sign of Jason. Figuring he may have been in the toilet, or elsewhere near the entrance, they waited for him. As the minutes ticked by, they became puzzled when he didn't appear. They started to look for him in the casino. 'We waited around, we looked everywhere, Michael and I,' says Jess. 'We were there for a couple of hours, but he didn't show. We thought, right – we're all pretty self-sufficient and able to walk home, and he's used to taking the bike track along the side of the city, so we just thought maybe he'd walked. But Jess did start to worry when she couldn't find him at the casino. 'He had no reason to go,' she said. When they couldn't find him, after spending hours searching inside and out, they caught a taxi back to Jo's house to see if Jason was there. They asked the taxi driver to take a particular route that they felt Jason would have taken had he decided to walk home. There was no sign of him.

Jess and Michael arrived back at Jo's house and told her that Jason had disappeared. 'Jess said to me that Jason should've been home by now, but that they couldn't find him,' says Jo. She's positive Jason would never have left his sister on her own at the casino. He was very protective of Jess and she's sure he would have also not left best mate Michael there without a word. Michael was also staying at Jo's home, so Jason would definitely have intended to go back there with him. They've considered all possible scenarios of what may have happened to him that night and none seem plausible. They're sure he would not have caught a taxi and left them behind, and if he'd started to walk home to Jo's, they or someone else would have seen him. The distance back to Jo's house from the Casino was around 10 kilometres and it would have taken a bit over two hours to walk. 'We all waited and waited and it just wasn't like Jason at all. He would always make his way home. When he didn't come home, we started to call the hospitals,' says Jess.

'We rang the police straightaway, but they told us we had to wait. We just had to wait,' says Jo. 'They told us, "Oh, boys do that"; they weren't very helpful at that stage,' says Jess. 'They told Mum he'd probably gone home with a girl. We said he just wouldn't have done that.

'We waited until the nominated time the police had said we could finally report him missing and called them back; we said he was still not home and still no word,' says Jo.

Jess and Jo knew immediately something serious must have happened to Jason. 'I knew something was wrong the minute he didn't come home,' says Jo. 'He always rang. Always. He'd say, "I'm not coming home, I'm staying at Michael's."' But Michael was at his sister's home – Jason had nowhere else to stay in the city. Jason didn't have his phone on him, as Jo had told him to leave it behind that night, but she is adamant he would have found a way to call her and let her know what was happening. 'He would have found a phone and rung me. He had every intention of coming home.'

Jason's bank accounts were untouched from that night onwards, which also made Jo certain something terrible had befallen him. 'He had no money; he was waiting for his study money to come through, and that's still sitting in his bank account today. I had a gut feeling something was wrong, so did my sister. The police said to us at the start, well, boys go missing all the time. There was a boat in dock at the time nearby, a navy boat, and they said that the sailors off the boats on shore leave go missing all the time. I told them, he wasn't on a fricken naval boat, so stop using that as an excuse and get out and start looking for him! They just didn't take it seriously.

'In fact, I don't think they ever have. They were asking us if Jason was mixed up with drugs, mixed up with bikies – he was so shy he wouldn't even help a lady with her groceries, so there's no way in hell he was mixed up with a bikie gang!' Jo says scornfully. 'I KNOW my brother. I kept telling them over and over, NO, he wouldn't have done that, just gone off. He wasn't trying to get away from anybody. It gets frustrating after a while. I know they have to ask these questions, but surely they can have a bit of compassion and start listening to *us* and what *we* say?'

'It was probably about a week after he went missing that the police started taking it seriously,' says Jess. Wrest Point Casino is situated right on the waterfront at Sandy Bay, on the River Derwent so police sent divers into the water around the immediate casino area, and also conducted land searches, but nothing at all was located. They checked CCTV from the shops along Sandy Bay Road but there was no sign of Jason. The weather was wild that weekend, which made the search more difficult. The family were angry and frustrated, feeling police were not doing enough to find Jason.

'They weren't doing what they do over on the mainland. They look for other missing people – why not my brother? A few months after Jason went missing a little girl went missing in the same area. They went out immediately, doorknocking and searching all night, it was all over the news, they took it seriously from day dot. We had to push for everything to be done about Jason and to me that showed [that they didn't care]…we were just so angry,' says Jo, clearly upset.

My sister and I printed up flyers and we walked around town, we handed them out, we put them on cars. We tried to find him on the internet, Googling, ringing the police – not that they would ever return our calls – we were just focused on trying to find him.

Jo says it was mainly she and Jess who led the search for Jason, as her other sisters were very young, and her mother also had the younger girls to look after. Jess says, 'Mum and I did a walk from the casino all the way into the city on the route we thought he would have taken if he had been going to walk home, handing out flyers and putting them in letterboxes all the way, hoping someone saw something that night. Nobody ever did.'

The family were disappointed in what they saw as a delayed response from the casino, considering the urgency and serious nature of the situation. 'It took three weeks to get the video footage from inside the casino,' says Jo. 'It's all digital and they should have had it within 24 hours.'

Jess says: 'TWICE the police were given the wrong tapes! About a week after Jason went missing they gave them the first tape from the foyer but it was the wrong tape, then a second time they gave them the wrong tapes; the third time they finally got the right tapes to them.' The casino was only able to provide police with footage from the foyer area of the building. There were no security cameras outside the casino at the time of Jason's disappearance. 'After Jason went missing the casino put up security cameras outside, everywhere, with signs saying "For your safety",' says Jo.

The CCTV footage shows Jess telling Jason to wait in the foyer, and after she leaves to look for Michael there's nothing remarkable on the footage until Jason leaves. Jo thinks it's possible Jason went to check his bank balance at the ATM, and that could be why he left the foyer, but intending to return there to wait for Jess and Michael. 'The ATM was inside the venue around from the Birdcage Bar, on the surveillance footage you can see him walking in that direction before coming back towards the main entrance followed by the security guard, and then walking out the front door never to be seen again,' says Jo.

Casino management said in explanation of the footage that the guard was not, in fact, ushering Jason out, but they merely happened to be walking out at the same time. Jo, who has seen the footage, does not believe this to be the case. Jess also feels the guard would have been escorting Jason out of the building. 'I've seen the tape myself, and he was ushered out the door,' she says firmly. 'The guard approached him and Jason would have probably said, "I'm just waiting here for my sister and friend to come down and then we're going". Because he had a goatee and wasn't really a suit-and-tie–type person, Jason felt they gave him a bit of a hard time each time he came in. He looked rough, but he wasn't. He had a missing front tooth and that probably wouldn't have helped. I mean, everybody has their own opinions of people at face value, but it wasn't right. The casino doesn't shut until 4 am so there was no other reason for the security guard to be walking him out the front door at that time. It was only 2 am, they weren't closing.'

Jason had been drinking that night, but was not drunk. He was not the type of guy to drink to excess, and Jo can tell by the way he's walking on the CCTV footage that he was not drunk. She said: 'He was walking a straight line, no swaying, no missed steps.' Jo is sure that the casino staff would not have had cause to eject him from the premises for any type of unruly behaviour or drunkenness – that was just not Jason. Jo says Jason really only went to the casino that night to dance, not to drink. He'd had a few drinks throughout the day at the hockey but when he came home, before leaving for the casino, Jo could see he definitely wasn't drunk. Given Jason's meek and reserved nature it's very unlikely he would have been the instigator of any violence; he would have simply done as he was told and followed the security guard's directions to leave the foyer. What happened after he left remains a mystery.

'Apparently no-one saw him walking away from the casino,' says Jess, 'and he had no reason to leave. I just don't know what happened outside. The police have always felt it was foul play, but they don't have anything to go on.' Jo thinks it's possible Jason saw something in the carpark of the casino that he shouldn't have seen. She recalls being told, possibly by police, that there had been a stabbing in the casino carpark on the same night, and wonders if it was connected in some way to Jason's disappearance.

We found out about the stabbing later. I don't know whether he's seen something, maybe on his walk home. Maybe someone tried to steal his wallet and then something's happened to him. Someone knows something. Someone would have seen him that night. I mean, it's Tasmania! Everybody knows everybody! Somebody knows something.

It was a busy Saturday night at a popular casino, yet not a single person has ever come forward with any information about what happened to Jason that night.

Jo is still angry about the initial police response when Jason went missing. 'I know it was hard for them; they didn't know him, but we do. That really upset my family, when they kept saying that it was usual for boys to just go off. We knew he wouldn't. I was just about to get married at that time, and there was no way in *hell* he would not have been at my wedding.' Jo's wedding was a particularly emotional day for her. Jason went missing in September and Jo's wedding was the following February. She admits she did think about calling it off, as Jason was not there to share it with her and also her former husband, who had been close friends with Jason. He was meant to be their best man.

To make the day even harder for Jo, on her wedding day, before the ceremony, she went to the casino to place a wreath of flowers at the spot Jason was last seen. Her mother had given her a card that she had written on behalf of Jason, a memory that brings Jo to tears. After laying her wreath, casino staff approached Jo and advised her she would have to take the wreath with her when she left; they would not allow her to leave it on casino property. 'I jumped up and down. I said to them, "You leave that where it is. Don't you touch it. I don't care what you do with it after I'm gone, but whilst I'm here you will leave it. I am leaving it here." There's still a lot of anger there, in me.'

Jo feels like the original police who worked on the case gave up on Jason a long time ago. 'It was the 10-year anniversary of Jason going missing in September 2012, and we heard nothing from the police. There was a body found a few years ago in

Claremont, but we didn't hear from them then either. We were really stressing then, thinking it might be Jason, but they didn't contact us, so we contacted them and they said, "No, no, no, it's not him". But we were like, thanks very much for the heads-up. I hear nothing from the police. I haven't heard from them for many years. I just feel the police in Tasmania didn't know how to handle it properly. There was no-one senior enough to deal with a missing person. They weren't trained enough; we don't have enough missing persons that are murders for them to have the experience.'

Jo feels other cases have been dealt with as a higher priority than Jason, and this is very upsetting to the family. She would have liked experienced Homicide officers from the mainland to have travelled to Tasmania to review Jason's case. Police asked the family, after seven years, if they wanted a Coroner's inquest into Jason's disappearance. Their mother decided to say no, as she felt that would mean Jason's file would be closed forever. 'She felt it would have meant that no-one was looking for him anymore,' says Jo.

Like many families who have a missing person, Jo has been to psychics, and several of them have told her a similar story – that Jason is no longer alive. 'Something happened to Jason; he was in the wrong place at the wrong time. They think he was hit on the head and died as a result of that. They seem to think he's then been dumped somewhere. One said in the water, one said near Pittwater area. My guess is water. I just have to find a body and find who's responsible.'

Jo felt that when the psychics told her what they felt had happened to Jason, it helped her somehow.

'I was on the radio recently and this lady didn't know me from a bar of soap, but she told me things.' Jodie's radio reading was with psychic Charmaine Wilson, and although she did not get all the details regarding Jason correct she did pick up that his name was Jason, that he died in the ninth month and Jo's partner's name; and she told Jodie she felt Jason had 'passed quickly'.

Jess also had a friend who had a psychic reading and Jason was mentioned. 'She said, "Your friend has a missing person", and she told my friend that Jason isn't in Tassie anymore, he's in Darwin. But I can't hold those kinds of things as true. I mean, this lady did know that my friend had a friend with a missing brother, but I still can't go off on that. There is that possibility that he could be out there somewhere. You never know. But in my heart, I don't think that's true. When people [psychics] come up to you and start talking about those kinds of things, it does get you thinking about the whole thing again, it makes you go through it all again in your head.'

The lives of all the Mazurek sisters changed forever that night. They have no answers, and as Jo says, it would have been easier had Jason been killed in a car accident, because they would have had closure.

We would have had something [like a grave] to go and visit, not be stuck in limbo. We have a memorial for him every year, we get upset over his birthday, but it's different … we, as a family, know he's not coming home, but it's just not having the closure. We don't know what happened to him. We have no clue. Who hurt him, why did they hurt him, where is he? It plays on your mind. It was so hard for us, as a family. We've

*always been a really close family, still are, but Jason going
missing pretty much killed us.*

Jo's first marriage started to deteriorate after Jason went missing,
and a serious illness put extra pressure on her life. She's certain
Jason's disappearance contributed to her marriage breakdown,
being the trigger for many arguments. 'He was just as upset as I
was about Jason, and we were young and just didn't know what
to do, how to react. There were many factors, but I know Jason's
disappearance had an effect on our marriage. Jason wouldn't
have left his friends without a word, and especially not my ex-
husband, as they were so close, like brothers.'

Jo now has a new partner who has been a tower of strength
to her. He didn't know Jason, but knows how upset it makes
her when she thinks about what happened, and he tries to
protect her. He's helped her come to terms with living with
Jason's loss, as it was starting to affect her entire life, including
Jo's overprotectiveness of her children. 'I wouldn't let them out
of the yard, I wouldn't let them walk to school – and it's only a
few hundred metres down the road. I still really worry about the
kids. It's those sort of things that travel with you for the rest of
your life.'

Her new partner has encouraged her to let go of the fears that
built up after what happened to Jason, and to let her children
have a little more freedom. He's helped her get to a point where
she can cope much better. 'He shook me up a little bit, saying,
"Come on, you've got to live your life," whereas I wasn't, really,
before. My headspace wasn't right. My whole world was trying
to find Jason and I put my life on hold for about two or three
years. It got to the stage where six years ago, Steve said, "Nup,

come on, you've got to snap out of it. Your brother's gone, and he's not coming back. You're still here – keep going." It was the harsh words that he said that I needed to snap me out of it. I thought, yeah, he's right, I've got my kids, I've got to focus on *my* family now.'

Jason was especially close to Jo's daughter, who still gets very upset at the subject of her missing beloved uncle. She was four when Jason went missing, and it has affected her deeply. 'I know he didn't leave of his own accord, because he wouldn't have left my daughter,' says Jo. 'Those two were just two peas in a pod. I remember one time, he wanted to buy her a present. I told him she wasn't allowed to have a pair of boots, she'd only just turned four. Jason said, "Okay, then, I'll take her shopping and I'll buy her a birthday present." So, he comes back with a pair of bloody boots for her! She thought he was the bee's knees!' Jo laughs at this wonderful memory. 'That's just the kind of person he was. He adored her.'

It's been especially difficult for Jo as she still lives in Hobart and sometimes passes the casino. 'For a long time, I just could not go near the place. Then Mum and I started visiting the casino, frequently, to try to find out any information we could.'

Jessica does not currently live in Tasmania due to her work commitments, so finds it hard to continue to physically search the area for Jason.

We all do our own little searches here and there, when we can.
We make an effort to go to the casino when we're there.

Jo breaks down when she tells me she's been unable to bring herself to sell her house, because it's the last place she saw Jason.

She can't let it go. 'It's a stupid way of thinking. But I kept thinking maybe he'd come home one day and walk through the door. I don't like the house, but I had to keep it. Maybe this was the only place he could remember and know, if he lost his memory or something. Stupid things you think of.' She tried to put it on the market, but changed her mind, and still lives there today.

After Jason's disappearance, Michael and Jess shared a flat for a while before Jess joined the army. Jess and Jason had once shared a flat together, and had planned to also share with Michael once the boys had joined the navy. But Jason's best friend, Michael, who had been with him the night he disappeared and who had planned to join the navy with him, withdrew his application. He could not face going through with it without his mate by his side.

Jason's mum coped by keeping much to herself. As Jo says, 'She was a bit lost. She didn't know what to do. It was her son – I mean, he was our brother, but he was her *son*. We need to know what happened, not only for our sake, but for Mum.' All Jason's belongings were still at his mum's house and when she moved she kept some of them; that was also her way of coping. Some of Jason's clothes were passed down to Jo's son, and that was a way of keeping his memory alive within the family. Jo's son was born after Jason went missing and Jo remembers when she found out she was having a boy she was upset – after Jason, she didn't want any more boys in her life. Her son has grown up to look very much like his uncle, which is bittersweet for Jo. 'He's the spit out of Jason's mouth. He's scared of the dark like Jason was, he's soft; you tell him he can have a lolly and he'll get three, one for each of his sisters too; he's exactly the same as my brother. That's why I think Mum dotes on him, because he's so much like Jason, even to look at. I've got a daily reminder of him, living with me.'

One of the areas I wanted to explore when writing this book was whether the siblings took more of a role in dealing with the many issues that arise when a family member goes missing or whether it remained the parents' job. In Jason's case it seems to have been very much a family affair.

'Mum had little kids at home at the time, so it was really hard for her to deal with that and with Jason being missing as well,' says Jess.

With Rose and Emma still being so young, Jess and Jo found themselves being the ones in the family who spoke to the media most often. 'I felt like I needed to step up,' says Jess. 'I needed to be stronger for everybody else. I didn't deal with it. Everybody around me was crying but I wasn't, I just couldn't deal with it at the time. I didn't know what emotions I should be feeling. The only thing I could do was step up and try to do something about it.'

Most of the phone calls in the early days of the investigation came to Jo's house, but Jess would answer the phone. She felt that she was the one who could talk to people about it without breaking down. Jo says that being the eldest child in the family, the role of dealing with police and the authorities naturally fell to her much of the time, and she tried to ease the burden on her distraught mother. Like Jason, she wanted to protect her mum as much as possible. 'I'm the mouthy one of the family,' says Jo with a chuckle. 'I do try to get things done. I'll jump up and down a hell of a lot to get my way sometimes; other times the quiet approach is probably better – but that's not me. I'm just so sick of talking to the police, and they put new people on and I have to answer the same questions over and over again. The answer's never going to change.'

Jess says, 'It went through so many people in the police – just kind of handballed to each other. We dealt with so many different people in a short amount of time. It was confusing, especially initially when they weren't taking us seriously. We wanted things to happen but they weren't happening.'

Jo tries to keep Jason's name out there. I have a page for him on my website and I post his profile regularly on my Facebook page. She says there are a lot of Jason's friends still out there supporting the family and hoping for answers. When I spoke to the sisters in 2013, Jo said she felt the relationships between the remaining siblings – all girls – were not as close as they were before Jason went missing, but Jess disagrees and feels they have been brought closer. The sisters didn't always agree with the way each other handled things with police, and they sometimes argued.

Jess and Jo have always talked over issues to do with Jason's case, but Jess' army career meant she could not be around as much as her sister. 'Jodie and I speak about Jason,' says Jess. 'We're all trying to deal with it, and sometimes it's really hard to bring it up.'

Emma feels her brother's loss keenly: 'I remember Jason watching a new release movie, and not letting me in his room, because he would say I would ask too many questions. We used to play the PlayStation together all the time, Tony Hawk was a favourite! He'd yell out to me, so proud, when the game would glitch and your trick would get caught, and your score would fly high into the millions; we'd always laugh because you could never land it and get out of it.'

The sisters are all conscious of protecting their mum when the dates special to Jason come around each year; Jo takes her mum out to lunch on the anniversary of Jason's disappearance, to help take her mind off it. Jess always calls her mum to make sure she's okay, before and also afterwards. 'I end every phone call to Mum with "I love you". So do Jodie and Emma. I think that's just brought it to reality; you never know "when",' says Jess.

On the anniversary of Jason's disappearance each year Jo goes to the casino on her own and sits for a while, thinking about her brother's last evening. 'I go over the "what-ifs". What if I hadn't taken his phone off him? What if I hadn't let him go out that night? If he'd had his mobile on him – what if? Could we have tracked his mobile? Stupid things like that, but they've played over in my mind for years.'

Survivor guilt is a theme that plays out in almost every missing person case I deal with, including Jason's. Survivor guilt is a recognised condition experienced in cases where one person survives an event that another person does not. It's common for those returning from war, and it's common in missing person cases. The families left behind almost always feel they should have been able to stop it from happening.

Jo felt guilty about not being able to protect her brother from whatever happened to him that night.

I did feel guilty, for a very, very long time. I bet Jessica feels the same; I bet she feels guilty for not being able to do more that night. It's a natural thing to feel, and it's taken us a long time to get back to the stage where we're not blaming ourselves anymore.

Jess agrees. 'You don't get past it. It's always there, you've got no closure. Every couple of days I think about Jason. It's a constant thing. I do feel a little bit guilty about that night, but that's self-guilt stuff. I know there's probably nothing I could have done. I mean, he was in the foyer and I was upstairs but still...' You can hear the pain in her voice. I remind her that if she'd been with Jason and had gone outside with him they might both be missing today. She says: 'Sometimes I feel like I should have been there, like I was needed. How could you lose someone that's right in front of you?'

'We used to be a very trusting family but now we're always second-guessing people, which is not right but that's how we've become,' says Jo.

Jess has found it very difficult to trust people since Jason disappeared. 'I give people a wide berth. I sit back and watch for a while and I don't tend to let too many people into my life. I do have mates, but as far as relationships go, you don't want to lose somebody, you don't want to go through that hurt again, so you tend to stay away from it and not let anybody in. The things people take for granted like Christmas and holidays and Easter – they don't feel the same to me now. When I'm on holidays and not working, that's when my mind will go over it again and again and again. Just trying to think of anything I saw that I might have missed,' says Jess. 'There's probably somebody out there who knows what's gone on but it's just really frustrating that you can't access that. It's like it's right there, but you can't see it. Like it's sitting in a black box somewhere.'

Being the spokesperson for the family, Jo reflects that she didn't take much time to grieve for Jason. She was too busy trying to push police into investigating his disappearance as well as looking after her young family.

Sometimes as a family we don't like to talk about it because all this stuff is going through our heads about what could have happened to him. It upsets us because we didn't want him to suffer. We just want to be told, you know, he died...

Jo breaks down in tears. I know what she's trying to say is she needs to know Jason died without any pain. She can't bear to think of any alternative.

Jess thinks the people who know what happened to Jason – and she's sure they're out there – would have lived with the guilt for years and hopes they can unburden themselves by coming forward and clearing their conscience and give her family some peace. 'At the moment we're visiting photos. We don't have a grave we can go to. I'm sure somebody saw something. The smallest thing always helps, the tiny things that people just don't think are important at the time.'

I asked Jo a hard question – does she think they'll ever find Jason. She thinks about it for a while. 'My gut says no. But my head says there might be a chance of finding who did it. I don't think we'll ever find a body. I don't know where to go from here. I'm at wit's end.' But Jo has a determined strength to her and she says, 'I won't stop, though; I won't ever stop until I find out something, find out who did it. Whoever did it, I feel so sorry for – because there are a lot of angry people.'

In 2019 Tasmania Police released an appeal for National Missing Persons Week that included Jason. The sisters say the information in that appeal is not entirely accurate. The appeal says: *Before he went missing, Jason had moved from Bushy Park to Glenorchy and was unfamiliar with Hobart and suburbs.*

This same information appears on Jason's profile on the Australian Federal Police missing persons website. However, Jason had not moved at all; he was only visiting Hobart, he still lived in Bushy Park with his mum. He did know the area he was in well, having visited his sister many times, he went to high school in Claremont in Hobart, and he had been to the casino on several previous occasions.

The appeal also says: *Jason's last known movements as he walked out of the casino were captured on CCTV footage, as shown in blue on the map provided.*

The map shows a blue trail from the entrance of the casino, walking out to the left of the circular road, north along Drysdale Ave, past a service station, then where the road curves around to the left, the blue trail makes a right, which leads directly over to the water's edge of Sandy Bay. It's a completely open area, no fences, just grass and a walking path in front of the water and a few large rocks on the shoreline making a small breakwater. Yachts are neatly moored behind, not far away.

This CCTV footage, which was not from the casino but from the nearby service station, was shown to Jason's sisters. Neither of them felt the person in the footage was Jason, and it was too small and blurry for anyone to make a positive identification. Besides this, why would Jason leave his sister and mate and walk far away from the casino, almost 300 metres, towards the water's edge? The sisters told police they didn't think the person was Jason, and police would not have been able to tell if it was or was not Jason from the grainy footage, so it seems strange that in 2019 they worded this appeal to state that the person in the footage walking from the casino to the water was Jason.

In 2022 I contacted Tasmania Police and sent them this chapter on Jason, asking them to please let me know if there were any inaccuracies. This is their reply:

The below information, sourced from the missing person file, provides a summary of the police response and investigation:

- Tasmania Police commenced investigations regarding Jason's disappearance on the same day he was reported missing (15/09/2002)
- Tasmania Police made enquiries with Wrest Point Casino re CCTV footage on 15/09/2002
- Wrest Point Casino initially provided Tasmania Police incorrect CCTV footage, but correct CCTV footage was provided by 19/09/2002
- The Wrest Point CCTV footage captured Jason at the foyer, taxi rank and staff car-park
- Tasmania Police was obliged to report Jason's disappearance to the Coroner per the Tasmanian *Coroners Act 1995*
- In 2008, the Coroner delivered his findings regarding Jason's disappearance and commented 'I am satisfied

that a full and detailed investigation has been carried out regarding the disappearance and subsequent suspected death of Mr Mazurek'

- The Missing Person Report, and a file note, states that the family believed Jason was unfamiliar with the area

May I add that missing person cases, including Jason's, are not closed until they are located. This includes situations in which the missing person's disappearance is reported to the Coroner (as is the case with Jason).

Any further information received by Tasmania Police regarding Jason's disappearance will be assessed for investigation.

There seems to be contradictory information about the CCTV footage. In 2019, the police released the map showing Jason's trail extending far along Drysdale Ave and out towards the water. Yet in 2022, in their email to me, they say the CCTV footage only shows him at the foyer, taxi rank and staff carpark; in other words, immediately surrounding the casino entrance. The taxi rank is right next to the island that forms the circular driveway in front of the casino building. Jess has only seen the CCTV footage from inside the lobby and was under the impression that the casino did not have any cameras outside. It is unclear how the cameras captured Jason outside the building.

Jess and Jo also both disagree with some of these statements by police. 'It annoys me that this information in their files is incorrect,' says Jess. 'They didn't start looking for him until a week later. They told Mum he probably just went home with a female. It took a week of us contacting them before they actually started doing anything. It was a mess from the start by police. It took three weeks to get the correct CCTV tapes, and Jason was very familiar with the area. My phone number has never changed, but they didn't have it on file – I had to give it to them again just last year.'

Jodie is equally frustrated by what she believes to be inaccuracies in the files. On reading the police response she said, 'I've got lots to say about that, and none of it good.' Jessica called her mother and read her the police response, and Eva Mazurek agreed that, in her opinion, the police files are incorrect. She said the family have all tried to correct this with police for a number of years, without success. 'It still keeps astounding us that they have it all incorrect. I have no idea who made these records … were they made up? It just doesn't make sense to us. Mum said every time she asked about it the police would tell her nothing and just pass her on to the next person.'

The information in the email about the Coroner's finding was confusing to Jason's family. They were not invited to attend the inquiry, nor had they been given any copies of the Coroner's report. It was only when I asked them if they'd read it did they all realise none of the family knew anything about it. I advised them how to request a copy from the Coroner's Office. Eva says she was told Jason would have a 'closed inquest'. It is not a term I'm familiar with – the very reason for an inquest is for there to be a public inquiry into an unexpected or unnatural death, or disappearance that is a suspected death. They are usually not 'closed', and certainly not to the families of the subject of the inquest. They can be valuable in uncovering more information from the public about a possible crime.

After I advised the family how to contact the Tasmanian Coroner, they discovered the office did not have Eva's correct address, email address or phone number. A couple of days later Eva received a copy of the Coroner's finding into Jason's death. No-one in the family had seen the document before. I emailed the Coroner's officer to ask what a 'closed inquest' was and they responded that no inquest had been held at all for Jason, and that the Coroner had conducted an in-chambers finding. The family, again, had no idea that this was the case. When they received the copy of the finding, 14 years after the case went to the Coroner, they learned the Coroner, Christopher P Webster, had directed the finding *not* be published on the Tasmanian Magistrates Court (Coronial Division) website. The family have no idea why this would be.

The finding is sparse, to say the least, just a one-page summary of the basic events of Jason's disappearance. There is no mention of the CCTV footage. There is no mention of the security guard who walked out of the building with Jason. The Coroner details Jason and Michael's bus trip from Jo's house into Hobart, with them attending some other nightspots before arriving at Wrest Point Casino at 11.40 pm. The report goes on to say: 'Mr Mazurek was on the dance floor dancing with a female when [Michael] went to the bar to get a drink and was only gone for a few minutes. When [Michael] went back to the dance floor both Mr Mazurek and the female were gone.'

Until today, 20 years after her brother disappeared, Jess had never before heard those facts, and knew nothing about a girl dancing with Jason. Did police identify her? Was she ever spoken to? I spoke with Michael recently after reading the report, and he said: 'He was dancing with a girl, but I can't remember what she looked like. I was never questioned by the police or asked about the girl.' Once again, it's a potential lead that was not followed up, and who's to know if it might have been vitally important?

If the girl Jason was dancing with that night is reading this now, please come forward. You might hold that piece of the puzzle.

The Coroner stated that Michael looked for Jason but could not find him, then met up with Jess at 1.45 am. Jess told Michael that Jason was downstairs. The report says Jess 'asked him to get him', as in, Jess asked Michael to go downstairs and get Jason. This account differs from what Jess recalls, who said she told Jason she was going upstairs to find Michael in the nightclub, which she did, in order to bring him downstairs so the three of them could go home together.

The report concludes with Coroner Christopher P Webster saying: 'Based on the available evidence I am unable to state with certainty the cause or location Mr Mazurek's death; however, drowning in the Derwent River as a cause of death cannot be excluded.' He also stated: 'The evidence before me does not allow me to find that any other person was involved in Mr Mazurek's death.'

However, despite their clear frustrations with the initial police response to Jason's disappearance, all the sisters agree that police efforts have greatly improved in recent years. In 2021 the National Missing Persons Coordination Centre released an age-progressed image of what Jason may look like today, and a video. Jess says the police who are currently handling Jason's case are doing a much better job than their predecessors: 'There is a really good Missing Person team in Hobart now, who are going over old cases like Jason's and fixing things.' It gives the family a little hope, and it's certainly good to see Jason still being included in appeals and age progression images.

Jess, Jo and their other family members have all continued to work with police to make sure Jason's case is still being investigated, and it's encouraging that police have stated that his case will never be closed until he is found.

It was almost Christmas 2013 when I first interviewed Jodie and Jessica, and during that Christmas break Jess was astonished when she was swimming in the ocean and a fish with a hook already in its mouth swam past her three separate times. On the third time, she caught it with her bare hands – just like Jason caught the fish in her favourite memory of him. She then told me how she'd found an old VHS video tape her grandfather had made, who passed away in 2007. None of the family had any idea what was on the tape which was labelled 'Mazurek Family'. Jess sneakily took the tape from her mum's house, intending to have it converted to DVD to give to her mum and sisters for Christmas.

When it was ready she took it home to watch. 'I knew that if Jason was on it then that's probably the only video footage we have of him. It turned out that it was footage my grandad had taken from between 1989 and 1992 or just after. It shows us at the national park in Tasmania, then Jason's eighth birthday ... amazing. Then it goes into a Christmas. Then a trip at the beach. It's wonderful ... but I had to tell my sisters that they need to watch it with Mum, because I didn't want her to be alone, because I know it will make all of them tear up. I was able to put a copy of it on my phone too so I can watch it anytime. It just reminds me of our childhood... And I was pretty much joined at Jason's hip the whole way through the video footage,' she says with a big smile. 'I just want people to know what a lovely person he was,' says Jess. 'He wouldn't hurt a fly. He was a fantastic brother. One of the best.'

On the night he went missing Jason Mazurek was wearing stonewash blue jeans, a white short-sleeved button-up shirt and sandy-coloured Colorado shoes. Jason was 175 centimetres tall, with dark brown hair, brown eyes and an olive complexion. He was 20 years old.

As I put the finishing touches on this chapter, in September 2022, a few days ago was the 20th anniversary of Jason's disappearance. We are no closer now to finding him than 20 years ago.

If you have any information about the disappearance of Jason Mazurek, please call Crime Stoppers on 1800 333 000. You can remain anonymous if you wish.

CHAPTER FOUR
Lisa Govan

Lisa Govan was last seen at the Club Deroes bikie clubhouse on Boulder Road in Kalgoorlie, WA, early morning on Friday, October 8th 1999. She was 28 years old.

Every missing person needs a voice. I started off knowing very little about Lisa until I spoke to her lovely family. I read what was in the media about her case, and the information police released at the time of her disappearance. What I learned made me angry and sad that her life was cut short. I wanted to be Lisa's voice.

This is Lisa's story. The butterfly.

As well as Lisa's sisters, I spoke to her mother Pat while I was writing this book. Sisters Ginette and Sharon speak with a delightful lilting Lancashire accent, evidence of the family's early years in the UK. Mum Pat's accent is even more charming – she speaks with almost a sing-song quality to her voice – and when I spoke to them it was hard to remember the tragedy these amazing women have gone through. Pat is a delightful lady, more than happy to talk about her beautiful daughter. However, I get the sense she keeps a lot of her pain inside. Pat says husband Ian is the strong one, but this family of mostly women are extraordinary in their combined strength against some of the most fearsome criminals in the country.

There were four sisters in the family: Sharon is the eldest, then Lisa, then Jacqueline, and Ginette is the youngest. There are seven years between Ginette and Lisa, so her memories are those of looking up to a big sister who she admired tremendously. 'We had a very happy childhood, growing up in England. We'd all go and play with all the kids in our street; our sisters all played together, we all got on really well. I used to tag along after Lisa and the older kids, and she didn't mind that, not that she had much choice!' Ginette chuckles.

Sharon says that as Lisa was her next youngest sister they tended to play together more than with her other sisters. The girls' mother Pat went back to work for a year when Ginette was about three and relied on her daughters to look out for each other. As the eldest, Sharon took on most of the responsibility. 'It was not long ago that I was talking about this with Mum. I said, "God, you worked me hard!"' she says with a laugh. 'They used to get me up in the morning and go off to work, then I'd get myself ready [for high school], then I'd get the three of them up, get the two ready for primary school, get their breakfasts and do their hair, make sure their teeth were brushed. I'd put Ginette in the stroller then I'd walk Lisa and Jacqueline to school, drop them off, then I'd walk Ginette to daycare, put her in there, then I'd walk round to my school. Then in the evening I'd reverse the route, pick them all up then get home and start dinner!' Pat cut back her work hours to part time and was able to spend more time with all her girls.

Lisa had a very rare blood disorder called Abetalipoproteinemia, or Bassen-Kornzweig syndrome. It's so rare that at the time Lisa was diagnosed there were only around 20 people with the condition, and there are currently only 100 cases worldwide. The illness means the body is unable to absorb nutrients from food and as a result Lisa had to take massive doses of vitamins in order to keep her body healthy and functioning, as it affected her nervous system. She was also unable to eat anything containing fat or it made her violently ill. 'She didn't grow and develop as a baby,' says Pat. 'When she was nine months old she wasn't much heavier than when she was born. She couldn't sit up, as she didn't have the strength.'

She was treated at Great Ormond Street Hospital in London, spending quite a lot of time there. She had to take a large quantity of medication all her life to keep the condition under control, and Ginette recalled she hated taking it. She would often spend a week at a time as a child being tested and treated. Without the medication, Lisa's eyes would have rapidly deteriorated, and on her trips to London she would also have to see an eye specialist. Older sister Sharon remembers she had an overwhelming feeling of wanting to protect Lisa when she was a child. She thinks Lisa saw her as more of a mum than a sister, as she looked after her when her parents were working, and helped Lisa with her medications. Sharon says it was an unusual role that continued as Lisa grew older and became more able to manage her own condition; they never really became like sisters. 'I was always, "Have you got your tablets?" "Yes, okay, have you taken your tablets?" I took on a motherly role with Lisa. I was always making sure she was eating right, telling her what she couldn't eat, looking after her. That's what I remember most.' Sharon recalls with a smile Lisa becoming indignant at her constant reminders and questions about what she was eating; she'd say, "I can eat that. I've had it before!"

Pat says from time to time Lisa would rebel and refuse to take her medication, and try to tell her mother she'd taken them. Pat always knew when she hadn't. It wasn't long before Lisa realised that if she didn't take the medication she would become very ill, so she resigned herself to the ordeal. Pat remembers at Easter she used to give Lisa more than her other girls, to make up for Lisa not being able to eat chocolate. She would have boiled lollies instead.

Because of her illness Lisa was always very slim and slight.

'The biggest thing I remember about Lisa was her little chicken legs,' says Sharon with a laugh.

A couple of weeks ago I was looking through some old photos and all these memories came back. We used to go away in the caravan to Wales and we used to have to climb this blinking big hill. I remember her in the car, complaining that her legs were aching. On these long trips, Mum would buy a bag of lollies for the six of us, but no-one could have another lolly until the last person had finished theirs. I always used to shove mine up to the side of my mouth until it dissolved. Everybody else would be crunching and sucking on theirs and they'd all call out that they'd finished, then they'd all look at me and say, 'Sharon...?' And I'd stick this big lump of lolly out on my tongue, and they'd all be fed up with me because I hadn't finished.

The thing that really sticks in my mind is having to cut the fat off the chicken and making sure she didn't get egg yolks or chocolate, making sure she had her own separate food. Making sure she was safe.

Sharon feels cheated that the family took such good care of Lisa, only have to her ripped away from them. 'We did everything right; for her to survive all that, then to be just taken...'

Pat tells me a story that she recounts with delight, which demonstrates Lisa's cheeky sense of humour. The family were in London for one of Lisa's appointments and bought kebabs. As they stood outside the shop eating, a low-flying pigeon deposited an unwanted surprise all over dad Ian's jacket, narrowly missing the kebab. Lisa thought this was the funniest thing she had ever seen and laughed for hours and hours, every time she recalled it. 'She saw the wickedly funny side of every situation,' says Pat. 'And she had the most gorgeous blue eyes, and her skin was so soft, like velvet. She was so good at doing her hair and makeup, she always looked so good. She took hours to get ready to go out. I remember she just used to laugh and laugh. When Lisa was about 13 or 14 she went to the cinema with friends. She used to wear a brace for her teeth, and she hated wearing this, so she took it out and put it into her pocket, but lost it! We had to get another one. She would laugh her head off now if she was here; she had a wicked sense of humour.'

The Govan family emigrated to Australia in 1988, settling in Perth. Pat's parents and her sister had already moved out to Australia, so it seemed a natural move for the family. Sharon, the family's eldest daughter, is five years older than Lisa and was already married by the time the family emigrated, so she stayed in the UK with her husband, but five months later they too moved out to join the rest of the family in Perth.

Ginette recalls she was not at all happy about the move. 'I didn't want to come; it was the worst thing in the world to come to the other side of the world, but Lisa was okay about it.' Lisa was 17 when the family came to Perth. She had left school and probably saw the move as an opportunity to spread her wings. 'She was more outgoing, she would have just gone with the flow,' says Ginette. Lisa continued with her medical treatment in Australia, but the doctors here knew very little about her very rare illness. She had to keep taking the medications and vitamins all her life.

Pat recalls when they first moved to Australia it was difficult at first for Lisa to make new friends, as she was no longer at school. She started meeting people through her work. As Sharon was married and Lisa's other sister left home at a young age, it became just Lisa and Ginette at home and the two sisters became close. Ginette remembers Lisa taking her out for the day to Fremantle, and they loved going to movies together. Lisa would also drive Ginette to school when she got her licence, not because she was asked to, but she enjoyed driving her little sister around. 'She just loved going out and she didn't mind me tagging along. She was very outgoing, very friendly. She'd talk to anybody, would help anybody. I recently posted her photo on a Facebook group for WA and I had lots of people respond to that, lots of messages from people who knew her and used to go out with her, hang around with her, people from Kalgoorlie too. Everybody had something nice to say. Even friends she had in England remember her. She just affected people.'

Sharon says: 'She could walk into a pub or club with any sort of people and she'd be in there, mixing, absolutely at home. I could walk into the same pub and think, "Ugh, get me out of here." She and I had different views of people. I could look around and think, "They're not really the kind of people I would associate with" whereas she would go in and it didn't really matter what the people were like.' Lisa would give anyone a go, she was happy to talk to absolutely anyone she came across. 'She'd befriend anyone, she really enjoyed life, where I would be like, "I wouldn't trust him", or "Oh, my God, I'm not going near that one",' says Sharon. 'She was bubbly and outgoing, but I wasn't.' I suggested that it may have been that carefree attitude towards the world, her refusal to regard anyone with wariness or suspicion, that ultimately cost Lisa her life, and Sharon sadly agreed.

Sharon and her husband lived just around the corner from her parents and sisters in Perth and saw them regularly, but says she and Lisa still never had a traditional sisterly relationship; Sharon was still looking out in a protective, motherly way for her sister, and making sure she was handling her illness. Lisa worked at a few different jobs in Perth, including bar work, as a care assistant in a nursing home, and in a factory that manufactured football uniforms. Pat says she was like a butterfly, going from job to job and meeting lots of different people.

Lisa had a few boyfriends but no-one special until she met Tim, in Perth. Tim got a job in Kalgoorlie at the mine, so he and Lisa moved there together. They set up house and Lisa worked at a couple of jobs in Kalgoorlie, in a gift shop and also at night at the mine as a spotter, guiding the enormous trucks. Lisa wrote a poem about her work at the mine which showcases her wicked sense of humour.

NIGHT SPOTTING

The moon is bright
And the air is still

The clouds are moving
But it isn't raining

I'm sat here all alone
Wishing I was back home
I'm thinking of my old man
Oh what a lucky girl I am

My job here is Spotter

The trucks reverse in
And my job is to stop her

All the trucks are loaded with dirt
Off falls a rock but I didn't get hurt

The truck drives slowly up to the dump
When they toot the horn it makes me jump
I spot them in to the dump their load
Then off they go down the bumpy road

There's lots of noise I can hear
Ooh oh, there's dust in my eye
And out runs a tear

I can hear the digger
Toot it's horn
As it digs and digs
From dusk till dawn

Here comes the truck
Called the water truck
But the water in it
Smells like a fart

It sprays all the dust
To keep it down
The smell it gives out
Makes me frown

I use my torch to spot at night
So the driver can see
As I swing my arm
From left to right

By Lisa Govan. The spotter.

Ginette thinks Lisa liked living in Kalgoorlie, but it was hard at times. It couldn't have been more different to her life in Lancashire, and it was also difficult living so far from her family and friends in Perth. It was the first time she'd been away from them, and she was now almost 600 kilometres away. Lisa called her parents every week, and when Ginette got her first mobile phone she and Lisa would text each other all the time. Pat remembers with a laugh ringing Lisa and saying, "What time is it in Kalgoorlie?" It felt like 10,000 miles from suburban Perth.

Lisa and Tim were happy in Kalgoorlie, but Ginette didn't think Lisa would live there forever. 'I don't think she'd have wanted to stay there,' she says. 'We kept in touch a lot and I think she would have been happier at home in Perth. Whenever they came home to Perth we'd catch up, but it wasn't the same as her living back in Perth, all together. The family would have preferred to have her at home where we could see her more, but she loved Tim and wanted to stay with him.'

Unlike Ginette, Sharon doesn't think Lisa would have moved back to Perth. 'She was always doing her own thing. It never surprised me what she was doing because that was *her*, she was like a free soul, not somebody who would conform.' She thinks Lisa would have settled in Kalgoorlie and eventually had children. She loved her sisters' children and Pat knows she wanted her own children one day. Pat recalls that at one point Lisa did want to move back to Perth, but Tim's work kept the couple near the mine. Sharon was happy to see Lisa living in Kalgoorlie. She knew Lisa was happy with Tim, and she could see Lisa had made a home for them and was settling into life out there. Sharon felt that Tim and Lisa's dog would keep her safe.

Lisa loved dogs and adored her huge Rottweiler named Devil. She used to take him to a large stream in Kalgoorlie for a paddle. I remarked to Sharon it was ironic that she had a huge, protective dog who could have kept her safe from anyone, yet he wasn't with her when she needed him. Pat remembers Devil as a very affectionate dog who would lick and cuddle people constantly, but he was a giant, butch dog and she doesn't know how the very slightly framed Lisa could have possibly managed to control him when she walked him. Her love for, and devoted attachment, to Devil was another reason why her family were certain something terrible had happened to Lisa, as she would never have left him behind if she'd left Kalgoorlie of her own accord.

'Tim seemed to look after her, and although we didn't know him very well, the family liked him. We knew Lisa could be … a handful,' Sharon says with a laugh. 'She didn't like being told what to do, but I knew she'd be okay with Tim.' When Lisa went missing, she and Tim had been together four or five years. Lisa was her same happy and outgoing self, living in Kalgoorlie as she had been in Perth, with lots of friends. 'She was a little social butterfly,' says Ginette.

Take a Google Street View walk through Kalgoorlie; it has the most amazing historic buildings and is reminiscent of old Wild West movies with ornate storefronts and second-storey balconies on the numerous hotels, paying tribute to the town's goldrush origins. The town, founded in 1893, is 595 kilometres east-north-east of Perth. It has red-earth-stained wide streets and a thriving community, but not too much further past where Lisa disappeared the landscape changes dramatically to one of isolation, and you begin to understand how someone could be lost here and never found. The land is flat, with the vast Super Pit mine dominating the landscape. This is where Lisa worked. The mine itself is extraordinary, vast and cavernous, and extremely productive. The largest gold open pit mine in Australia, it produces 850,000 ounces of gold each year. This is a town where the summer temperatures regularly climb high into the 40s, and it's hard to imagine how different that would have been for Lisa to her home in Lancashire, England, where the average January temperature doesn't get above 3 degrees.

On Thursday 7 October 1999, Lisa went out with some work friends. Tim was at work at the mine, doing a 12-hour shift. Lisa had dropped him there in the ute, as it was pouring rain at the time he started work. She started her night out at the Exchange Hotel, where she met a work colleague. Lisa moved on to the Safari Nightclub in Hannan Street, Kalgoorlie. CCTV shows her mingling with other patrons inside and outside the club. Lisa left the Safari with that work colleague, known as 'the bald man', at 4.45 am. They caught a taxi, which took them a short distance, but Lisa asked the taxi driver to take her back to the Safari, as she wanted to see her female friend, who had been out the front of the club. That man told police he was expecting Lisa to meet him at his home that morning, after she left the Safari, and when she did not turn up he rang her repeatedly. This information was not known by Lisa's family at all until very recently. Police have interviewed this man extensively and have stated he is not a suspect.

Tim had been phoning Lisa throughout the evening, unhappy that she was out having a good time without him while he was stuck at work, and he asked her to please go home. This resulted in the couple arguing, and perhaps to spite Tim, Lisa switched off her phone.

The next sighting of Lisa was at around 7.30 am, on Friday 8 October 1999, outside Bunnings, then across the road at the Foundry Hotel[3] bottle shop, on Boulder Road. The hotel is next to the clubhouse for the Club Deroes bikie gang. Witnesses have told police Lisa was then seen inside the clubhouse at 7.45 am, playing pool.

Police believe Lisa's last known location was at the Club Deroes clubhouse. There is no evidence that anything happened to Lisa at the clubhouse or hotel, but she was never seen again after going inside.

To Ginette, it's a mystery how she came to be last seen at a bikie clubhouse. 'Her boyfriend had a bike, but he wasn't a bikie. Lisa never talked to me about anything to do with bikies, so I don't know how she came to end up there.' Sharon, however, was aware that Lisa regularly went to the bikie clubhouse. Her initial reaction was one of horror. 'I was like, "Oh, my God, what is she doing?"' When Sharon confronted Lisa about what she saw as her sister's risky behaviour, Lisa couldn't see what all the fuss was about. To her, these people were just her friends. To be granted access to the clubhouse, visitors had to be associated with the club members and be invited in, so it seems clear Lisa knew some of the bikies. 'I told her to be careful,' says Sharon. Lisa shrugged it off.

Pat thinks it's less unusual than people may think that her

3   The Foundry Hotel was frozen under the proceeds of crime legislation in 2003 after its co-owner was convicted of drug dealing. The hotel was damaged by fire in suspected arson attacks in 2008 and 2009 then burned to the ground in 2012.

daughter went to the clubhouse. 'A lot of the young people in Kalgoorlie went there. When the pubs and nightclubs closed, they all used to go to the bikie club. We were even speaking to one of the reporters about Lisa and she was a lovely girl, expecting her second baby and she told us that she often went there.' It wasn't regarded as a dangerous place, and in a town where the main source of employment – the mine – operates 24 hours a day, seven days a week, the clubhouse was just another venue for shiftworkers to go to when they finished work, when the usual pubs were closed, if they knew someone to invite them.'

I asked Pat if she thought Lisa was being rebellious when she decided to ignore Tim's pleas for her to head home, and deliberately stayed out longer, and Pat said she thought she probably was. 'I've been stubborn like that, in my day, too. If someone says don't do it, I'll do it.' Lisa lived about 10 minutes' walk from the Foundry Hotel. Pat isn't sure if Lisa would have chosen to walk home or hailed another taxi. That decision may have been fateful.

When Tim finished work he came home to find no sign of Lisa. He was immediately worried and tried to report Lisa as missing to Kalgoorlie Police. He called police on the Friday morning but police told him they were unable to do anything about a missing person for two days.[4] Tim rode around Kalgoorlie on his motorcycle, looking for Lisa. He was panicking, and while he was out searching he fell from his bike, injuring himself, and went to Kalgoorlie hospital.

---

4 It is not standard practice in Australia to have to wait a specified amount of time before you can lodge a missing person report with police. When there is genuine concern for someone's safety and welfare and their disappearance is out of character then a missing person report may be made at any time. In most cases, the earlier someone is reported missing, the greater chance there is of locating them safely.

Ginette remembers driving home from work at about 5 pm when her mobile rang. It was Tim. He asked if Ginette had heard from Lisa. The fact that Tim was calling her at all rang alarm bells for Ginette, as she didn't speak to Tim very often. Ginette told him she hadn't heard from Lisa at all and suggested he call her mother. A short time later Tim phoned Pat to say he could not find Lisa. Pat recalls Tim sounded 'absolutely petrified'. She, too, was concerned that Tim had phoned, as it was quite rare for her to speak with him on the phone; it was usually Lisa she spoke to when she called them. 'My stomach turned over and I thought, "Crikey, what's wrong?"' says Pat. Lisa had arranged to phone her mother to discuss a recipe that day, so Pat waited for that call to come. It never did. Pat tried to call Lisa multiple times throughout that day and next, with no answer. She contacted Sharon to let her know something was wrong.

Tim waited the two days he'd been told to and then rang police again on the Sunday. They took the missing person report from him, but the report was not given to detectives until Tuesday, a full four days after Lisa was last seen. Four days wasted. 'Anybody could have done anything … disposed of Lisa … they had plenty of time,' says Pat sadly. It's frustrating, to say the least, that even though Lisa's last known location was at a bikie clubhouse, the report was not acted on for several days. 'It's disgusting,' says Pat firmly. 'Not just because it was Lisa. Now I think they're beginning to change things, they're starting to look for missing people sooner. But if you're told something by a policeman you just take it.'

By this stage Tim and the Govan family knew something terrible had happened – there had been no activity on Lisa's bank account and no answer from her phone. Because Tim's last contact with Lisa had been an argument, this may have made police think Lisa had gone off in a huff and would come back when she'd cooled down. Tim was questioned extensively by police but was just as much in the dark as everyone else as to Lisa's whereabouts. Lisa had stayed over with friends before but had never stayed out this long without telling someone where she was.

At first, Sharon was not overly worried.

I thought perhaps they'd had a row and she'd gone off, so I thought, yeah, she'll be all right. She's just gone off with a friend or something. Then the day after that, we were ringing again and Tim was saying no, nothing yet and that's when it all started; the police became involved and Mum was getting updates from them. We were piecing together the puzzle; okay, so she was here, then she was there. Mum was on the phone daily. It was just waiting by the phone, hoping something would come out of it, getting the daily updates. Then it went from daily to weekly. We checked the obvious, her bank account, her phone, what about this, what about that, and we were double checking and double guessing everything – have we done this, have we done that?

Lisa's parents and aunt drove to Kalgoorlie when the police finally looked at her missing person report. They found Tim in a state of distress; he was very frightened that something terrible had happened to his girlfriend. The family tried to ask him what had happened, but he was very upset. 'He was absolutely fearful,' says Pat. The family visited police several times during their stay in Kalgoorlie, trying to work out what could have happened, but there was simply no trace of Lisa. Pat started to question everything and recalls grilling the police about whether they'd done enough to try to find her. She asked the police about rugs that might be missing from Lisa's home and whether they'd questioned anyone in relation to the case.

I wanted to know all the ins and outs, all the nitty gritty. They [the police] were good with us, they did tell us a lot. But it feels like the police in Australia are undertrained. My husband and I both used to work for the police in the UK; he was in the garage workshop and I was in the kitchen canteen, so we saw how the police worked every day. I think over here they're not as thoroughly trained as they are in the UK.

Pat feels that Kalgoorlie, being a regional town, may not have had the resources or experience to handle a murder case. The police were, however, accommodating to Lisa's family, driving them all over Kalgoorlie and pointing out the locations significant to the case.

As Lisa's case progressed, or failed to, Pat and her family learned more about how the law worked, and what initially seemed like a case that was easy to solve became far more complicated and difficult. The bikie clubhouse attached to the Foundry Hotel, being the last place Lisa was seen, was thoroughly searched by police, but nothing was found. Tim had to move out of the home that he shared with Lisa for a few days while police sprayed the entire place with luminol (a chemical that detects traces of blood) but again, nothing was found.

After a few months, Tim moved out of their Kalgoorlie house permanently, and brought all Lisa's personal belongings back to her family's Perth home along with Lisa's car. Sharon remembers it being an awkward situation for Tim, who she could see found the experience distressing. He wanted to deliver her things and leave as quickly as he could, as it was upsetting for everyone. Lisa's car was eventually sold, with her father organising the sale, but Sharon remembers seeing the car parked outside the house, a constant reminder of her missing sister. She was glad it was sold quickly.

It was seeing Lisa's car and belongings returned to the family that made Sharon start to believe Lisa would definitely not be coming home; it was a turning point for her. Lisa's beloved dog was given to a friend. Tim moved to Papua New Guinea for work, and kept in touch with the family for a while, especially with Lisa's mum, Pat, but he eventually needed to move on with his life. Although he was an obvious initial suspect in Lisa's disappearance, police and the family are confident that Tim was not involved in any way.

The thought that something terrible may have happened to her sister was too overwhelming for Ginette to consider. She was still living in Perth with her parents and was working in 1999. She was 22 when Lisa went missing, Lisa was 28. Ginette carried on going to work and going about her usual days, always thinking that Lisa would turn up soon.

It took a while to actually face that she wasn't coming home. For a long time, I thought, 'She'll turn up; something's happened but she'll turn up.' It was a long time before I realised she wasn't going to. My workplace was great and said I could take

time off and be with my family, but I didn't want to. I kept
working just so I didn't have to think about it. It was too hard.
I think I was a bit in denial.

Sharon agrees. 'I think it took a while for Ginette to accept what happened. I was a little bit like that, at first; I would say to Mum, "Oh, she'll be fine, she'll be somewhere, you know what she's like, she's probably just gone off somewhere."' But then it became, "Hmm … I don't think she has…' But you try to convince yourself that it will be okay. As time goes by you start to realise something *has* happened. But you still try to hold onto that little thread of hope that she's going to walk in one say and say, "Sorry, got lost walking around." You've always got that hope, even though you know it's probably not going to happen.'

I asked Sharon if she still holds onto that hope today and she is quiet for a long time. 'No,' she replies reluctantly. 'All I want now is just to bring her home. Especially for Mum.' It's very distressing to Sharon that her mother has had to endure so many years of pain. 'Mum just wants to bring her home as well. It hurts me to see Mum hurting. She's learned to deal with it, but her wish really is to bring her home and put her to rest. If she could do that, then she'll be okay.'

As the years went on, the family tried any means they could to work out what had happened to Lisa. Pat was contacted by many clairvoyants keen to help try to locate Lisa, including one from the USA. She was, however, unable to provide enough information to pinpoint Lisa's location. Many of the clairvoyants mentioned the number three. One said Lisa would be near three telegraph poles or palm trees. Another said she was in water near three bushes. Pat contacted well-known psychic Debbie Malone, who was willing to help her but the police would not discuss the case with Debbie, as is their standard policy. A family friend of the Govans came to them saying he had a 'strange feeling' about a particular location, so the family went to a disused mine shaft on the outskirts of Kalgoorlie. The police did accompany them to check out this shaft and they lowered a camera down, but it hit water and the operation had to be abandoned. They told the family even if they drained the shaft, the water would come in some somewhere else and find its natural level again.

The sisters' greatest wish is for Lisa to be found. 'I think with the right equipment she could be found,' says Sharon. There was another recent search of a mining town for a long lost girl: 16-year-old Karen Williams, who went missing in Coober Pedy, South Australia in 1990. There has been a huge dig for her remains, with an extraordinary amount of heavy machinery being brought in to search deep mine shafts. It's difficult and frustrating work and so far has not been successful. A similar search has not been done in Kalgoorlie. 'I'm just hoping they've got the resources one day to go back out there with the right equipment and have a proper look,' says Sharon. 'But if she's out there and has been in water for that long I don't know how … what the … what effects it would have…' Sharon's voice trails off as the grim reality of her words sink in.

It was difficult for the family being in Perth and a long drive from where Lisa went missing, a journey they had to make many times. Ginette says, 'Mum and Dad have been to Kalgoorlie a lot since it happened. They were in close contact with the detectives all along; they spoke to them a lot and were kept up to date with everything.' A couple of years after Lisa's disappearance Ginette, Sharon and her parents made an emotional journey to Kalgoorlie to visit the spot where Lisa was last seen. They laid flowers near the bikie clubhouse, 'But the next day they were gone,' says Ginette angrily. 'Somebody had taken them. I was so sad and disappointed, because we don't have anywhere like a grave to go, so to put flowers there and for that to happen...' The memory clearly still upsets her. Sharon was angry when the flowers were taken but later thought, 'You know what? It doesn't matter. If that's what you want to do, do it.' The family felt they were fighting against something unknown to them. 'I thought, you can do that to the flowers, but you haven't won. It was a bit like a silent battle. You can take my sister, you can take the flowers, but that's all, I've still got everything else. You haven't won. You'll never win.'

Pat recalls the flowers were actually taken twice; it also happened on a separate trip she made to Kalgoorlie with her sister. Ginette says: 'There was a lamp post directly outside the clubhouse, but we couldn't just put the flowers there, so we put them on the lamp post on the opposite side of the road, outside a vet surgery. We wanted people to notice the flowers and say, "Oh, yes, I remember that happening." The first time, the flowers were taken within a couple of hours. Lisa had a good friend in Kalgoorlie and she's become close to us since Lisa went missing. She picked flowers out of her garden for Lisa, and we bought flowers from the florist, and wrote her a card. The next day all those flowers were gone again. I got in touch with the police and they got in touch with the media and we did an article about it saying how awful it was that the flowers had been taken. It was obvious to me who had taken them. The police said, "Well, perhaps they were nice flowers and people wanted them for themselves," and I said, "Oh, come on! People wouldn't take flowers like that!" And some were out of a garden.'

Sharon says she's like a dog with a bone – she can't give up or let things go – and on the trip with her family she wanted to physically search for Lisa. However, the vastness of the terrain was daunting. 'If someone's lost something, I'll methodically look for it. My dad would often say, "If anyone's going to find it, Sharon will find it. She's so bloody nosy she won't give up,"' she says with a laugh. 'So, when we were there it was the four of us and we thought, this time is never going to happen again, with us all there together, we have to find her. It was almost like we have this huge, huge mountain in front of us, but even me, this time, I thought, I just don't know where to start. I felt like she was happy the four of us were there. We did have some good laughs out there, and yes, I do think she was there, but as much as I wanted to get out there and have a look and search, it was almost like I had something wrapped round my arms, a bit like a straightjacket, and I was being patted on the head and told, "It's not going to happen." I did feel frustrated, but I also felt that it was okay that we didn't find anything, or that we didn't get out there and search, it was okay. We came away as a stronger unit, the four of us. I came away appreciating Ginette a little bit more as well. That's what I got from it. It gave me a lot of other strengths. It made me what I am today and allowed me to change for the better. Before all this I wouldn't have been able to do anything, but I picked up her strength.'

Ginette had never been to Kalgoorlie before the family trip. 'It was hard, but it was good to see where she had lived and her house, to know that she'd been there.' Lisa had talked to Ginette about all the places she visited in Kalgoorlie, so Ginette appreciated getting to see them in person. The trip was very painful for her, though, and today as she recalls her sister and the life events she's since missed out on she breaks down. 'We got married in 2003 and we've got the three kids now, and to know that she'll never see them, that they'll never meet her...' Ginette's tears start to flow. 'My older two, I've told them about her and shown them photos, so they know basically that she's missing and that we don't think she's alive anymore. My oldest daughter's middle name is Lisa. Lisa will always be a part of our lives.' Ginette's husband also knew Lisa, as they met a few times before she went missing, and Ginette says he's been a wonderful support to her. 'It was only the other day I was saying to him it would be nice if we could have her come round for dinner; she was the sort of person we'd get along well with, to just sit back and have a drink and have dinner together. She was just like that.'

Sharon's children remember and miss their aunty too. 'I had to explain to them that Aunty Lisa was missing. They'd ask, "When is she coming back?" and we'd have to say, we don't know. We had to explain that she might never come back. It was hard for them to accept that what I was saying was true, because they couldn't understand how you lose someone. You can lose a book or whatever, but how do you lose a person? My daughter would say, "Well, are you sure? She must be coming back." We'd have to say no, she's not, we think something's happened. Then you have to try to explain that maybe someone's murdered her, but without scaring her. My son was only three when she went missing so he didn't really understand. When my seven-year-old daughter used to see the news reports on TV she'd say, "Oh, that's my aunty," so she did sort of get to grips with it, but now and again she'll still ask me. It's been quite hard on the kids.'

Sharon's first marriage ended and she now has a new partner. It was difficult explaining to him that she had a missing sister. 'He was overwhelmed by it at first. It was hard having to go back and explain it all. He understands now, though.' Sharon told her partner about Lisa early in their relationship, as it was a natural part of the conversation to talk about their families. When he asked her how many sisters she had, she hesitated … but then answered three.

'When she went missing, it was around the same time as the Claremont murders and also when Hayley Dodd went missing, a few weeks before Lisa,' says Sharon. 'I remember seeing it on TV and thinking, "That would be so horrible." I think that's why I took a while to accept it. Some people at work were chatting about the search for Hayley Dodd and one of them commented, "Oh, they never find people who go missing." I just said, "Is that right?" They said, "Yeah, it would be good if they found her, though." I said, "There's nothing worse than having somebody go missing and not knowing where they are." A few people at work know about it, but not many.'

About a fortnight after Lisa disappeared, Pat broke down. 'I lost the plot completely,' she says. Her voice falters as she tells me that this is when she realised the worst had happened.

I just kept living in hope, but I've got used to the fact now. The hope is gone. I still dream about her, and I still have nightmares about her. It gets easier to cope with, but it never leaves you.

Pat and Ian have since been to Kalgoorlie with metal detectors, scouring the red dirt in the hope of locating Lisa's remains. If her clothes had something metal attached, like a zipper, belt buckle, buttons, bra wire, jewellery, then the metal detector just might pick that up. Ian would locate something of interest with the detector then Pat would get down on her hands and knees and dig at the dirt, searching for her buried child. It's an image that moves me to tears.

'I used to have lots of dreams, and in my dreams, she'd always turn up,' says Ginette.

I know that she's not going to, but in my dreams, she'd always turn up. It's hard not knowing, and it's hard not having anywhere to go, not having a grave. Just not having a proper farewell to her.

'When you look at people on TV who have committed murders, they just look so normal. You think, how? How did you murder someone, or two or three?' says Sharon. She wonders about the person who killed Lisa, still walking around free. 'It could be anybody. It's not someone with two heads, it's just a normal looking person who could have done it. It could be anybody in the whole world. I look at people and think they just look normal, and Lisa probably would have thought exactly the same about whoever it was that she met that night.' Sharon struggles to make logical sense of how someone can go missing without a trace. 'If some*thing* goes missing, you've got to find it. Nothing ever really goes missing, you can't just lose something; if you lose something in the house then one day you'll find it, it'll be in a safe place. But with this ... how can you lose a person? How can someone bury someone or hide them, never to be found again? I mean, I know it's happened for years and years, forever, but you think, how can you just hide someone? If it's in a shallow grave, or left to be found then fair enough, but to hide something, never EVER to be found – how can people never, ever be found? That's the hardest part. Accepting that she might never be found.'

Sharon thinks she's now a stronger person emotionally and she acknowledges she's built up some barriers around her feelings about Lisa. 'Before, I was a bit of a "yes" person. I think a lot of young girls are, you'd get shouted at in the workplace and you'd just take it. The people Lisa associated with I would have cowered away from, but now I could just walk up to them and talk to them. I've learned to stand up for myself and, I suppose, now I'm on a par with Lisa ... she would just leap in but I'd go in gingerly. It's like when we'd go in the swimming pool, she'd jump in the deep end whereas I'd dip my toe.'

Ginette has this plea to anyone who might know what happened to Lisa.

I hope she's found one day. If someone just comes forward with something, just that tiny little bit of information – that's why

I keep sharing her photo on Facebook. I did it on quite a few pages that were really popular, and the amount of people who liked and commented and shared her picture ... it's just going to have to reach somebody, somewhere, who's got something. I want to find out what's happened, and I want justice. I want the person caught. Knowing that somebody out there does know something and they're just going on with their lives, and we're left never knowing...

'We just want her home,' says Sharon. 'She is here with us, I know she is, and she's passed her core strength on to me. But we need her home.' Pat has a tattoo of a butterfly on her back, for Lisa, and when I spoke to each of the Govan ladies they all separately mentioned that Lisa was just like a butterfly. It's a beautiful way to remember her. 'Life isn't fair. The people who hurt her are all living their lives and we are left with broken hearts wondering where Lisa is and what happened to her. She was harmless, and a fun-loving girl,' says a heartbroken Pat. 'Please just tell us where we can find Lisa.'

Someone out there knows exactly what happened to Lisa that day. I'm sure it's a daunting thought, coming forward and telling such a huge secret, but her family need to know. They need their girl home, they need to lay her to rest. Lisa Govan did not deserve what happened to her, she'd done nothing wrong. She survived a rare, life-threatening medical condition only for her life to be cruelly taken. That's what you've taken, a beautiful girl, full of life. That's what you've taken away. The butterfly.

In 2021 *The West Australian* newspaper released an investigative series about Lisa's suspected murder. Detective

Sergeant Shane Russell of the Special Crime Squad, Homicide unit was asked by Ben Harvey if he knew how Lisa Govan died. Without hesitation he replied, 'Yes, I do.' He then went on to emphatically state: 'Lisa Govan did not leave the Club Deroes clubhouse.'

Despite their frustrations with the original police investigation the Govan family say they now have faith in the cold case team reviewing Lisa's case. A few years after Lisa disappeared a call was made to Crime Stoppers. Police are keen for that person to call back as they feel their information may be vital to Lisa's investigation. They felt the person had more information to provide but the call was rushed and then cut short. If that's you, please call them back today. It's time to put things right. Police have also asked the public to help locate a white 1985 Toyota Landcruiser ute that was seen at the Club Deroes clubhouse on the morning Lisa was last seen. The ute was seen at the clubhouse, left, then returned and police say it was 'quite extensively cleaned', then disposed of in late 1999 or early 2000. Police know who owned this vehicle. They feel the ute might still hold some forensic evidence, even decades later. If you bought a ute that fits this description, police want to hear from you.

A year after Lisa's disappearance the Western Australian government posted a $50,000 reward for information that would lead to her suspected killer. In 2017 that reward was increased to $250,000. To further put pressure on those who police suspect are involved, properties owned by the Club Deroes were raided in Kalgoorlie and Perth. The Cold Case Homicide Squad went back to Kalgoorlie and re-interviewed their persons of interest. They say they have received 'very credible information' in relation to Lisa's suspected murder.

Detective Sergeant Shane Russell was asked by Ben Harvey if he believes he will find Lisa's body.

'Yes, I do,' he firmly replied.

As I concluded Lisa's story in 2021, the Western Australian government announced the reward for information about Lisa's disappearance and presumed murder has been increased to $1 million.

If you can assist police, please contact 1800 333 000. You can remain anonymous if you wish, and you can even claim the reward money anonymously.

CHAPTER FIVE
Norman Lawson

Norman Lawson, aged 16, disappeared while on a camping trip near the South Alligator River, Kakadu National Park, NT on October 21st, 1986.

It would be distressing enough to have a missing brother for the last three decades. But what if you thought his body might have been found, and no-one will tell you whether or not that's true?

That's the situation facing brother and sister Murray and Susan Lawson. Their brother Norman was last seen in 1986, when he was just sixteen years old. In 1990 a body was found, with a gunshot wound to the head, but since that time various government departments have told the Lawson family conflicting information about whether this body is Norman. They've now been waiting more than 30 years for that answer.

Norman Lawson was born in Melbourne. Older sister Susan and younger brother Murray completed the Lawson children, but they were not a happy family. Murray and Sue speak about constant fights between their parents, which resulted in them frequently moving. Their parents separated and Murray lived with his mother, while Norman and Susan stayed with their father, Henry. 'I was passed round the family,' says Murray. 'It's very hard to talk about. I had an abusive childhood. We were all together when we were younger, but Mum kept taking me away, and we ended up in the Northern Territory.' His father, Henry, was Aboriginal and his mum was white. Murray recalls people were critical of his parents' mixed marriage, making their childhood difficult.

Susan was 13 when the family moved to Darwin. 'Our dad was a bit of a gypsy,' she says. 'Murray went up before us, with Mum, and Norman and I went up later. Norm was about 12 months younger than me. We were lucky to spend six months in one place. Sometimes we'd be chucked in the car in the middle of the night and off we'd go to the next place. We used to camp on the riverbanks in Queensland. The highway was like our home; we travelled all over Australia.' The family lived a nomadic lifestyle, with Murray and Susan saying they have lived in too many places to remember them all.

'Susan did well at school, but school was never any good for Norman and me,' says Murray. 'As soon as we could, we were out. We were skilled bush kids. We grew up in the bush all our lives, we knew what to do, how to handle ourselves, how to find food. All the uncles and cousins used to take us out to the bush.' Susan recalls their father being strict with them. 'All of us were made to work from a very young age,' she says.

'Norm was a quiet worker, but he was a happy-go-lucky larrikin,' says Murray. 'Into athletics and fitness; he won some major awards. He was a good kid, had a lot of friends, very skilled at martial arts, he had a black belt. We were brought up doing martial arts and boxing. We got on good. He was very kind hearted and well respected by the people he grew up with. Everyone liked him.'

Murray and Susan describe their brother exactly the same way, almost word for word. Susan remembers Norm's generosity and compassion for others.

You couldn't fault him. If he saw someone struggling across the road, carrying groceries or mowing the lawn, he'd be the first one there to help. He was a good kid. He wanted to leave school, and Dad said if he wanted to do that he had to get a job. He wanted to put himself through university; he wasn't sure if he wanted to be a lawyer or a doctor. He wanted to go and help all the underprivileged people. That was his goal; to save his money and put himself through university.

Norman left school at 15 and started working as a ringer on cattle stations in the Northern Territory. He then started his own timber-cutting business, which became very successful. He was 16 years old, had never had a permanent home, and not only had his own business but was employing staff. Sue remembers her brother's success with great pride. 'Up in the Territory, when treated timber first came out, he was shipping out the green logs to Gove and other places. He was doing really good for himself. Then some mongrel came along and stole him.'

Norman used to go fishing and camping frequently, at least every second weekend. He'd usually take his best mate, Johnny, but this time was different. On 21 October 1986 Norman went on a trip with a group of four older people who he didn't know well. Susan doesn't believe the group intended to fish, and she doesn't know why he was with that group of people nor why they travelled to that location. Murray also isn't sure how Norman knew these people, other than one of the men in the group who worked for Norm in his timber business. The group of five were camping on the Old Jim Jim Road in Kakadu, near the South Alligator River, about three hours' drive from Darwin. Rather than alligators, the area is well known as being well stocked with fearsome saltwater crocodiles. The road is 4WD only and is a short cut from Cooinda to the Arnhem Highway. It's closed during the wet season, when it floods. It's breathtakingly beautiful country. The end of October, when Norm went missing, would have been the very end of the dry season, with the wet starting in November.

The official police information about the incident, and the one I have been using for many years to make appeals for information about Norm, was that the group was on a fishing trip. Murray and Susan say this is inaccurate; he was actually camping with the two men and their wives. Police also said he is thought to have drowned, information I included in my 2020 appeal during Missing Persons Week, and that's how I met Murray – he responded to that appeal, letting me know it was wrong.

'People get the wrong impression, that they were in a boat – there was no boat. They were on land. It was a big muck-up. They said that he'd run away, when it was proven that he didn't run away. There's a lot of untold stories, untold truths.'

What is known is that Norman Lawson went on a camping trip with two men and two women, and disappeared on that trip. The people he was with did not report him missing to police.

Norm's family knew straightaway something was wrong when no-one had heard from him by the end of the weekend. 'Norm was supposed to be home on the Sunday, but he didn't come home,' says Susan. 'Dad said, "There's something wrong here," because he always taught us to be where we were supposed to be either before or on time, never late, so if we were late he knew something was wrong. On Monday, still no word from him, and by Tuesday, Dad said he was going to the police station. He reported Norm missing.'

Murray says he will never forget the moment he learned his brother hadn't returned from the trip: 'I was at Henry's place when Mum came and told us Norm was missing. I was very shocked, and sat by myself for quite a while.' The family could not understand what had happened, but immediately thought something was very wrong.

The four people Norm had been with scattered to different parts of the country immediately after the disappearance. 'One went to Western Australia and was picked up at Wave Hill, as you go through Katherine, on the border,' says Susan. 'His woman went to Queensland. The other fella and his woman went back to Darwin, and not one of them reported him missing.'

None of the four people who were the last to see Norman Lawson were ever charged with any crime. Police did question them, and their stories about what happened were inconsistent. Their story – that they had an argument with Norm and he walked off down the road without his shoes, hat, rifle or swag but only took his swag cover – was not believed by Norm's family.

Rumours and stories eventually filtered their way through the Darwin community and reached the family, and little by little they pieced together the probable events of that day, even though the stories were slightly different. Murray says: 'The partner of one of the men told me that they had a fight, a punch-up; she said Norm slapped the man around, then Norm walked off with his gun. She said the man ran him over and shot him with his own gun. Then they moved the body and fed him to the crocodiles.'

Susan heard a very similar account. 'At the time there was a story going around, that Dad's brother was told while we were out searching for Norm. They said Norm was hit over the head with his gun, wrapped in a swag cover and chucked in the billabong for the crocodiles. We only found that out about eight months after he went missing.' Susan believes if there was an argument amongst the group, it might have been triggered by alcohol, and Norman's disapproval of it. 'We grew up with an alcoholic father,' she says. 'He bashed us, and Norman said to him there was to be no grog in the house. Dad thought the argument with Norman and the others could have been about grog, because they were all drinkers.'

Police, finding no trace of Norman on Old Jim Jim Road, collected the rest of his possessions from the group he had been with, and took them back to the police station. Susan says police should have realised at that point that something was amiss.

When the police rang Mum and Dad and asked them to go to the police station to collect Norman's belongings, Dad asked them if Norm's swag cover was there, and listed what Norm was meant to have, and the police said, 'Yeah, we've got everything here, Mr Lawson.' But when we went to get the stuff, there was no swag cover and no rifle. Dad asked the police where they were, and they said they didn't have them. This was not long after Dad heard the story [about Norm being wrapped in the swag cover], so when we found the swag cover was missing, we thought that story was possibly true.

Police told Dad the men said that Norm had jumped off the back of the truck, took his swag cover but left his swag. You can't tell me someone's going to unwrap the swag, take the cover and leave the swag behind. Wouldn't you grab the whole lot?

My brother, when he went to sleep, always put his shoes beside the swag, and when he got up in the morning the first thing he did was put his shoes on. He did that ever since he was little. And he never went anywhere without his hat. So, for him to walk off up the road without his hat or his shoes, that's just straight-up lies. No. I know that for a fact.

Norm's .22 rifle was only later found by chance. His father, Henry, had gone to Kakadu to speak to the park rangers and was telling them about the missing rifle. By an amazing coincidence, one of the rangers Henry spoke to told him that some months before he had purchased a .22 rifle from one of the men Norm had been camping with. It turned out to be Norm's rifle. 'The gun was jam-packed with yellow clay, and that clay could only be found in a certain part of the area, in a billabong,' says Murray. Sue believes the clay became wedged into the gun because it was used as a digging tool. It's possible Norm was initially buried, in a grave dug with his own rifle, but then later moved to the billabong, so his remains would never be found.

'We think he was buried in one spot, then moved to another spot, with crocodiles,' says Sue. 'I don't know if any of that is true, but that's the story I have been told from people.' Even with the evidence of the rifle sale, no charges were laid against anyone.

In 1989 Stan Tipiloura, the Labor member for Arafura, asked the Chief Minister in the Northern Territory Legislative Assembly:

> *Can the minister offer any comfort to Henry Lawson and his wife Val after what would have been the nineteenth birthday of their son Norman last week? As we all know, Norman disappeared from Kakadu National Park. Has the minister any discretion which would allow him to seek a coronial inquest into Norman's disappearance given that the police think he was taken by a crocodile and his parents believe he was murdered?*

ANSWER

Mr Speaker, this is indeed an awkward and sensitive matter. I have met with the Lawsons to discuss the matter with them. I have also held discussions with the Commissioner of Police on the matter. The honourable member said that the police believe that the missing person 'was taken by a crocodile'. I do not believe that that is so. The police do not know what happened to this person who is officially listed as a missing person. I appreciate that the parents of the boy are firmly of the belief that he is dead and was murdered. I have discussed with the Commissioner of Police whether or not we can refer the entire matter to the coroner, with all the available evidence, and ask him to inquire into the matter so that he can make a ruling. Whilst I am uncertain about the terminology that I should be using, I can say that that matter was investigated. I am informed that the matter cannot be referred to the coroner under the law as it stands at present. To answer the honourable member's question, I am unable to refer it to the coroner. I can assure him that I would be pleased to do so in an effort to have this matter cleared up. I understand that that cannot be done. It is not a matter of will.

In the late 1980s or early 1990s, journalist Derryn Hinch did a story about Norman's disappearance for television, and organised for Norman's best mate to be filmed walking down a road in Adelaide, posing as Norman. Susan says he looked exactly like Norm in the footage. No leads came from the story.

In 1990 skeletal remains were found at Lake Bennett, a 300-kilometre drive from Old Jim Jim Road. The body had a bullet wound to the skull, believed to be from a .22 rifle, the same as Norm's gun. Police told the family they had found Norm's body. Susan remembers when her parents learned about the Lake Bennett body. 'Me, Mum and Dad were driving out there, as Dad had heard a man had something to do with this body, and Dad wanted to go and see him about it. Meanwhile, the police had gone past us, going out there too.'

'It was a botch-up,' says Murray. 'The body was sent to a medical centre in Adelaide for testing and they said it was definitely Norman. They sent the body back to the Northern Territory, and they tested it again, and they said no, it's inconclusive. They said there was animal blood found but it was actually human blood. So, Adelaide said it was him, and Northern Territory said it wasn't him. Yet I've got a death certificate. I'm not sure what happened to that body. Last time I spoke to someone about it was three years ago and they said it's a closed case, as far as they're concerned.'

This is alarming. Not only have authorities told this family conflicting information about the identity of the remains, they have also told them they are no longer investigating what clearly seems to be a homicide. If the remains are not Norman Lawson's, whose are they? And if that body had a gunshot wound to the head, who is investigating that crime? I contacted the Northern Territory Coroner's Office in 2021 to ask if the Lake Bennett remains had ever been identified and they simply referred me to the new National DNA Program launched in 2020. It really didn't answer my question as to whether the remains had been identified at any time in the last 30 or so years.

In 2009 journalist Rebekah Cavanagh of the *NT News* wrote an article about Norman:

> *Police said yesterday Norman's disappearance was still an open missing persons case. They said the Coroner's Constable would be conducting a project, overseen by the Major Crime Division, where a number of old unidentified skeletal remains, including those found at Lake Bennett, would be tested by new technology. But they said the results are not expected to be known until next year.*

That was 13 years ago.

After going back and forth with police, and the authorities giving conflicting information about the Lake Bennett body, Murray has accepted that his brother is still missing. 'I don't believe the body is Norman,' says Murray. 'They did say they thought that body was older than Norman. When they first told us that body was him, I did believe them, and I was overcome with emotions. You just want to have a body to bury, but then we didn't. I think after they took my DNA they did say that the body wasn't him, but I'm still not too sure. At the time, in 1990, only two people were able to give a DNA sample for testing, that was me and our father. Our father refused to have the test done. I was the only person able to give a sample. To get Mum's DNA, they would have to exhume her.'

Susan has also had her hopes raised many times by police who told her they'd found Norm, only to call back and dash those hopes.

> *There were times the police went to the markets where Dad worked and said to him, 'We've found a body and we're 100%*

sure it's Norm.' That happened four or five times. The last time it happened I was living in Brisbane, about six years ago. Murray rang me and said some lady from the police rang him and said that they'd got a body, and asked me about DNA, then she rang back and said it's not your brother. No-one has ever taken my DNA. I'm very confused about that. Mum and Dad were in the police station once being interviewed and they heard someone say if the truth ever came out about this it would be a bigger thing than the Lindy Chamberlain case.'

There was an inquest held into Norman's disappearance and presumed death in June 1990. The Coroner was unable to find a cause of death. The four people who were with Norman on the camping trip did appear at the inquest, but Susan says they were physically protected by police and her family were prevented from speaking to them. 'It was a circus, it was ridiculous. One of them was drunk on the witness stand. They just gave Mum and Dad a coronial inquest to make them shut up I think, that's all it was.'

Susan believes the men who were on that camping trip with her brother have since passed away. 'One of them was in his 60s or 70s back then, and the other one was around 48 or 49. He'd be in his 80s now if he was still alive.'

Murray agrees: 'Unfortunately the bloke who I believe murdered my brother is dead now, I think, as I can't find him anywhere in Australia, and if I can't find him then no-one can.'

In 2022 I contacted NT Police to ask them whether the suspects in this case were still alive, but I received no response. Sue and Murray know little about these men, except by reputation. 'People said one of the guys was really violent,' says Susan. 'He used to bash people, and he'd apparently killed someone before, a woman, somewhere like Anthill. When I was living in Brisbane I thought I saw him once, but by the time I turned the car around to go and look he was gone. Goodness knows what I would have done if I'd caught up to him.'

Susan's mention of Anthill rang a bell with me. A young woman named Catherine Graham was found murdered, bashed with a rock, at Anthill Creek, west of Townsville in Queensland, in 1975. Her murder has never been solved. Tony Jones, a young hitchhiker, was also last seen at Anthill Creek in 1982. Eerily, the last sighting of Catherine was when she phoned her mother from a telephone box in Townsville. The last sighting of Tony Jones was when he phoned his mother … from a telephone box in Townsville.

Norman's loss has had a devastating effect on Murray and Susan. Murray was 14 when Norman went missing. Within six months of his brother's disappearance Murray dropped out of school. 'Norm was never in any trouble; I was the one who got in trouble with the law,' says Murray. All that started after Norm went missing.

His disappearance had a major impact on me. I was the outcast, no good for nothin'. Unfortunately, I was skilled at crime. I'm not proud of it, but I did it for a reason. I would break into houses, put the money into an envelope and put on the front: 'Mr and Mrs Lawson, this money is to help search for your son Norman' and put it under our front door. I did that for years, and they didn't ever know it was me. Even the copper who busted me said, 'As far as I'm concerned you did it for the right reasons' and all charges were dropped.

I ask Murray if he thinks his life would have been very different if he'd still had his brother around and he quietly says:

Yeah. To this day, I'm still beside myself. This stuff belongs in a movie or a horror story. I've had some bad experiences with coppers. I suffer from lots of illnesses. I have post-traumatic stress disorder. I've had a really bad life. I have chronic pain. Major mental illness. My body's been through quite a bit. I attempted suicide many times. I blamed myself — why couldn't it have been me instead of someone who was so good, who'd never been in trouble? Now I can't even walk out the door, I don't like going outside, I don't like going into town. I hate coppers with a passion; every time I see them I have a breakdown. My Aboriginal skin name is Strong Warrior. I like that.

Susan thinks Murray has been trying to deal with the pain of losing his brother the only way he knew how.

'We're both damaged. I dealt with it a different way, I guess,' she says.

My aunty said to me that Norm wouldn't have wanted us to feel guilty, he would have protected us. That's what he did all through my childhood; even though I was the oldest, it was like he was older. This sounds weird but if he had to die I would rather someone had come up and stabbed him or shot him, at least that way there would be closure and we'd know what happened. Even though I know in my own heart he's dead, believe me, you're still looking. I want to go back to the Northern Territory, as our mum is buried in Katherine, and maybe have a go at the Northern Territory government or something, to try to get Norm's case back out there. Thirty or forty years is way too long.

I know what happened, but it's too late. The coppers botched it. All the people who should have been brought to justice are dead now. That's the worst part about it all, not having answers. I see all these other cases on TV where the families are finally getting answers, and I'm so happy for them. It would be such a relief. It would just be nice to one day find out what happened to him, because it's been a long time. Out of our family it's just me and Murray left now, both our parents are gone.

Murray reflects on what their mother went through, losing Norm. 'It affected Mum terribly. She went through hell. And I've had a lot to deal with in my own head the last 20 or 30 years.' Susan agrees. 'Norm's disappearance has wrecked our family. It's agony to live with every day, it's cruel. It's messed me up in the head a lot too. It affects my relationship with my children and my grandchildren, because I can't let them go anywhere without knowing where they are. It's had a ripple effect; it hasn't only affected my generation. I named my baby Norma Jane, after my brother. I have anxiety, depression and PTSD, all these years, since my brother went missing. Sometimes I am screaming in my sleep, trying to run, to get to him. I've tried all my life for something to be done.'

Susan says her first thought when she found out Norm was missing was that someone had killed him. 'I believe that deep down in my heart. There was many a time that me and him ran away together, and we looked after each other, he looked after me, and he would never have gone anywhere and left me behind.

There's no way in hell he ran away and left me. We were very close, we went through everything together. He was building me a big greenhouse so I could start my own nursery business. That was the type of brother he was. I lost my best friend.'

It was not easy for Murray bring back all these painful memories when I spoke with him. 'I find it really hard to talk about him, but for Norman I will do anything,' he says. Murray says if he could find Norman's remains that would bring him some peace, as he could lay his brother to rest with their mother. Susan says the thing she misses most about Norm is his company. 'And his smile. He'd say, "No worries, sis, it'll be good, we'll be right." He always said that to me. It would just be nice to put him to peace. So, he can rest.'

If you have any information regarding the disappearance of Norman Lawson, please contact Crime Stoppers on 1800 333 000.

CHAPTER SIX
James Crocker

James Crocker, aged 27, was last seen as a patient in the Royal
Adelaide Hospital. On the night of May 27th 1994 he discharged
himself and was seen walking down North Terrace.

How does a man just vanish in the middle of a city? People ask me all the time: 'How can someone just disappear?' and in many cases I can answer: very easily. We live on a really big island, surrounded by sea, covered vastly by bushland. There are a million ways to go missing and never be found. I know of one missing man who curled himself up under a shrub on a suburban street, and his remains went undiscovered for months, despite being in a populated area. You'd be amazed how easy it is to hide yourself away. But in the city? Concrete and bricks? Paved roads? How do you go missing in the city? Yet that's exactly what happened to James Crocker on the evening of Friday 27 May 1994, in Adelaide city, South Australia.

James' sister Tracey is a lovely woman, quietly spoken and calm. There's the faintest hint of her pain in her words, and you get the sense it's been kept well hidden and covered over in layers for many years, and that began with her and James' childhood in suburban Adelaide. Ron and Val Crocker had two children: James was born first, then three years later Tracey came along. The photos Tracey has sent me of her and James as children are charming. They could be any Aussie kids growing up in suburbia; there are Christmas parties, splashing in the backyard paddle pool, James on his first day of school, two seemingly happy little children, a close brother and sister.

'Mum and Dad used to take us on train trips,' Tracey remembers. 'My brother and I used to get on great, and muck around. We'd go to little towns like Port Pirie and stay in hotels. We were very close, growing up. We'd stay up all night talking after Mum and Dad went to bed.' However, their happy times came with a dark undercurrent at home. 'Dad was very strict,' says Tracey. 'What Dad said went, and Mum went along with Dad. It was a pretty tough childhood.'

James coped with his stern upbringing by withdrawing into himself, but also by disappearing as a young teen. 'He was very, very quiet,' says Tracey. 'He would go … we'd call it walkabout. He'd go for a couple of days, just to get away, clear his head, but he'd always come back.' James was around 13 years old when he started running away. He never told his family where he'd been. His mother worried when he was gone, but Tracey says he'd do it so often the family became used to his strange disappearances.

As James approached his later teenage years, his need to escape escalated. 'Something changed in him,' says Tracey. James didn't like school, and had few friends. 'He was intelligent, but he was a loner,' says Tracey. 'He was a very withdrawn sort of person. We got along really well when we were young, but the older he got, the more he withdrew into himself. He was not a very social sort of guy. I'm quiet as well, a bit more outgoing than he was, but James was much quieter.'

James left school after Year 11. After leaving school he was unemployed for a long time, and he would sit in the lounge room at home all day, watching cricket. His father would get angry with James and they frequently argued; it was clearly a fractious relationship. Finally, James found a job in the mailroom at the Australian Taxation Office, a job he was still at when he went missing.

Tracey thinks their strict upbringing had a definite detrimental effect on James. When he was in his late teens he was diagnosed with depression, and was taking medication for the illness. 'It was a chemical imbalance,' Tracey says. 'I think it started in his late teens, early 20s, something like that. He also had a problem with alcohol, and he was on tablets for that as well. He was about 18 when he started those. I came home from high school once and James was passed out in his room, from drinking. He was against the door, and we couldn't get in. As soon as I walked in the front door I could smell alcohol. I'm surprised Mum and Dad didn't smell it.'

James also had therapy for his alcohol addiction. He never discussed the problem with his sister, and Tracey only discovered what James had been going through from conversations with her mother.

James moved out of home when he was about 19, and lived alone for a while. He would phone Tracey, wanting to check that his younger sister was coping okay still living with their authoritarian father. To the family's surprise, James began seeing a woman who was 20 years older than himself. Tracey thinks she was James' first ever girlfriend. The woman had a daughter the same age as James, and his parents had concerns about such an unconventional relationship.

'James wanted us to go out and meet her, so we drove there,' says Tracey. 'I thought she was quite nice, but Dad didn't like her at all. It didn't last all that long. James moved in with her, but I think that was about the time he started drinking heavily. His girlfriend was the one who helped him with all that, and took him to the doctor.' James had his girlfriend's name tattooed on his arm, but when they broke up he had the tattoo replaced with a wolf. 'He was a one-eyed West Adelaide supporter, and their mascot is the wolf, so maybe that's why he chose that tattoo,' says

Tracey. James also had a small tattoo of a dragon on his back, but Tracey is unsure of the significance of that.

After the relationship ended, James lived on his own once again. He was 22, and after the break-up with his girlfriend he didn't have any further relationships. When Tracey left home her relationship with James was not as close. 'We'd talk on the phone and I'd come and see him, but we started to drift apart a bit,' she says. The siblings would phone each other on birthdays, but didn't have much to do with each other's daily lives. The conversation often revolved around their father, with James asking his sister if she had spoken with their dad, and what was said. She is wistful in her recollections of her brother. 'He had a lot of problems, I think.'

The last time Tracey spoke to James was when he called to wish her a happy birthday. The day James went missing was his mother's birthday, and James had been to see her earlier.

James was still working for the Tax Office at the time he went missing. He rarely socialised with his colleagues, but on this night – Friday 27 May 1994 – he agreed to go out with one of them for a drink after work. However, James' problems with alcohol meant he had little self-control, and once James started to drink, the evening was headed for disaster. Tracey thinks the man from James' workplace was not really a friend, only a colleague he didn't know very well, who may not have known about James' alcoholism. James had not previously been out with his work colleagues, preferring a more solitary lifestyle. 'He wasn't one for being around a lot of people,' says Tracey.

They were drinking at a nightclub in Pirie Street, which

Tracey thinks was The Tivoli, and it was about 9 pm when James collapsed. 'James got drunk and the other man apparently just left him,' says Tracey. James was discovered unconscious in the street, and was taken to nearby Royal Adelaide Hospital by ambulance. Tracey is unsure who called the ambulance, whether it was his work colleague, or a stranger, or the hotel staff.

The details about James' time at the hospital are unclear, as the hospital initially said James had not been a patient there. It's possible James may not have had identification on him, which may have led to the confusion. It was not until James' watch was discovered left behind in the emergency department, reportedly a week later, that they acknowledged James had indeed been brought there. He stayed in hospital for a few hours, then discharged himself. His next movements remain a mystery. Did he call anyone to pick him up? Did he try to call his dad?

'I think he would have called Dad,' says Tracey, 'because he really didn't have anyone else to ask for help. But Dad said he didn't call.'

The medication James was taking to treat his alcoholism would have caused him to feel nauseous and vomit if he drank even a tiny amount of alcohol. The medication warnings state even spraying an alcohol-based cologne on the skin can cause a reaction. James must have been feeling absolutely horrendous as he drunk himself to the point of unconsciousness. It is unknown exactly which medication James was taking but it was likely a drug such as disulfiram. Worryingly, the manufacturers warn the drug should not be prescribed to someone with a mental disorder. As James was also on medication for his depression, should he have been taking both medications? If James continued to drink with the alcohol-abuse deterrent drug in his system, the reaction to alcohol may have caused flushing, nausea, thirst, abdominal pain, chest pain, dizziness, vomiting, fast breathing, fast heartbeat, fainting, difficulty breathing, or confusion. Even if James had last taken the drug up to two weeks before he had a drink, he could still have had the reaction. 'He would still have been groggy and feeling pretty crook when he discharged himself,' says Tracey.

James was last seen walking from the hospital down North Terrace. This route would have taken James past Government House, the State Library, South Australian Museum, Adelaide Convention Centre, Adelaide Casino, the railway station and Parliament House. It was about a 15-minute walk from the hospital to the train station – did he catch a train? Where to? James lived in Richmond, an Adelaide suburb about 20 minutes from the CBD. He frequently caught the bus in and out of the city. The nearest bus stop to the hospital was a four-minute walk. I don't know about the bus timetables in 1994, but today there are no buses or trains between midnight and 5 am.

We don't know what time James discharged himself from hospital, but it is thought to have been after midnight. If he intended to try to catch public transport home in the night, he would have found it very difficult. He rarely caught taxis and didn't carry much money on him – and we know he'd had a big night drinking so may not have had cash for a taxi – so his options for getting anywhere were very limited. If the hospital didn't have a record of him, he might not have had his wallet on him at all and therefore would have had no money at all for a ride home. Ron and Val lived in Plympton North, a suburb not far from Richmond, where James lived. If he was heading home that night, he would have reached his own home sooner than his parents.

So, where did James go that night?

A short walk from the hospital, a comedy theatre production called *Jokers at the Mercury* was on that night. Another couple of minutes' walk away, at the Centre for Performing Arts, was the world premiere of a performance called *Sticks and Stones*, performed entirely with Aboriginal clap sticks and singing stones. Did you go to either of these performances? Perhaps you remember seeing James walking the streets nearby? Or were the streets deserted late at night?

It is unclear how his parents discovered he was missing, but they are the ones who reported him missing to police. The police questioned patrons at the hotel James had been drinking at, and spoke to James' work colleagues and the hospital. James had a car, and more importantly a dog that he left behind at his home. His dog was a Pomeranian named Cashew. If James had decided to go away, he would probably have taken his car and certainly made arrangements for the care of Cashew. Police and his family are sure he did not return to his home the night he went missing.

Tracey didn't discover her brother was missing for a week, when her mother finally called to tell her. 'To be honest, I didn't take it all that seriously,' Tracey says. 'When we were young, he used to go away and come back, so I didn't really think anything of it; I thought, yeah, he'll come back. But the more time that passed, I realised something was wrong.'

It was about a month before Tracey started to worry that something terrible had happened to James. 'I thought he'd just packed up and gone away, but then he doesn't know anyone, so where could he go?' As time went on, it became clear James had not just disappeared for a few days like he used to. Despite their strained relationship it was clear James' parents were deeply concerned for his wellbeing. They made up 5000 flyers and walked the streets of Adelaide searching for their son.

A 1995 newspaper article from *The Adelaide Advertiser* reported that Dutch psychic Gerard Croiset Junior had approached an Adelaide journalist named Dick Wordley to pass on a letter and sketch he made after apparently having a 'vision', showing him where James Crocker's body was. Dick passed away in 1995, not long after Croiset contacted him, but I tracked down Dick's children to ask them about the letter and sketch. Dick's son Mick does not remember his father speaking about James Crocker but does remember both Croisets, Senior and Junior, speaking with Dick, and Mick remembers seeing sketches amongst his father's correspondence with the Croisets.

Croiset Sr was a Dutch parapsychologist, psychometrist and psychic. Psychometry, it is claimed, is the ability to 'see' crimes that have happened by holding objects associated with the victim. It is unclear whether his son used the same technique to produce his theory about James. Croiset Sr had his own infamous involvement with a South Australian missing person case when he came to Australia in 1966 to search for the remains of the three missing Beaumont children. He was unsuccessful. There is also no evidence that Croiset Jr was ever successful in his own psychic abilities. It is curious that Croiset would choose such a very different cases to focus his interest on – the Beaumont case is still Australia's longest running child abduction case that continues to garner great interest today, but James Crocker's case is relatively unknown in comparison.

Why did Croiset Jr have a vision about James?

Croiset Jr said that in his vision, James crawled into a large hole in the ground covered by an iron or bronze plate. In *The Advertiser* article, Croiset is quoted as saying, 'He opened it, got inside and never went outside. He wanted peace, he wanted to recover himself from the shock.' Croiset claimed James crawled into a space on the hospital grounds, possibly into a pipe, and died there. He drew a strange sketch of where James' body was concealed. The Crockers reportedly felt Croiset's theory was 'quite credible', and they searched the hospital grounds extensively, but failed to find any trace of James. The newspaper article quotes Ron Crocker as saying: 'We've searched creeks and drains all around the hospital, because we don't think he ever left the grounds. If he had gone anywhere, someone would have to have seen him.'

The police did investigate James' case thoroughly and the family were happy with their efforts. 'There was one detective, Sid Thomas, who was really good,' says Tracey. 'He worked with the Sturt Police, and he used to come and have a chat to me about things. He had talked to Mum and Dad, and he knew they weren't telling me what was going on, so he'd come and fill me in. He was really nice.' Sid Thomas is now a highly respected detective senior sergeant, still with SA Police, and has been acting chief inspector.

One line of enquiry police followed, and one that has occurred to Tracey also, is that James may have been harmed by someone close to him. 'At the back of my mind I do wonder about things. Things that I hope would never be the case, but I do think down that line sometimes. I know that he hasn't just wandered away and started a new life anywhere, I know that,' she says. 'Maybe he hitched a ride and met the wrong person, and that's it. He used to hitchhike all the time when he was younger. Maybe he did that, trying to get home, still feeling seedy and crook.'

Tracey also considered the possibility that James kept walking from the hospital, looking for somewhere quiet to rest until he felt better. 'If he'd wandered off, the hospital is right next to the Botanic Gardens, so he could have wandered into there. I don't know if that was ever searched.'

In *The Advertiser* article, Ron is quoted as saying:

Every time they drain the Torrens, or find a body somewhere, our hearts are in our mouths, wondering if it's him. People say we have done everything we could, but we feel we owe it to him to keep looking.

But when Tracey visited her parents, they would never discuss James' disappearance with her. Even today, Tracey is in the dark about many of the details surrounding the case. 'It was really hard for me when they wouldn't talk to me, as I had no-one else to talk to about it,' says Tracey. 'I don't know if they didn't want me involved. They did do an article in *The Advertiser*, not long after James went missing, and Dad told them my brother was an only child. I was a bit hurt by that.'

Because of Tracey's strained relationship with her parents, she doesn't know what they thought happened to James. It's something they never talked about, and now both her parents have passed away. 'It knocked Mum around,' says Tracey. 'She died of breast cancer a few years ago, and I think James going missing really led to that.' Ron Crocker died eight months after his wife. I asked Tracey if, now her parents are gone, she feels the responsibility of continuing the search for James now falls to her. 'Definitely. I contacted Missing Persons and told them Mum and Dad have gone, and could they please keep in contact with me about James' case. A lady from Missing Persons rang me asking for my permission to put a flyer up at the railway station about James. I said yes, definitely.'

Tracey has been waiting for almost 30 years to find out what happened to her brother that night.

It's tough. When my own son goes out, it's natural to worry, but I get really paranoid. I worry that something's going to happen, or he's going to go missing when he goes out. I'm very protective of him.

Losing her brother took a terrible toll on Tracey. 'I did start drinking quite heavily when he went missing,' she bravely admits. 'But I sorted all that out, and my husband's been really great, he's helped me through it. I'd only been seeing him for six months when James went missing. He hadn't even got to meet James.'

As I'm writing this story today, I've just shared a new missing person case to the AMPR Facebook page; a 33-year-old man who has disappeared around midnight from Canberra

Hospital. Just like James. We have a much better chance of finding this man than they had of finding James back in 1994 because today we have social media. I wish I'd been able to make James' disappearance public back then. There has never been a coronial inquest into the suspected death of James Crocker, but I think there really needs to be one. Not only to investigate his disappearance, and provide much needed answers and information for Tracey, but also to look into the medications James was taking when he went missing. James Crocker was in serious trouble that night, and several different people had a duty of care to make sure he was okay.

James Crocker must not be forgotten, but I tend to think he's the sort of man who would be astonished that someone has included him in a book. I don't think he felt he was worthy of that.

But you are, James. Where are you?

If you have any information about what happened to James Crocker, please call Crime Stoppers on 1800 333 000.

CHAPTER SEVEN
Marcia Ryan

Marcia Ryan was last seen walking beside the Princes Highway Victoria, at Moe on 19th August 1996, walking towards Morwell, 1 km before the Yallourn turn off. Her car was located abandoned by the side of the road about 1.5 km away. Marcia had been travelling with her Smithfield Heeler/ Border Collie dog Ziggy. Marcia's wallet was later located on the roadside near Darnum, 20 kms from her vehicle. Marcia was 33 years old.

Marcia Ryan grew up in a large, noisy, happy Catholic family – there were five children in five years. Marcia was the baby. Eldest was Paul, then Dianne, Mark, Tony and Marcia. 'One of my happiest memories of Marcia was when she was born,' says Paul. 'I doubt Tony or Mark would remember, because they were only one and two at the time, but we really wanted a girl. We had three boys and one girl, and all this focus was on wanting another daughter, and we got one, so we were really happy, we felt great. She was a lovely girl.'

Just before Marcia was born, Paul remembers the family of six buying a house and moving to Melbourne with all their possessions and furniture in a big truck, and Mum about a week away from giving birth. The family turned up at their new house to find someone else living in it. They'd paid a deposit but been gazumped, and the agent hadn't bothered to let the Ryans know. They had nowhere to go. They very quickly had to find a house to rent that was big enough for seven. The family moved around various Victorian towns in the early years, with the children born in Bendigo, Shepparton and then Melbourne.

When Marcia was about 10 years old they moved to Box Hill. They had a typical, happy Aussie childhood. 'We played together, fought together – all the usual sibling stuff,' says Tony. Paul remembers the five children always being together, playing and doing things as a family. 'We made our own billycarts and rode them around the streets,' says Tony. 'We didn't go inside until the sun went down. We visited our grandparents on Sundays, had holidays on farms and at the beach. When we were kids we went to Bermagui every year; they had a place called the Blue Pool, a big rock pool on the edge of the sea, we'd swim in there. That is a happy memory. It was a very good childhood. We were given every opportunity by our parents. Dad worked hard, we always had food on the table.'

Tony says Catholicism was an important part of the Ryan household. 'But as teenagers, all the kids walked away from it. We were no angels,' he says with a chuckle. 'Marcia was the youngest and didn't get in trouble at home, just at school. She was a talker, we all were. When there's five kids in the family, you've got seven of you sitting down to a meal every night – because we always ate together as a family – you learn to talk. Not much listening; you just learn to talk loudly to get heard. Marcia was the littlest, and always Dad's favourite. She was reasonably clever at school.'

Tony says that it was when Marcia became a teenager that she started to change and become a little more rebellious. 'Through her teenage years, I thought she was a normal teenager,' he says. 'No problems, no drama. Maybe a bit of hanging round with the wrong people, but then again my parents regarded any child of a divorce as "wrong people".'

Marcia and older sister Dianne were always close. 'In our teenage years the four of us drank, smoked, got up to stuff at parties,' says Tony. 'One didn't – my brother Mark. Marcia was rebellious, she used to fight with Mark a bit, he'd pull her hair. She used to get invited to these parties by Dianne – Marcia was about 14, Dianne 18. They were so close that Dianne was happy to have her younger sister hanging around her friends. She was protective of her too. After Dianne's accident, things changed.'

Tragedy struck the Ryan family on 28 September 1980 – grand final night – when eldest daughter Dianne, aged 20, left a party with four friends in her car. She got about 200 metres down the road when a 16-year-old kid, joyriding in a stolen car, on the wrong side of the road, hit her head on. Dianne was killed instantly, her injuries horrific. Marcia was at the same party. When others rushed inside to tell people there'd been a terrible accident just down the road, Marcia went outside, and said, 'That's my sister's car.' She ran to the car, arriving at the crash scene before police, and helplessly watched her sister die. It's an unimaginable thing for a 17-year-old girl to have to go through.

'She looked into the car. She saw the worst of it,' says Tony sombrely. Tony was at a girlfriend's house when his brother Mark arrived to tell him the news about his sister. The death of their sister was a shock to them all. 'Dianne had her career mapped out; she was doing really well in it. She was studying physiotherapy in Melbourne,' says Tony. Her life was cruelly taken before it had even begun. The family came together but were helpless to try to comfort one another. 'Mum and Dad had to identify the body, to see their child smashed up,' says Tony.

The trauma that comes out of that ... how a person deals with it ... we just tried to cope as best we could. I don't think that we really coped. You wake up the next day and think, was that real? Yes, it was real. Okay, we've got a funeral to organise, we have to let all the family know – we have a huge family. Everybody's devastated; we had people constantly knocking on the door. These days they have trauma counsellors and support, but back then, that didn't happen. Marcia would have just been told, there's a funeral in two days' time, be ready for it.

As kids we just thought, stay out of Mum and Dad's way, they're upset. Don't do anything to upset them more, they've got enough on their minds.

Marcia's trauma at witnessing her sister's horrific death went largely unchecked, as her parents dealt with their own grief and the practicalities of their daughter's death. Older son Paul was living in NSW at that time and returned to Melbourne for the funeral. Tony thinks Marcia may have spoken to Paul about what she went through, but he doesn't recall her speaking to anyone at the time. All her pain and grief, and the violent experience, was bottled up inside her.

'Marcia changed after Dianne died,' says Mark. Tony agrees, noticing his sister's emotional decline. 'Things went a bit haywire with Marcia,' he says. Marcia, at 17 years old, left school and decided to move to the small town of Dondingalong, west of Kempsey, in northern New South Wales, perhaps as a way of physically distancing herself from the horror she had witnessed in Melbourne. The whimsically named Dondingalong – Aboriginal for 'wild apples' – is a small community of less than 700 people. A glance over real estate listings describe it as a 'retreat from life', 'peace and privacy', 'rural seclusion'. It probably looked like a good place to hide and heal, and Marcia moved in with a man she met there.

'She lived out in the bush in a dingy old house for a few years,' says Tony. 'They were living pretty rough,' says Paul. 'It was just a little shack out in the bush, no power or facilities.' Tony was worried for his little sister, and went to visit her. 'A mate and I went up the coast and met up with her in one of the country towns,' says Tony. 'We spent a few days camping in tents, swimming, and we'd drive to the local pub for tea. One funny memory was driving back from the pub one night, we'd all had far too much to drink. The police pulled us over and took Marcia back to the station, leaving me and my mate on the side of the road. An hour later she was back – "Oh, they let me go," she said. She'd talked her way out of it. I said, "You've got the gift of the gab, you have!" But she probably just cried,' Tony says with a laugh.

But Marcia's carefree, relaxed life in the bush was about to take a sour turn. The relationship with the man she'd moved in with was not a healthy one. Tony painfully recalls the events that changed her life into a nightmare. 'Around this time Marcia got into some drugs and stuff that she shouldn't have gotten into. I think it was LSD, or something like that. She had a psychotic episode – she had these hallucinations and she was running through the bush, naked, chasing a guy with an axe. That's when the police got involved and locked her up. Marcia was not a violent girl; she wasn't the sort of person to chase someone with an axe.'

Paul lived in Byron Bay, about 360 kilometres away, close enough to visit Marcia and try to keep an eye on her. 'Someone rang me,' he says. 'They said Marcia was in a bad way. Basically, she and her boyfriend were stoned day and night, not eating, not looking after themselves. She probably felt pretty trapped in the situation. They said Marcia was in the women's refuge in Kempsey. Her partner had been knocking her around a fair bit. I went to try to see her, but I had difficulty because her partner had long dark hair, and so did I at that stage, so when I turned up they thought I was her partner, trying to pretend I was her brother. When I eventually saw her, she was bruised. But when I saw him, he had both arms in plaster. When I spoke to him to ask what was going on, he told me he'd been trying to knock some sense into her. I thought, that's not going to bloody help, you idiot! Some people have some strange ideas.

'He later moved to Greece to live, and he's only ever been back to Australia once. He wasn't here when Marcia went missing. I picked her up from the refuge and took her back up to my place. She'd be up in the middle of the night, she wouldn't stop cleaning, she was having auditory and visual hallucinations.'

Paul took his sister to Lismore hospital to try to help with her extreme mental health issues. He contacted Tony to let him know what was happening. 'She ended up in the psych ward at Lismore hospital,' says Tony. 'She was off her nut, completely and totally. She was in the secure area of the psych ward; she was so bad that we didn't know who she was anymore. We could see Marcia somewhere inside her.'

Knowing that Marcia would need ongoing treatment, Paul asked his parents to come and get her to take her back to Melbourne. 'Mum and Dad had been on the Gold Coast and about to head back to Melbourne, and they came to my place to pick her up,' says Paul. 'She was quite psychotic. I have dealt with a lot of people with mental health issues, and she was off the planet at that stage. It was exacerbated by the violence, but it was drug-induced psychosis.'

Tony travelled to northern New South Wales to help with Marcia. 'Mum and I went up there to try to bring her back to Melbourne, but the laws in New South Wales were different to the laws in Victoria; in New South Wales a patient could only be transported to another state by car, with a nurse in the car, then when you get to the Victorian border they're no longer allowed to be transported by car, they have to be transported by *plane*, with a nurse in the plane. I was up there for about a week with Mum, trying to get Marcia into a psychiatric facility in Melbourne so we could take care of her. The system was saying, "No, you can't do that," and we were saying, "YES, WE CAN, AND WE WILL!" By this stage I'd had to go back to Melbourne, and Dad went up there to be with Mum.

'Eventually we got one doctor to agree that as long as we had a nurse in the car who could administer the drugs she needed in case she went off the rails, we could drive her all the way back to Melbourne. We got her into a place called Willsmere [formerly known as Kew Asylum] for about 18 months. She was about 22 years old by this stage. When I went to visit her there all this stuff came out about Greek mythology, numerology, all these "ologies" – all this spiritual stuff, and none of it was taught in our family. I don't really know where it came from. Mum would be in tears on the way home after listening to it all, saying, "That's not my daughter."'

It was traumatic for the Ryans to see Marcia committed to a psychiatric hospital, but they knew they had no choice, as her mental health was so bad. 'One of my big feelings that I've had since the beginning was that she wanted to go missing because she didn't want to go back through those years,' says Tony. 'Those years were horrific. We used to go and visit her, and everyone else in there was a nutcase too; some were drug induced, some not, and Willsmere had a hundred of them in there, all living together. They're just not nice places.'

Marcia was very young and vulnerable; it's not hard to imagine how frightening the experience must have been for her, to not only have a serious mental illness but to be living with so many others who were also very unwell.

'We just had to keep going back there until she got better,' says Tony. 'It took a long time to get her back.'

But they did get Marcia back, and she responded well to the treatment in Willsmere. 'When she came out of Willsmere, things were back to normal,' says Tony. 'She was good. She got a job with our uncle, who ran a trucking company, and she worked there for the next 10 years, in the office. She worked with truckies who were as rough as guts, but she could hold her own with them. She sometimes used to drive the pilot vehicles in front of their trucks. They all thought very highly of Marcia and were actually all devastated when she went missing. She lived with Mum and Dad for a while, and then she bought herself a house and a motorbike. She went out with a couple of guys, but then became engaged to a man named Neil. They were engaged for a while, but both eventually realised that they were not meant to be together. The break-up was amicable and they parted on good terms.'

Marcia and Neil were together for three or four years. The family had been very happy that Marcia was settling down, but Tony felt the relationship may have been a little volatile towards the end, on Marcia's side. Marcia lived on her own, even when engaged to Neil, and Tony thinks this caused her to cope with life differently to other people. She led a quiet life, going to work each day, not earning a very high wage, paying off her mortgage and motorbike loan.

Marcia had a dog, a Smithfield cattle dog named Ziggy, who was her constant companion. She went everywhere with Marcia in the car. They'd go for walks along the beach and Marcia would throw sticks into the ocean for Ziggy to fetch. Marcia seemed happy. She started taking a belly dancing class that she really enjoyed, and she would ride her motorbike to visit friends and family. Two months before she went missing Marcia had added a large deck to the back of her house. She was on such good terms with her former fiancé, Neil, that he actually built the deck for her. They had broken up about 18 months before Marcia went missing, and were still friends.

Marcia was diagnosed with Graves' disease when she was in her 20s. This is an autoimmune illness that affects the thyroid, and when Marcia was examined she was found to have diffusely enlarged thyroid glands. The Coroner's report states that Marcia was first diagnosed with Graves' disease in June 1995, about a year before she went missing. She was told by her doctor that she needed to take medication for this for the rest of her life or she would likely suffer from mood swings. However, Marcia's father reported that she didn't take her medications as directed. She required surgery to remove a goitre, and Tony says the illness also played havoc with her hormones. Part of the recommended post-operative treatment is radioactive iodine, which can lead to sterility, and Marcia made the decision not to take the medication, so she could one day have children.

The prognosis after goitre surgery is 'lower quality of life for 14 to 21 years after treatment, with lower mood and lower vitality',[5] so could the thyroid surgery and Graves' disease have contributed to Marcia's distressed state of mind at the time of her disappearance? 'I believe that it had something to do with her going missing,' says Tony. 'The things that she wanted in her future, like Neil and having children, were disappearing. She was 33 years of age, she was meant to be on medication that can make her sterile, she was no longer in a relationship ... but she knew she wanted to have kids – the biological clock's ticking. Today it might be different as you can do IVF and there are other options available, but not in 1995. With our Catholic background too, there were all sorts of issues surrounding IVF[6] and the Pill and I don't know where Marcia's head was at with all that.'

Tony is honest about his sister's behaviour during her erratic mood swings. 'She wasn't an angel,' he says. 'She had lots of siblings, and you grow up learning to stand up for yourself, pulling hair or scratching. I remember a story she told me: she'd been out walking Ziggy along a track and a bloke jumped out and flashed her. Marcia found a stick and she and Ziggy chased him with it. She said it was so funny watching him try to pull his pants up while she was chasing him down the path!'

A few days before she went missing, Marcia took a lodger into her home. Marcia had never previously done this, but she was only just scraping by financially, and decided it would be a wise move to bring in some extra cash. She was keen to go on an overseas holiday, but hadn't been able to afford it. Marcia's parents had paid for the deck on her house so Marcia wasn't

---

5 (Abraham-Nordling, Torring, Hamberger, Lundell, Tallstedt, Calissendorff, Wallin). Graves' Disease: A long-term quality-of-life follow-up of patients randomized to treatment with antithyroid drugs, radioiodine, or surgery, Thyroid 15, no. 11(2005), 1279–86)

6 Artificial insemination is not permitted by Catholic teaching.

stressed about finances, but she wasn't really getting ahead in her life. Her mortgage and motorbike repayments took most of her small income. Tony recalls that Marcia advertised for her lodger and her ad was answered by a young man who Marcia had never met before. He duly moved in. However, the experience was not a positive one for Marcia, who quickly became suspicious and annoyed with her new housemate.

'We think that tipped her over the edge,' says Tony. 'She got really stressed about it. In her words, "He was a bit odd." She thought he was strange. It was her house, just her and her dog, and now suddenly there's this third person there.'

'She wasn't with it, all weekend, that weekend she went missing,' says Mark. 'She came here, to the family home, on her motorbike, two days before she went missing. She was all over the place. She was worried about the boarder, and didn't know how to handle having him there. She didn't trust him. She hadn't slept, so she lay on the couch here and slept. She went home, but on the Sunday, she came back here and I asked her if she'd eaten. She said no. She picked at a peanut butter sandwich for about an hour. I knew she wasn't right. I rang Mum and Dad and told them Marcia was all over the place, and they asked me to go over and see her the next day.'

On 18 August, Marcia had also been calling her parents. Mrs Ryan told the Coroner's court that Marcia was 'hyped up, having panic attacks, was paranoid and delusional'.

On Monday 19 August – the day Marcia went missing – she left work early, telling her aunt and uncle, who were also her employers, that she was not feeling well. Her uncle noted Marcia looked pale. Marcia had told them about her worries surrounding the new boarder and they assumed this was why she was unwell. That day, Tony received a phone call from their mother. John and Johanna Ryan were on holiday in Queensland at the time. They usually spent the winter months on the Gold Coast instead of in chilly Melbourne. Johanna said to Tony, 'I don't think Marcia's right … there's something wrong.' Tony asked why she thought that, and Johanna replied that she'd been speaking with Marcia on the phone and she didn't sound well, and Mark had also expressed his concerns to his mother.

Johanna asked Tony if he could drive down to Marcia's home in Larool Crescent, Seaford to check on his sister. Tony said he was at work and couldn't leave just yet. Johanna said she'd already spoken with older brother Mark, who was on his way to Marcia's. To ask both her sons to check on their sister, it seems Johanna was truly worried about Marcia's state of mind. Tony says:

> I told Mum that if Mark was on his way, he could deal with it, why did I have to go as well? Mum said Marcia just didn't sound right, so I said, okay, I'd go down too. Mum said Marcia was at home, and I asked why she wasn't at work. Mum said that she'd gone to work in the morning, said she wasn't feeling well, and went home about 10 o'clock. It was unusual for her to take time off; she wasn't the sort of person who took sick leave, so they were a bit worried about her at work. They told her to go home and have a good sleep.

It was also during this conversation with his mother that Johanna told Tony about Marcia's boarder. After speaking with his mother, Tony rang Marcia at around 2 pm and spoke with her for a while. Their conversation worried Tony; Marcia started off seemingly rational but she became more upset during the call. Marcia told Tony that the boarder's dog had left faeces all over the backyard, but the thing that disturbed her the most was finding some bones and feathers in the backyard, which to Marcia's mind meant the boarder was putting a hex on her. In reality, it was likely just a bird that Ziggy had killed.

Tony was worried about his sister, but as his brother Mark and another friend were already on their way to Seaford, he decided not to go. Mark arrived in Seaford in the afternoon. 'My best mate came with me,' says Mark. 'We got Marcia to come back to my home. I tried to get her to sleep for a while. She finally dozed off on the couch, but it was really hard to get her to sleep, because she was worried the boarder was going to steal all her stuff. So, I drove her back to her place and I managed to get her to sleep in her bed there, which was bloody good. I was watching TV and a friend of Marcia's came to the front door. She wouldn't believe I was her brother. She just didn't have any idea of what Marcia was going through. I even pulled out my driver's licence to show her, but she said she didn't care, she wanted to see Marcia and she started shouting out for her.'

Marcia's friend was upset that Mark would not wake Marcia. Marcia had told her friend she was worried about the boarder, so her friend came to check Marcia was okay. Paul can see both points of view. 'I understand Mark being angry, but I can also understand what she was thinking; that she didn't know who Mark was, and she knew Marcia had concerns about the boarder. For all this girl knew, Mark was the boarder, she'd never met him. She was suspicious. I think Mark felt the same way I did when I tried to see Marcia in the women's refuge; they didn't believe I was her brother either.'

The friend was a girl Marcia knew from her belly dancing group. Mark says the girl pushed her way past him into Marcia's home, and woke her. 'I didn't want her to wake Marcia, because I had finally got her to sleep and she was stable, and I wanted to have time to deal with the boarder when he came home,' says Mark. 'When she woke up, she was worse than what she was before – paranoid about the boarder and all his stuff being in the house. So, she picked it all up and put it out on the nature strip.' Marcia wanted the boarder to leave. He was not home when this happened, so Mark told his sister he would wait for the man to come home and explain to him what was happening, so Marcia wouldn't have to. Mark's priority was his sister's health, and she clearly wasn't well, so Mark didn't hesitate to take control of the situation and ensure the man was no longer going to be living there. Tony recalls that Mark said, 'Right, you want him out, he's gone.' Mark and Marcia didn't always have the best relationship but he wasn't going to let her be upset by some stranger.

Mark spoke with his sister for a while and assured her that he would be there to confront the boarder when he got home, but instead of this calming Marcia down, she continued to become angry and irrational. 'This boarder had a dog as well,' says Mark. 'Marcia collected all the dog turds and put them all over his stuff.' Meanwhile, Marcia's belly dancing friend was alarmed by Marcia's behaviour and told Mark she couldn't handle it and was leaving.

'I said, "You've done all the damage now, so piss off!"' says Mark. 'She should have left her asleep and left me with it.' Marcia's friend left and Mark continued to try to calm his sister down. 'Marcia was all keyed up then,' says Mark. 'I had my car parked behind hers in the driveway, and she said, "I've got to go!" I asked her where she was going, and she just said, "I'm going!" She said she was going to drive to Queensland to see Mum and Dad. I said, no, you don't have to. I told her I'd deal with the boarder. She said she was heading north. She put on blue jeans, a black top and a leather short sleeve bike jacket, and looked for Ziggy. She said to me, "Move your car, or I'll ram it." Marcia and I never used to get on, we used to fight like cats and dogs. So, I knew if she said she was going to ram it, she was. I backed my car out of the driveway, and she just took off.'

Mark was understandably concerned about his sister suddenly wanting to drive more than 1760 kilometres interstate, late at night, especially when she was unwell, and tried to stop her by standing in front of the car in the driveway. However, Marcia was adamant, and jumped into her car. She packed nothing, only Ziggy. 'She didn't take anything for herself, but she did take dog food. It was the only thing she put in the car,' says Paul. She was so determined to leave that she drove the car straight towards her brother, and Mark had to jump clear or be struck. She took off into the night. Although he'd been concerned about her leaving, Mark at least knew where she was heading. 'It sounds like it was pretty spontaneous,' says Paul. It was around 10 pm.

Mark waited at the house for either Marcia to return or for the boarder to come home. Marcia's boarder was seemingly unaware his presence in Marcia's house was causing her so much distress. He returned home on the Monday evening, but Mark would not allow him into the house. He told the man his sister did not feel safe with him, and he told him to collect his belongings and leave. Although not happy about the situation, he did leave. 'He was upset about all his stuff being thrown onto the nature strip,' says Mark. With Marcia gone and seemingly not coming home, Mark decided he had little choice but to go home himself. 'I stayed around until about 1 or 2 o'clock in the morning,' he says. He locked Marcia's house and left. Tony spent the night at home with his family, unaware of the strange events that were happening at his sister's home in Seaford.

The following day, Mark called Tony and told him he was going back to Marcia's to see if she'd come home the previous night. When he got there, he found Marcia hadn't been home. Her next door neighbour was a police officer, and Mark called in to tell him what had happened and to see if he'd seen Marcia. Mark was extremely worried about his sister because of her behaviour the previous day. 'Her neighbour asked me how long she'd been missing, and I said since yesterday,' says Mark. 'He asked me where she was going and I told him up north. He asked if she went in the Sigma and I said yes, so he got the rego and said he'd put an all-points bulletin out for the car. I rang Mum and Dad, and told them Marcia had left and said she was driving to see them.'

Mark spoke to Tony again, and they worked out if Marcia was heading to Queensland to see their parents, she'd probably arrive the following day. Tony called his parents and told them to expect Marcia. 'They didn't want to leave the Gold Coast,' says Paul, 'in case she turned up there.'

By Wednesday, with no sign of Marcia in Queensland, the family began to get worried. Johanna rang Tony, expressing her concern that Marcia hadn't turned up, and Tony tried to reassure his mum that Marcia had probably just stopped off somewhere along the way. When another day went by with no word, Tony drove down to Marcia's house at Seaford. He listened to her answering machine, but there were no messages. By Friday night, Tony was worried enough to report her missing to police. He went to Boronia Police Station, near to where he lives.

'This is where *my* trials start,' says Tony. 'I went to Boronia Police and they told me that as Marcia lives in Seaford, I should be reporting her missing at Seaford Police Station. I told them that I lived near Boronia. They said, "Well, her car's been spotted in Moe and Morwell." I thought, "That's good! She's been spotted! I wonder who she knows around there?" I thought I'd go and find her or the car, as they're only small towns. So, the police logged that I'd been in, and I decided to go and see Seaford police the next day. I went to Seaford and told the police my sister was missing, she lives around the corner, blah blah, and they told me that if the car had been spotted in Moe and Morwell, I should go and speak to the police there.

'I left there and went back to Marcia's house, and on her answering machine was a new message from a man. He said, "Hi, Marcia, my car broke down. I pulled up on the side of the road and I found your wallet. My name is such-and-such, here's my number, if you want your wallet back give me a call." I thought it was a bit odd.

'Then the next message was from VicRoads saying, "Marcia, your car's been on the side of the Princes Highway for the last four days; if you don't move it today we're going to impound it." It was then that I went, "Oh, shit. That's not good." Because in my head, I thought she was driving between two towns looking for somebody or something in those towns, like a friend or someone.'

The realisation that no-one had actually seen Marcia since the night she went missing, that her car had been abandoned and her wallet had been found on the side of the road, was horrific to Tony. 'I had a different vision in my head to what was going on as opposed to reality,' says Tony. 'I now had a problem. I've got Marcia's car on the side of the highway that has to be moved, I've got to pick up the wallet in Darnum ... and I ain't got a sister,' he says grimly. 'I had no idea where she was; she wasn't in Queensland on the Gold Coast where she was supposed to be.'

'Even when the car was found, we didn't know if she'd just broken down or run out of petrol,' says Paul.

Maybe she decided to hitchhike, which sounds a bit weird these days, but in those days we used to hitchhike quite a lot. I hitchhiked from Byron Bay to Melbourne many times. I wasn't really concerned about her; you hadn't yet had your Ivan Milats and the sort of people who mean a hell of a lot less people hitchhike these days.

There's about 15 kilometres of highway between the two towns of Moe and Morwell. It's an area Marcia knew quite well, as her fiancé Neil's family had a house near Darnum, where her wallet was found, and Marcia had been to the house a few times.

Tony was still hoping Marcia had simply gone to stay with a friend in this area. He says, 'I took a mate with me and we drove down to where the car was found. We went to Darnum first to get the wallet and the guy told me where he found it.

I didn't understand how it could have been there, and I didn't understand how he could have possibly found it within the last couple of days, in a spot where no-one would pull up in a hundred years, but he's pulled up there within two days. We drove back to the spot and it did seem to check out, what he'd said. Then we drove to Moe Police, who said to go to Morwell Police. We went to Morwell Police and they basically said, "Oh, we're not going to deal with it. Here's a coat hanger – if you want to, go and break into the car and see what's inside." So, we did!

'We went and broke into the car with the police coat hanger. There was no-one in the car – no Marcia, no dog. We thought, what if someone's stuck her in the boot? So, we broke in through the back seat as we had no other way of getting into the boot. We smashed the back seat and the firewall, but there was nothing in the boot. I thought, well, it's good she's not in the car. But where is she?'

Marcia's wallet contained her driver's licence, Medicare card, diving certificate and her address book. Tony rang a tow truck and arranged for them to tow Marcia's car from the highway, and he drove home. When he arrived home, St Kilda CIB phoned him to say they'd received Marcia's missing person report and wanted to know what was going on. Tony filled them in.

'They said, "Well, we know where the car is…" and I said, "No, you don't, because I had it moved today. And I've got her wallet." They said, "What are you doing with her wallet?" I explained what had happened, and they abused me for interfering with an investigation. I thought, hang on, I've been to FOUR police stations, at any one of them they could have said, "It's okay, we'll look after it," but because nobody would help, we did it on our own. I've never felt guilty about that, though. There's a level of frustration with whether people believe you or not, whether they're listening. I actually felt guilty about using the resources. I felt like this was our family's issue, like you know it costs police money to do stuff and you think well, they've got enough to do, it's only Marcia heading up the road. I felt ridiculous reporting a 33-year-old woman missing. She was living on her own, with her dog, she was in her own car, we thought she had her wallet in her pocket, and I'm reporting her missing? Am I insane? It took Mum and Dad four days to convince me to go and report it.'

When the CIB (Criminal Investigation Bureau) became involved, things started moving more quickly. Police interviewed Tony and Mark, and phoned their parents, who were still in Queensland. Meanwhile, Mark found himself the prime suspect in the disappearance of his sister. 'The police interrogated for me for about six hours,' he says. 'They were thinking I had something to do with it. They fingerprinted the whole house, and questioned me three times, and at St Kilda Road as well.' Tony's story and his own enquiries to date were verified, and police started to take Marcia's disappearance seriously. Police relocated the car, from where Tony had it towed, to their own yards so it could be forensically examined. 'The detective from CIB – John – was very, very good, very helpful,' says Tony. 'At this stage, Mum and Dad were stuck because they wanted to come back to Melbourne, but I kept telling them to stay in Queensland in case Marcia turned up there. We didn't know if she was on foot, or if she'd caught a bus or train. I just assumed she was still on her way to Queensland. Not having a car was no big deal for Marcia; when we were teenagers we used to hitchhike everywhere.'

A widescale search was started for Marcia near where her car was located, which included officers on horseback and hundreds of searchers on foot. No trace of her or Ziggy was found. A headquarters was set up at the Darnum pub and public appeals were made for anyone with information to come forward, and it made the newspapers in Victoria, Tasmania and Queensland, but not New South Wales, to Tony's dismay.

Crucially, a truck driver did come forward to report he had seen Marcia, about 100–200 metres away from her car, walking along the Princes Highway. He reported that she was walking in the left-hand driving lane, and he was worried for her safety. The truck driver pulled over his truck on the road ahead of Marcia and asked her if she needed help or a lift. He said Marcia appeared to be in a distressed state, but she told him she didn't need any help. The truck driver was still worried, so he drove on a little further and pulled over again. In his statement to police and the Coroner he said he was 100 per cent positive it was Marcia he spoke to, as the truck lights enabled him to see her well.

Notably, Ziggy was not with her, or at least that information has never been given to the family, and the Coroner's report states Ziggy has not been seen since Marcia left home with her. This means the truck driver didn't see Ziggy at all, only Marcia. The truck driver, who was a delivery driver for a large supermarket chain, had a GPS attached to the truck that recorded his movements. Examination of the GPS records tendered to the Coroner show there was 'no delay or deviation in the route of the truck', so the truck driver is not a suspect in Marcia's disappearance. His truck was examined forensically and there was no evidence that Marcia had been inside it. The truck driver warned Marcia how dangerous it was to walk on the road, but Marcia crossed the highway and continued to walk along it. The exact spot in which he spoke to her was just past the turn-off to Moe.

A timeline of events on the night Marcia disappeared was established. Marcia left her home in Seaford around 10 pm. At 10.50 pm, Marcia called her parents from a public phone box to tell them she was on her way to see them in Queensland. We know the time, because the call was made reverse charges. It is not known where this call was made from. The Coroner speculated it was around Bunyip or Yarragon. It would have taken around 50 minutes to get to Bunyip, so that is a likely location. An hour later, Marcia was spotted by the truck driver. The truck driver's GPS logged his stop by the side of the road as being at 11.48 pm, so it was in that hour between the phone call and the truckie finding her in distress that Marcia abandoned her car. She was not far from the car when spoken to by the truckie, so if we assume it took maybe 45 minutes from Bunyip to the Moe turn off, that leaves 15 minutes for something to happen to cause Marcia to leave her car and for her to start walking along the highway.

Where did she make the phone call from? It would be almost impossible now to find out where public phone boxes were located in 1996, but the township of Bunyip was not on the highway; she would have had to turn off at an exit to get there. There isn't much at all along the Princes Freeway, just bushland. Was it at a petrol station? Is it possible that someone was at the petrol station, listening to her conversation? But if it was at a petrol station, and she knew she was almost out of petrol, and had just told her parents she was headed to Queensland, why didn't she fill the car?

At 12.30 am that night, Marcia's car – a tan/cream Mitsubishi Sigma station wagon with Victorian registration DUP 002 – was spotted, pulled off the road, on the M1 (Princes Highway) between Moe and Morwell. The car was then logged by police as being there at 2.48 am on Tuesday 20 August, and the police had checked on it four times in the days before Tony reported Marcia missing, unaware it belonged to a missing person. The car was locked. Moe is more than 120 kilometres from her home in Seaford; it would have taken around an hour and a half for her to drive this distance, so it suggests she drove directly from Seaford to Moe/Morwell without going anywhere else, apart from her stop to make the phone call. If Marcia was intending to drive to her parents in Queensland, it's possible for her to have taken the route she was on, driving via Canberra, but that way takes around two hours longer than if she had headed north on the M31 (Hume Highway). Why did she head east instead of directly north?

Marcia's wallet was located on the highway at Darnum, a small town in West Gippsland more than 25 kilometres from Moe – but back in the opposite direction to where Marcia's car was found, towards Melbourne. It appeared to have been tossed out of a car. Did Marcia throw her wallet out of her car? And why? Was she intending to start a new life somewhere? Or was her wallet thrown away by someone who had taken her, and who was heading back to Melbourne? Police said the wallet appeared to have been thrown out of the driver's side of a car onto the nature strip in the centre of the highway.

When the car was examined it was found to have run out of petrol, yet Marcia would have just driven past a 24-hour petrol station only a couple of kilometres before. Marcia had a BP fuel card that had been issued to her from her uncle and aunt's transport business, so even if she did not have any cash for fuel, she had her card. However, her wallet was on the road back at Darnum. 'If you know you're running out of petrol, the last thing you do is throw your wallet away,' says Tony. 'This is why I have a different theory to the police. The police say she let her car run out of petrol, and then has met with foul play. But I think she's said, "I don't want anyone to know where I am, I want to start my life again, I don't want anyone to know who I am, I'll discard everything that identifies me – my wallet, my car, my cards. I'm going to get out and hitch, and I'm going to go … who knows where." But that's where I get stuck, as I have no idea where she'd go.

'The only thing is, we spent a lot of time in New South Wales as teenagers, around Bermagui, Merimbula. She'd lived in the bush at Dondingalong, and she had a brother in Kempsey on 40 acres. The bush didn't scare her, the darkness and the night didn't scare her, being on her own and dealing with stuff didn't scare her. My theory is that she's started hitchhiking, somebody's picked her up, someone headed up the coast of New South Wales and she's asked to be dropped off somewhere a few hundred kilometres up the road, and she's told them, "By the way, you don't know me." They've dropped her off in the bush somewhere, and they have no reason to tell the police, as Marcia was perfectly okay when they last saw her. She goes off and makes her own life – not easy in this technological life, but I imagine people can do it – and that's my theory. I don't like the police's theory. I like mine better.'

Marcia's story about fearlessly chasing the flasher tells us how she might have reacted to being accosted by a stranger in the night. Tony says, 'If somebody on the side of the road threatened Marcia, she wouldn't have backed down. She worked with truckies, so being confronted by someone on the side of the road wouldn't have worried her too much. But this is where my brother Paul and I differ. To go out there at midnight on a rainy night – the chances of a psychopathic killer driving along that little stretch of road at that particular time of night on a Monday, and just when Marcia's in that state of mind – the odds of that, to me, are phenomenal. How can you possibly believe that? It's beyond my ability to reconcile. But then my brother says, well, what about Ivan Milat? A killer who finds women on lonely roads? There are Ivan Milats out there and that's what they do – drive around looking for victims. And he's got me there, I can't argue with that. But there are two problems with that – either the person gets really violent and takes you out, or the person pisses off. I don't know.'

If somebody tried to attack her, she'd attack back and that would have left a whole evidence trail. If a man and a woman were having a fight by the side of the road, a major highway with lots of cars going past, somebody would have stopped, or at least reported it later. There were no signs of violence, and we had no reports from the public about a fight.

Tony also finds it strange that no trace of Ziggy was ever found. 'You'd think if someone attacked her, they'd just kill the dog and leave it on the side of the road,' Tony says. 'If he threw the wallet out, we don't know if he threw the dog out too. There were possible sightings of Ziggy near a farm my uncle owns in Longworry. We've got relatives all along that road, Longworry and Koo Wee Rup. These are all places on the way to Darnum, all places Marcia knows. She might have thought, "I'll leave him on Uncle Tony's property and he can look after my dog." I can imagine Marcia doing something like that. But probably not with Ziggy; she and Ziggy were best buddies. There were reported sightings of a dog around that area but because Ziggy was a Smithfield heeler (stumpy tailed cattle dog), there were lots of cattle dogs in that area. Finding a cattle dog isn't very difficult if you're in a cattle area.' Ziggy had virtually no tail, which was natural in her breed, and would have made her memorable if she had been spotted.

In the first few days after the search for Marcia began, Tony went to her bank to see if there had been any activity on her account. Marcia worked for her aunt and uncle, who were holding her most recent pay packet. They told Tony that Marcia would need her pay to make her mortgage payment, and they were concerned the payment wouldn't be made while she was missing. Tony collected the pay packet and took it to Marcia's bank to make the mortgage payment for his sister. The bank was reluctant to give Tony any information about Marcia's account, until he told them he worked for a bank himself and asked them to give him the information he required. He told them he wasn't leaving until they told him what he needed to know.

'I spoke to the manager and I told him my sister was missing, and that she owed the bank a mortgage payment and a motorbike payment, and I had the payment in my hand, but they would not see a cent of the payment until they told me what I needed to know,' says Tony. 'They finally agreed. I was able to look at her account and found the last transaction was on the Monday night, the night she disappeared, from a comedy club in North Fitzroy. I thought that was really odd. But at last I had some information. I rang the comedy club and they told me there'd been four tickets ordered but only two were picked up. So, I wondered who she was meant to be going with? I got the names of the people the tickets were for and I tracked down the guy she'd bought the ticket for. He said that it was really weird. They were supposed to meet up; there were two couples – Marcia, this guy and another couple. The three others all turned up; the other couple picked up their tickets and went in, but the man Marcia was meant to meet waited outside for her for an hour before giving up when she didn't arrive. He went home, not wanting to see a show that was half over. The other two tickets were never picked up. The comedy club didn't process the credit card payments until the Monday night. It made it look like she was using her credit card that night but she'd booked the tickets the week before, and never turned up.'

Tony believes these friends who Marcia was supposed to go out with that night are friends from her teenage years. Paul tells me they were old friends of his. He is certain Marcia would have kept the date if she'd been able to. 'If she'd organised to meet with people and do something, generally she was pretty reliable and she'd be there to meet them, or at the very least she'd have called and said she wasn't feeling well and wasn't coming.'

After she was released from the psychiatric facility, Marcia didn't touch drugs again. Tony has concerns that these old friends may have had a detrimental effect, coming back into Marcia's life. 'The previous few times I'd seen Marcia we'd gone for walks on the beach near her house and we'd had a few conversations ... some stuff had come out. She said, "Some of the people from my past are on my beach. It's no longer my beach, these people are hanging around." I was thinking, what people from your past? Marcia was talking a bit about Jesus, there was some Christian stuff coming through. I was trying to figure out if what she was talking about was new, or what from her past was she talking about.'

Tony is a born-again Christian, so that may be why Marcia felt the need to discuss her spirituality with him. 'I was thinking, where in your past? Hopefully not the psychosis days of 10 years ago! But she'd started hanging around with the people from her belly dancing class and these people were into crystals and New Age-type stuff. If she was talking about her old wilder friends from her teenage years, she might have been worried she would go back to that lifestyle, if she was seeing them again. That's what led her into the psych ward. I think that's what she was telling me: that she was being pulled back into it, because the people from those years were now back in her life. They found her, contacted her, and started hanging around again. She could see that she was going to end up back where she didn't want to be.

'Maybe she just thought, I've got to get away. This is all in hindsight, though. At the time I just thought that Marcia wasn't a hundred per cent, but she just seemed a bit tired, I wasn't really worried about her. I didn't know who the people were that she was talking about. But there were some signals I was ignoring. I didn't think there was a problem. I couldn't see that it was going to be a problem in the future. Now when I look back, I think maybe those were warning signs I should have picked up on. Guilt's a funny thing; after an event like this you can always pile guilt on. You analyse your life to the nth degree and say what could I have done to have stopped her going missing. I should have gone down there as soon as Mum rang me, I should have done something the week before, maybe I should have listened more carefully when we were walking on the beach. Did I contribute to it? Am I part of the reason she went missing, because I didn't listen to her?

'My brother Paul went through the same thing, thinking he should have been in Melbourne, not living in New South Wales. It's crap, but we all do it. I think the families you're interviewing for this book will all say they went through a period when they tried to work out if they were part of the reason. And every sibling will have their own view of the same thing. Her head wasn't 100 per cent when she left, and that's an issue we have to deal with as a family.'

Mark finds it difficult to talk about Marcia, and I feel carries a lot of guilt for the way Marcia left, perhaps feeling he should have been able to stop her. 'I love my sister,' says Mark. He has no reason to feel any guilt; he was there when she needed her brother, and he dropped everything and went to her. 'I've learned not to "if" and "what" over the years,' says Paul. 'You just drive yourself crazy for no gain. You'll feel guilt and it doesn't help.'

I have known Tony for several years now and he is the epitome of the phrase 'think outside the box'. When thousands may assume one thing, Tony will suggest something completely different. It's a refreshing point of view, and one that has helped him greatly, I believe, in coping with Marcia's disappearance. Tony is candid and accepting about the events that followed Marcia's disappearance.

After Marcia went missing, of course Mark's a suspect, I'm a suspect, the belly dancing friend is a suspect, Mum and Dad are suspects, anybody anywhere around the whole arena is a suspect. The people from her work had to verify her story of going home from work early, the phone call to Queensland – police have to tie up all these loose ends and work out who's the most likely person to have done something. It was pointing at my brother Mark. Until they interviewed Mark, they didn't know about the boarder.

Mark was lucky, as he had Marcia's belly dancing friend at the house with him as a witness who could later confirm his story to police. The belly dancing friend was a relatively new person in Marcia's life, and Paul had only met her a couple of times. 'Marcia had only taken up the belly dancing less than a year before,' says Paul. Police looked at, and discounted, all suspects, especially as no-one could have possibly predicted where Marcia would run out of petrol.

Tony recalls it being a very difficult time for him personally, trying to hold down a full time job, spend time with his wife and three children, and look for his missing sister. 'I had Mum and Dad ringing me from Queensland all the time, and we were all trying to work out where the hell Marcia was, trying to track down any loose ends, and the police were trying to do their job as well. I did keep records of everything I was doing so I could give it all to the police. When I'd speak to them I'd say, "Oh, by the way…" but they usually already had the information anyway. At least I felt like I was doing *something*, rather than sitting at home doing nothing.'

Tony sent me his own personal 'Marcia file': a collection of newspaper and magazine clippings, copies of police statements and the Coroner's finding, and his own notes jotted on scraps of paper from the day his sister went missing – phone numbers and notes to himself. It's a privilege to be entrusted with something so precious. Something stands out to me in this collection – two dishonour notices from the bank, the first dated 22 August for $170 and one dated 23 August for $315. Marcia subscribed to a music club, who sent her a CD each month. Chillingly, the selection for the time she went missing was *The Best of Toni Childs*, containing the songs 'I've Got to Go Now' and 'Many Rivers to Cross'.

Like many families of the missing, it wasn't just the disappearance that they had to cope with; there are many practical matters that also arise when someone disappears suddenly.

'The missing person world is quite strange, and there are privacy laws to deal with as well as difficulties dealing with a missing person's financial issues,' says Tony. 'Marcia had a mortgage to pay, but no money coming in. So, Dad wanted to rent out her house just to pay the mortgage, but he was told he wasn't allowed to as he wasn't the owner. So, what do you do? Default and let the bank take the house, and if she comes home three months later, her house is gone? We went ahead and rented out the house for five or six years. We had no Coroner's ruling or death certificate yet, so we had to apply to the Supreme Court and get Power of Attorney so we could act in her affairs. Then when it came to selling the house there were capital gains tax issues that kicked in – because Marcia hadn't lived in the house for the previous six years and it was rented there were different laws. It got to five years and it looked like we were going to have to sell her house so Marcia wouldn't have to pay all that tax on it, if she ever came back. It was very involved and complicated.

'It's really hard when a person isn't classified as dead. If a person's missing, they're missing – don't make it worse for people. Since then the laws have been changed to make it a bit easier on the families. Mum and Dad gave Marcia's motorbike to her former fiancé, Neil, on the proviso that if she turns up, he has to give it back. He always hoped he'd be able to give it back. He took over the loan and paid it off. We kept everything going in case she came back. Mum and Dad kept all her clothes, shoes, everything in her cupboards, the pictures on her walls. We only got rid of it a couple of years ago. We've still got some of it in their house, which Mark now lives in. I'm happy for it to sit there, in case she does come back one day, I can give it back to her. Her clothes will come back into fashion,' he says with a chuckle.

Marcia's childhood best friend, Louise, still keeps in touch with Tony and he says she doesn't understand Marcia's disappearance at all. 'She practically lived at our house, growing up,' says Tony. 'I went to a school reunion and a guy I had not seen for 35 years was there. He used to knock around with me and Marcia, and he was on the Gold Coast at the time she went missing. We had a good discussion about it, and there were others listening in that cannot understand how it happened. There were also a couple of others there who had met Marcia back in our teenage years. All have good, fond memories of her.'

Tony goes through spells of reviving his search, and has looked into every possible connection with his sister he can find. He says he must have contacted 30 or 40 people he didn't know but who knew Marcia. They, in turn, would give him more names of Marcia's acquaintances to check out. Marcia had a friend who lived on Phillip Island, who lived a hermit-like lifestyle with no phone and in isolation. Johanna often wondered if Marcia had headed down to see him, thinking it would be the perfect place to escape life for a while. She urged Tony to track down this man and see if Marcia was there. This seemed an impossible task to Tony, who only had a name to go by. He managed to get directions from his brother Paul, and finally tracked the friend down, who wasn't even aware Marcia was missing, as he had little contact with the outside world. He was devastated by the news, as Marcia did often visit him on her motorbike before she went missing. Tony and this friend now keep in regular contact, sometimes going to the footy together. Tony's taken him to the spot where Marcia was last seen. They explored the area together, looking down every dirt track and under every bush. Tony recalls the friend being in tears at the thought of Marcia just vanishing. 'How do you disappear, on foot, from here?' was his question.

Tony made several extensive videos when he visited the spots where Marcia was last seen, where her car was found, and where her wallet was found, both day and night. They are eerie to watch. It's dark, treacherously steep, and lonely; you can't imagine Marcia choosing to leave her car there and walk anywhere at all. I think it was important for Tony to walk in his sister's footsteps, and experience what she would have that night. Tony holds the camera in front of him as he walks alongside the highway, just as Marcia did on 19 August 1996. It would have been only about 4 or 5 degrees when Marcia walked along that road, if that. It can get down to below freezing. It's very, very dark. There are no lights now on the stretch of road, and certainly wouldn't have been in the mid-1990s.

To walk into the bush, in the middle of the night, in winter, you'd have been walking blind, and literally freezing cold. The traffic along the highway seems to move at breakneck speed, and there isn't much room to pull over. The truck driver claims that after he spoke to her, Marcia crossed the highway – another two lanes of traffic going a 100 kilometres an hour – and started to walk up the hill. There is an old hay shed on the top of hill, but it's questionable whether Maria could have seen it in the dark. Alongside the crash barrier on one side is a steep embankment, and beyond it a fence that she would also have had to tackle. It seems extremely unlikely. The scrubby, thick nature strip down the centre of the highway features a steep 1.2-metre embankment that she would have to clamber up, had she crossed the road to there, closer to her car. If Marcia kept walking along the highway to the top of the hill, near the Yallourn turn-off, there was a flatter section of the median area she could have crossed at, but in the darkness it's doubtful she would have been able to make out any details of the landscape.

On 19 August 1996, there was only 35 per cent of the moon visible, so it would not have been well lit at all. However, if she did manage to climb the embankment she would have found herself on a wide, dirt farm lane, which she could have followed reasonably easily in the dark. There are thick blackberry vines everywhere, which Marcia would not have been able to see in the dark; she would likely have been horribly scratched to reach the lane. Today, there is an electric fence running along the lane, but it's unknown if that was there in 1996.

Tony thinks Marcia would have been able to easily get over it safely, being familiar with farms as a child. Tony has filmed himself walking down farm lanes to visualise what Marcia would have seen had she spent the night in the shelter of the hay shed and then woken the following morning. It was raining – why did she leave the security and comfort of her car to walk in the dark, rain and freezing cold, across a four-lane highway, up an embankment to the farm lane, then up a grassy hill? One logical explanation is that Ziggy ran off and Marcia was chasing her, which would have explained her distressed state, and why she headed off the highway and up into the farmland. But by all accounts, Ziggy would have never left her side, and the truck driver said Marcia was walking along the road, not running to chase her dog.

'Back then there was a lot more vegetation close to the road,' Paul says. Beyond the hill is the eerily named Haunted Hills Road, alongside Yallourn Cemetery. It conjures up images from a horror film. Is this where Marcia disappeared? *The Argus* newspaper reported in 1947 that cattle would not graze on the Haunted Hills, and legend has it the hills were named by stockmen who claimed to hear 'ghost cattle' stampeding across them. The hills also saw their fair share of tragedy, with a young woman named Maria Whitelaw being found murdered on the track to the coal mine in 1918, and her husband going missing. Two skeletons were subsequently discovered in the area, but it's still unknown whether either was Maria's missing husband. Seventy-eight years later, the exact same area was extensively searched for Marcia Ryan.

Tony says the various Ryan family members have different ideas about what they think happened to Marcia that night. 'Each family member has a different viewpoint, yet we're all looking at exactly the same thing.' Tony says he and Paul have spoken at length on many occasions regarding Marcia's disappearance, and they surprise each other even now about what they think. The brothers are very close and Tony says they can spend days on their conversations about Marcia. They swap their theories back and forth and often agree to disagree, and Tony looks forward to the day when Marcia turns up alive and he can say to Paul, 'I told you so.'

'He's the big brother, though,' says Tony, 'and I normally lose to him. You've got to bow down to the big brother.'

Paul's own toddler son actually went missing overnight on his 40-acre property in northern New South Wales after wandering away, several years before Marcia went missing. The boy was found safely the next morning, after spending the night cuddled up to the family dog, who stayed with him. The fact that Marcia also went missing with her dog would have played on the family's minds. 'Our other brother, Mark, has a different view again, but he's quieter, he doesn't say much about it,' says Tony. 'Mark doesn't know what to think.'

Mark does, however, believe his sister is no longer alive. 'After 19 years, I think she's gone,' he says. The police did grill Mark as a potential suspect, directly accusing him of murdering his sister, but they quickly realised he had nothing to do with it. 'He was dragged through the wringer a bit,' says Tony. 'He was the last one to see her before she left. The truck driver spotting her alive in Moe meant Mark couldn't possibly have been responsible, as he was back in Melbourne. He was under a lot more pressure from police. I was just the naughty boy for "interfering with evidence."'

Like most of the families I have spoken to, they did consider speaking to a psychic, despite Tony's objections. 'My brother Paul has a different view to me; he's been to psychics who have pointed out on a map where they can find her body, that sort of thing; he's been down that path, out of desperation. He wanted answers and he wasn't getting them, so he went to seek answers wherever he could get them. But they came back with, "Oh, you'll find her body near water." Oh, that's just great. Ninety-five per cent of the population of Australia is near water. Does that mean if I walk across a farm and there's a dam on the farm, then I'm near water? Or is it because she's lying underneath a tap? Is she on Bare Sand Island, 2000 kilometres up the coast of Australia? Because that's surrounded by water? Not much else there but sand and turtles. Now, if they came to me and said she was near turtles and we found her on Bare Sand Island I'd think that was a really good call.'

Tony is clearly frustrated by it all. 'That's like saying "there's air where she is". Oh, okay, I'll go and check every spot that's got air. It's ridiculous. Where she went missing is farmland, and there's a couple of dams. Nearby is the Hazelwood Open Cut Coal Mine, and it's got a lot of water in it. Anybody looking up where she went missing would see that on the map. Police went and checked it out, and I've been up there myself, because one of the theories was she fell in there. But to get in there you have to go over a big pipe that's about a metre above the ground and half a metre wide so you have to climb over it, then climb over a big cyclone wire fence, with barbed wire along the top, to get to the cliff where they suggested she fell into the water. It's not something you can do by accident. And she wouldn't have been able to hide herself – her body would have floated to the top. She would have been found.'

The trouble with it being so many years is you think a lot, and I have. If she was hitchhiking, and picked up by the wrong person, and done away with, now they've got a body to dispose of. Unless they're really good at it and had a plan, they would have dumped the body on the side of the road, and she would have been found. So, they would have had to bury her, or put her in a freezer out the back of a house somewhere, or something. They've got a dog to dispose of as well. More than 25 years have passed and this place where they've buried her or disposed of her body has never been located accidently by bushwalkers or whatever? Possible.

But the other theory is she was trying to commit suicide, and that's a whole different issue. She wasn't in the right frame of mind — she's got debts, can't pay her loans, life isn't worth living, she's struggling, doesn't want to work anymore, suffering depression, there's a freaky guy living in her house and the old friends turned up who she was scared were going to pull her back into a world she didn't want to be in. She'd started the belly dancing and maybe wanted to do that full time but couldn't get a job — I don't know what was going through her head. So, she decides to knock herself off. She's driving down the road, gets to Darnum, doesn't need her wallet anymore so she chucks it out the window. Runs out of petrol, so she walks until she finds somewhere to kill herself. Walking along the road, out in the middle of nowhere, 12.30 at night, cars and trucks going along the highway — if you're going to kill yourself, you jump in front of a truck. At 100 kilometres per hour they're not going to see you until they've hit you. So, she didn't do that.

Did she go looking for a mine? Hmm, where's a mine in this random place I've just run out of petrol? If you're going to commit suicide, you can't hide your own body. If you drown yourself, you're going to float to the top. If you jump off a cliff, they're going to find you at the bottom of the cliff. After you find a cliff. I just don't think suicide's really an option. And if she killed herself, she'd have to kill her dog — the one thing she treasured more than anything else on earth. When she got into that car, the ONLY thing she took with her was the dog. Are you going to sit there and look into the eyes of your dog and say, 'I'm so sad, I'm going to kill you first'? You're not going to kill your dog. If she'd killed herself and left the dog behind, the dog's going to be found and people would realise that's Marcia's dog, she must be in the area, and they'd find her body. I'd never heard her talk about suicide.

She did talk about wanting to get away, from the people who were trying to drag her back into her past. She'd been told by the doctors she could never, ever touch drugs again after what they did to her before. I think she wanted to run to Mum and Dad and away from her life. When she took off, I always felt she was trying to get away. I didn't know what she was trying to get away from until later but the more I found out later, the more I felt she wanted to get away. It may sound a really stupid thing to say now, but she was a survivor. She knew how to deal with stuff, she survived all those years and the drugs. She was an independent woman and she'd lived some really good life. She didn't take no for an answer, she just did it.

Tony believes that if it was a psychotic episode that caused Marcia to disappear, similar to the one that had happened more than 10 years previously that landed her in the mental hospital, she may even think she is her dead sister Dianne. 'If she thinks she's Dianne, she may have taken on her date of birth, her middle name … she knows everything about Dianne, so has she set up a new identity as Dianne? She might be so traumatised from Dianne's death and revisiting that, that she actually thinks she's Dianne.'

Mark thinks it's possible Marcia dropped out of society to join a cult. 'Like the one in Bairnsdale,' he says. 'I reckon that's the only way she'd be alive. Who'd pick up a 33-year-old woman with a dog? That's what we've been asking all the time. Even though Ziggy was a lovable dog.'

I suggested to Paul that when Marcia said she was 'heading north', she may have meant northern New South Wales, where she had lived before. Paul isn't so sure. 'My problem with that, with her having made herself disappear, is from talking to Mark, I don't think she was in the mental state to have been able to plan that kind of a disappearance where you become invisible; it's not that easy. You cannot use your bank account again. To set yourself up with tax and that kind of thing. I don't really know what happened, it's all just speculation, but I don't think, in the state she was in, she'd be able to plan. That's the only reason that I don't think that's what happened. Not impossible, but highly unlikely. That only leaves us with something untoward happening. Her mental health was poor, but according to the truck driver who did pull over, he couldn't persuade her to go with him. I'm a bit dubious about whether she would have gone with someone. But if you're stuck in the middle of nowhere in the middle of the night, there'd be some temptation to go. She had the dog with her as well.'

The coronial inquest into Marcia's disappearance was held on 10 October 2001 by Coroner Francis Hender. The Coroner agreed with the police theory about what happened to Marcia, finding that she died on or about 19 August 1996 as a result of suspected murder, by person or persons unknown. Tony knows there are aspects of the investigation into Marcia's disappearance that police have not revealed publicly, even to the family. 'I imagine they withhold information, as they should, in case they need to use it down the track against someone. I don't begrudge them that. I would like to go through her files and see what's in them ... then again, I might not want to see what's in them.

But the Coroner made his ruling based on all the information available, and to come up with that ruling I feel that there must be something in there that we don't know.'

Until the inquest John and Johanna had held onto the hope that their daughter was still alive, but the finding made them realise that perhaps she wasn't. 'It changed their thinking, and it really hurt,' says Tony. 'It probably aged Mum 10 years.' Paul says, 'They'd often stop the car, thinking they'd spotted her out of the corner of their eye. Of course, it never was her. They varied in their thoughts; sometimes they were convinced that she was alive and she'd turn up, and other times, less convinced. The first death *(of Dianne)* really put 10 years on them and the second one just buggered them. It was just too much. And I think that's part of the reason that for a while they wouldn't countenance anything other than she's alive, but then you'd listen to their conversation and realise they were really just trying to convince themselves. It was too much to face. Dad couldn't face losing two daughters. It was a protective mechanism.

'That was one of the reasons they didn't sell the flat on the Gold Coast – she might have turned up there one day. They'd go up every winter, thinking Marcia knew they spent every winter up there, so she might turn up. They were just thinking she might have been in a psychotic state and confused, and not knowing who she was or where she was, but I've had a lot of dealing with people with mental health issues on a daily basis for close to 30 years, and people who are psychotic have moments of it, but times of lucidness as well. It's fairly unusual to think someone was totally psychotic for over 20 years. At one stage we were checking all the hospitals and mental health facilities on the off chance she might have turned up there – anyone who fitted the physical description but wasn't answering to that name – but we didn't have any luck there.

'Then sometimes Mum and Dad would get an idea that a particular person may or may not have been involved in her disappearance, but no luck there either. At the time there was some speculation about the boarder, who had been treated very poorly. If you put yourself in his situation, he's paid his money and moved in, then been kicked out. She had to cope with having someone else move into her space. But Mark was still there when the boarder came back – how would he know where she'd gone? It doesn't pass the common sense test. The time the car was spotted and when she was spotted by the truck driver wouldn't have allowed her to have doubled back, go home and then go again. She couldn't have gone any significant distance. She'd done the trip a few times and sometimes she did take that coast road and sometimes she went the other way. The coast road does take a bit longer, but it's a more scenic drive, and there were some people she knew who lived further on along that route. One of them was the brother of one of the guys in the car accident with Dianne. They lived a fair distance from where the car was, though.

'There was a guy who I used to live with in Melbourne, he actually lived with Mum and Dad for a while, and he knew Marcia well. He used to live in the Morwell or Traralgon area. She may have intended to call in and see him on the way. I'm sure the police spoke to them all.' Paul, however, does think it was just coincidence that they knew people in the area where the car broke down.

Tony doesn't agree with the Coroner, still believing there's a strong chance his sister is alive and well, out there somewhere, and in his think-outside-the-box way he has a different perspective. His strong Christian faith has helped him cope. 'To this day I'm still stuck in my ways. Being a born-again Christian, I had a lot of people around me praying for Marcia to be found, but I didn't, I had the opposite prayer. My prayer was – if she doesn't want to be found, don't let her be found. It's what *she* wants that we should be praying for, not what we want. We're all caring about ourselves – it hurts that Marcia's missing, or I feel sad – and I say, well, think about Marcia! If she wants to get away, the last thing she wants is us out there bloody well looking for her. She doesn't want to be found, and here's these pesky people finding her! Maybe she's got a legitimate reason for wanting to get away, and we just don't know what that reason is. So, why should we assume that she wants to be found?

'So, I prayed, as if my life depended on it, that if she doesn't want to be found, don't let her be found. Twenty-five years later I'm still right. I'm quite happy to live in my delusional world that she's alive and living in New South Wales somewhere. I couldn't think of anything better than her living her own life, and if she doesn't want to talk to us as a family? Well, good on her. That's her choice, her life. You know, I'd love it if she wanted to come home and say she'd changed her mind. Or what if she thinks she's somebody that she's not? She may actually think she's the Queen of England or something, and she's living happily in her own little kingdom somewhere in the middle of nowhere. If that's what's happening, then good luck to her. I'd like to see her, like to have a chat to her and find out why, and give her a good kick in the arse for disappearing on us, but the reality is, if that's what she wants, good luck to her. Why should we interfere? That's been my view all along. But I'd love her to see my adult children, as they were only little when she went missing.'

> *Until her body's found, or until she's found alive, my prayer's been answered. It's her needs that are important, and God cares about her needs, more than the people who are coping okay. My greatest prayer is, let it be your will, not mine, and I think Marcia's taken me to that point by disappearing, that I'm comfortable to pray that prayer, and it's almost the only prayer I pray these days.*

Paul says he would welcome his sister back with open arms. 'If she turned up tomorrow, we'd all kick in the money and get her a house. I'd be wondering why, and there'd be a slight amount of anger there as well, which probably wouldn't help, but I'd think well, that's the way it is now. It would be good to have her back. The pain is only partially buried. Sometimes it sticks its head out.'

Family has always been very important to the Ryans, and Tony credits his wonderful wife Robyn with helping him cope through the years. 'She watched me tearing my hair out, and writing notes, and trying to get something to happen. We've been married more than 30 years, and I've been very, very fortunate with her. I had all girls – even my granddaughter and two nieces – I lost two sisters but got all girls. My three daughters were young when Marcia went missing. My work was pretty good, I'd say to them I needed to go and look around where she went missing and a couple of workmates came with me on those trips.

'I had a lot of support from family and friends. I've had a good life, I had a good job, three beautiful daughters, great wife. I had to get on with my life after Marcia went missing. The hardest thing was feeling like we should be doing something, all the time, to find her. When the police searched the bush, we could go and search with them and we felt we were contributing to finding her. But the reality is, there's nothing you can do. It got to the point where Mum and Dad needed more support than anyone else, so I made sure I visited them regularly, had dinner with them, sat down and talked.

'What it was doing to Mum and Dad was killing them, especially Mum. There are days when it was harder, like Mother's Day, her birthday, Dianne's birthday, grand final night *(when Dianne was killed)*, the anniversary of when she went missing. A few years after Marcia went missing, on Mother's Day, Dad decided to cheer Mum up and arranged for a big bunch of flowers to be delivered. The delivery guy walked up to the door and Mum ran out thinking Marcia had sent her flowers for Mother's Day. She was so depressed when she saw they were from Dad. Here's Dad thinking he's doing this wonderful thing and suddenly his wife's in tears. He was just trying to be a solid husband, a good person, but it was a mistake.

Mum never gave up. She would never sell the house in case Marcia came home. They had lost a second daughter and in 1996, the same as when Dianne died, there was no counselling.

Paul has tried to not let the loss of his two sisters impact his relationships with his own daughter. 'You can't smother people, it doesn't work,' he says. 'My wife was really supportive, and she and Marcia got on extremely well. They were the same age.'

'It's impacted my life,' says Mark. 'It's impacted the whole family. Both parents are deceased now, and they died not knowing what happened. I inherited the family home and I'm still living here, but I still think one day she's going to show up. I used to know a bloke who'd go walkabout and never talked to his family in 10 or 12 years, until I told him to talk to his brothers. Marcia didn't know who she was. The way she was talking on that Monday night, I knew she wasn't okay.' Mark doesn't believe Marcia's state of mind had anything to do with her previous mental health issues, and thinks it was purely her fear of the boarder that triggered her panicked response. He doesn't believe the boarder had anything to do with Marcia's disappearance. Mark has clearly suffered in the years since Marcia went missing. 'I pulled a guy out of a burning caravan in Kempsey, and after that I had a lot of trouble with alcohol. It's how I coped with the death of my sister. I drank a hell of a lot, but I haven't touched a drink since my mum died 11 years ago. I promised her I wouldn't.'

The day I interviewed Paul was Marcia's birthday. He says it is not a happy day for him.

There's a lot of pain, losing two sisters. And Mum and Dad now, as well. We've been reduced to a small family. I'm at the stage where I would just like it to be resolved, even if the outcome wasn't exactly what I'd want to hear. Just to have it.

Paul feels that living away from Melbourne has helped him cope a little better. 'I've been trying to analyse that lately,' says Paul. 'My wife, for some time, has wanted to move to Melbourne to be closer to family. But losing Marcia and Dianne has made me not want to go back. I think if I'm not actually in Melbourne, in my mind I can trick myself into believing that they're all down there and everything's still going well. But when I go and stay in Melbourne, I can't pretend. It's in my face a lot more. When I visit, I sometimes spend a night at Mark's, who is still in Mum and Dad's old house. I probably would have changed it if I lived there, but Mark's changed nothing. Everything's the same. There's a whole lot of Marcia's stuff still in the cupboard there, waiting. Her scuba gear is in the garage. There's a lot of reminders.

'And I'll often run into people who were friends of hers. It's not easy to just go on with life and pretend things are just normal. I can't do that. I find it all a bit much. The emotions are there, but I try to work through it in a logical sense. I work with homeless people and often have to deal with their deaths, and I'm quite good at coping with it all, burying it all, and I'm not easily shocked. In my job I deal with girls who are pregnant at 12, and all sorts of unsavoury situations, so I switch off to it a bit.

'I really believe she's probably deceased. Going through all the evidence that was presented to the Coroner, and speaking with the detective leading the enquiry, his belief was that she was dead, that it was foul play, but they didn't have a body so they could prove that scenario. Because there's no 100 per cent proof, I still leave a small area where she could be alive, but I think that's the most likely, that harm has come to her. Tony does believe she's alive and it probably hit him more than me. I was very close to Marcia, but he was closer.'

I remind Paul that he was a wonderful brother to step up and rescue Marcia from the violent situation she was involved in with the abusive boyfriend, and he reluctantly acknowledges that, but the survivor's guilt still plays on him, as it has with every family I have spoken with. He does realise it's a pointless emotion. He also thinks that it may have been too late for Marcia to avoid being damaged by her early traumas.

Tony is frustrated that once a missing person case goes cold, especially if there has been an inquest, police no longer actively investigate it:

Once the Coroner makes his ruling, you go off the books. They're no longer here; why dedicate resources to it, they're not going to find out anything until something new comes along, so the family doesn't matter anymore. I don't know where her file is now. I wanted to look at the records — they changed the system in Victoria, took everything out of the regions and centralised it in the city. But then they changed it again and sent everything back out to the regions, so when you try to track down a box of files, it's not easy to find. You go round in circles and try to find the right person to help find it and by the time I got there, I didn't have the motivation to find it anymore. I dropped it. But then I got a bit of encouragement from someone and I decided I'd go for it again; you get a bit of energy for a few weeks. I went out to where she disappeared and it's all changed; there's new barriers on the sides and the trees are no longer shrubs, they're 12-foot high trees, things

don't look the same, and you think, I can't even recognise the
area now. It's all moved on, so maybe I should too.

Paul is hopeful for any clue that might help solve the mystery of Marcia's disappearance. 'Anything we can do that might jog someone's memory about something they saw. Ten or twelve years ago I had a phone call and they asked if Marcia Ryan was there. It was very strange. It might have been someone who was randomly ringing Ryans, looking for her. They didn't ask any other questions. It was very random. At the time I thought it might have been significant, but now I don't know. The only other thing is that Marcia used to say if she was going to go somewhere and wanted to change her life and start again, it would be in Tully, in north Queensland. But as far as I know she'd never been up to that part of Queensland; it's a long way up and I don't think she knew a soul up there. But maybe that's the point.'

To this day, Tony still follows up leads about his sister. He's been contacted by people telling him stories of bodies buried in the bush, of possible sightings. He remains level headed and doesn't get too emotional, but Marcia's disappearance is still very much with him, every day. The Covid pandemic slowed down his expeditions into the bush to search. But he's back doing just that these days.

He recognises the importance of families being involved in making appeals to the public. In 2021 he said to me, 'I stayed off the system during Missing Persons Week this year. Interesting that when I spent time answering stuff the previous two years, people contacted me with information. This year, I did not get involved in any commentary, and no-one contacted me with any new information. I think when people see that someone is actually interested then they are more likely to come forward, regardless of any reward.'

Tony's DNA is on file with police, just in case it can one day be matched with Marcia's remains. Tony thinks the police also have his parents' DNA on file but isn't sure. 'As a sibling, I think the information about DNA testing should be readily available to us,' he says. 'Now that Mum and Dad have passed away, they should have taken the DNA of her siblings, but we were never informed.'

I asked Tony if he would be okay with never knowing what happened to Marcia, and he takes some time to think. 'Well, if she's never found, my prayer stays answered and my faith stays strong. If she gets found, what does that mean? My prayer is no longer answered, but I get to know where my sister is. What could be better than that? Marcia lives! We'd get her a house set up again ... the money we all got from Mum and Dad's will, my brothers and I will band together and buy her a house. We'll do whatever we need to do to get her back on track. Or she might be a multi-billionaire and she can help *us*,' he says with a chuckle.

In May 2022, as my book readied for publication, Tony met for the first time ever with 'the boarder', the man Marcia took into her home just before she went missing. This man has had to endure decades of suspicion, and it has greatly impacted his life. Like 'the truck driver', online detectives have wildly speculated that these men killed Marcia, despite them both being ruled out by police very early in the investigation. The boarder didn't even know his belongings had been discarded by Marcia until hours after she left her home, and could not possibly have known which direction she headed in, as her family didn't even know. He was grateful to Tony Ryan for reaching out to him for the meeting. He was unaware of Marcia's history of mental illness before he moved in.

'These days she would have probably been diagnosed with PTSD,' says Tony. 'She would have received proper support and treatment. Things have changed for the better in those circumstances. He was really appreciative that I explained everything to him and told him the family do not believe he was involved in her disappearance. He was very relieved and told me our chat has lifted a great weight from his shoulders, as each year when the anniversary comes up people make comments to him that are wrong and hurtful. Hopefully, he will now be able to move on a bit.'

Marcia's parents have since passed away. In 1996, not long after she disappeared, they gave an interview to journalists Martin Daly and Jason Koutsoukis. With Jason's kind permission I include part of the article here:

From *The Age*, 1996.

There is now increasing concern that Marcia Ann Ryan may not be coming home. Her mother dreads this: her father refuses to accept it. But for 47 days, there has been no trace of the 33-year-old Seaford woman who disappeared as she drove from Melbourne to visit her parents in Queensland.

Her parents, John and Johanna Ryan, talk of their missing daughter in a mixture of tenses. They refer to her in the past tense and then, as if to make amends, they substitute 'was' with 'is,' reinforcing a belief that Marcia might walk in the door and explain why she has been missing since the night of Monday 19 August – and why she did not call home.

They talk about their daughter under stress and great pain because, in doing so, they confront all the dreadful possibilities. But they know that publicity about the case may jog somebody's memory and help find Marcia. Her parents do not consider suicide a possibility and police have no reason to suspect it, although all options are still open. Her mother says Marcia would not do something like that to herself or to her family.

'She is the only daughter I have left,' said Mrs Ryan, referring to her eldest daughter, Dianne, 20, who was killed on grand final night, 28 September 1980, in a car accident. Marcia, then 17, was in a vehicle behind her sister. 'When Dianne died, a part of Marcia died with her,' said her father...

...Marcia rang her parents in Surfers Paradise and told them she was going to drive to Queensland to spend some time with them.

'The last thing she said to me was: 'Dad I just a need a break. Don't try to talk me out of it, I'm coming up and I'll see you in a few days',' her father said. She withdrew $50 from an automatic teller machine at Riversdale Commonwealth Bank and headed for Queensland. But police do not yet know from where she made the phone call to her father, except that it was not from her home....

...As the investigation continues, the possible loss of their only surviving daughter has drained John and Johanna Ryan. As they sat one day last week in Marcia's house they talked of their

daughter of Irish-Dutch extraction, who has 'beautiful, big, Irish eyes' and who was planning for life.

Her mother recalls conversations with Marcia about her life as a single woman and telling her she was beautiful and should have no trouble finding a boyfriend. Marcia would say: 'Mum, all mothers think that about their daughters.'

Her parents talk at times as if Marcia will come back and then, as if she may not. Mrs Ryan said: 'After losing one girl, you never, ever, think it can happen twice.' She pointed to two old chairs in Marcia's living room: 'We would like to throw them out but she would kill us when she gets back.'

Then: 'I have believed right from beginning that she is dead. I think somebody did something to her.' Mrs Ryan's hope is that Marcia is being cared for by someone or, if she has been abducted, is unharmed.

Her father speculates that Marcia may be suffering loss of memory, or be too distressed or embarrassed by all the media attention to return home.

During the conversation with Mr and Mrs Ryan, detectives Jim Cooke and Carl Stella from the Missing Persons Unit drop in. Mrs Ryan tells them she grows more hopeful that Marcia is alive because no body has been found, despite the extensive searches.

She asks Jim Cooke: 'Do you think she is still alive ... honestly?' There is silence, then Jim Cooke says: 'It is possible.'

As a tragic postscript to this family's painful story, Marcia's brother Mark passed away in August 2016, not long after I interviewed him. Paul's 'reduced family' that he spoke of is now even smaller; there's only the two of them left. Finding Marcia is now even more important.

If you have any information regarding the disappearance of Marcia Ryan please contact Crime Stoppers on 1800 333 000.

CHAPTER EIGHT
Billy Steffen

Billy Steffen was last seen on June 17th 1985 after he saw a
doctor in Elizabeth Street, Hobart, Tasmania. He was 32.

Some families just have more than their fair share of tragedy, and when you come to the end of this story you'll understand some of the pain the Steffen family has been through. Sadly, their grief has no end point, because Billy Steffen has not been seen for almost 40 years.

The Steffens grew up in Mount Gravatt, in suburban Brisbane. Susanne is the eldest, then Dianne, then Billy, and Raye was the baby. Their mother left nursing to become a full-time mum, and their father worked for the Postmaster General. 'We had a very normal, loving childhood,' says Susanne. Raye remembers their family Christmases fondly. 'Growing up, I felt closer to Billy, as we had more to do with each other. Dianne had married when I was young, and Sue was away, so Billy and I spent a lot of time together. I have a photo of me as a baby, and Billy was holding me.'

Susanne describes Billy as the apple of his family's eye. 'Because he was a boy,' she says. 'He was a tease – he teased my sister Dianne mercilessly.' Raye says with a laugh: 'He was the best tormenter out. I always tell people now no-one can torment me, as I had the best growing up. I didn't let him know I was annoyed by it.'

Dianne remembers Billy teasing Raye the most. 'He used to mock her, and give her a hard time.' Susanne says: 'He was a fun-loving boy. He had a whole group of mates at school. An average student, but he certainly was intelligent.'

Billy left school after his senior year, with no real career goals in mind. 'He liked a bit of a challenge,' says Susanne. 'After he left school he drifted around a bit, both in Brisbane and elsewhere. He really couldn't settle at anything. He ended up getting an explosives licence and worked at that for a while. He'd get bored with things quite easily. He used to drink with his mates and gamble and play cards; it was a single man's life.'

His bachelor days didn't last long, with Billy soon meeting his future wife. When Billy was in his early 20s, his girlfriend gave birth to their son, Adam, and Billy knew it was time to settle down. They married and set up home in Brisbane. 'Billy doted on Adam,' says Susanne. 'The whole family did. Mum and Dad were really happy when Billy got married, and we had their wedding at the family home.'

Billy and his wife had a second child and he named his daughter Susanne, after his sister. She's known as Susie. This shows the deep devotion these siblings had to one another. Billy was the best man at Raye's wedding, and the photo from this day is the one used as his official missing person photo. Raye says: 'Because I was the youngest, I wasn't really close to my family until I grew up. There's 10 years between Billy and I, so they were teenagers when I was a baby. I did know Billy better later on, because I was living in Brisbane at the same time he was. I was as close as he would allow anyone to get,' she says wryly.

Bill loved his young family and wanted the best for them, but he struggled with the financial burdens most young families are faced with when they start out in the world. 'I think money was always a cause for concern,' says Susanne.

Bill and his father were very close and they often worked on Bill's house together. 'Billy and his wife were always around at my parents' house, and Dad was very supportive of them,' says Raye.

Their happy family life on Brisbane's bayside sadly did not last, with Billy's marriage failing when the children were very young. 'It was all very traumatic,' says Susanne. Billy was hit particularly hard by the break-up. 'I'll always remember, one night Billy came round, and said his wife had left him,' says Raye. 'He was at the back door, crying. That really broke my heart.'

As difficult as the break-up of his marriage was, worse was yet to come. What ensued was a painful custody battle for their two children. 'Billy wanted custody of the children. It was bitter for many years; it was awful,' says Susanne. 'Billy got himself a flat at Coorparoo, so he could have the kids stay with him, but I remember going round there and we were knee-deep in fleas. Billy was unconcerned, saying, "Yeah, I'll have to get pest control,"' says Raye.

Billy's daughter Susie has some upsetting memories of this time when her parents were separating. 'I remember some court cases. I can't remember which parent I was living with, but I have this vivid memory of Dad kidnapping me, in a phone box, with police in tow. Dad went to make a phone call and I went with him; I don't know who he was calling. I remember standing in the phone box and hearing sirens, and seeing the police cars coming towards us. They flew past and I was quite scared; I wrapped my arms around Dad's leg. Dad put his hand on my head and ruffled my hair; he was still talking on the phone. Next minute all these police cars stopped in front of us and a policeman pulled me out of the phone box, and I was crying. When they walked me over to the police car, Dad was in the back. I went in the police car with him, and then that's all I remember. I assume that was something to do with custody. Sometimes I wonder if that memory is one that I created, because it's never been spoken of.'

I have asked all of Susie's aunts about this incident and none of them recall it, but it was so vivid to Susie that when she made an art project at school based on the theme of 'emotions', she drew this memory.

Billy's mental state was beginning to deteriorate, made worse by the death of his father. Billy didn't cope well, as they'd been very close. It was 1980, and the phone call came from the hospital that his father didn't have long, but Billy's mother didn't pass along the message to him until it was too late. Billy didn't get to say goodbye. He was very angry at his mother, not understanding why she hadn't let him know earlier. Life changed dramatically for Bill after his father died, as his mother's mental health also worsened and her health deteriorated in the years following.

To the family's surprise, Billy decided to move himself and the children 2300 kilometres away, to Tasmania. 'No-one knows why Tasmania, as he didn't know anyone there, he just picked Tasmania,' says daughter Susie. 'I don't know whether he was meant to have us, but we were going on an adventure. I remember we had to exchange some glass bottles for money, and then we went on the big ship. We didn't have a cabin so we sat in the seats, and we slept underneath them. Then we were in Oatlands.'

Oatlands is a very old town in Tasmania, built in the 1800s, 83 kilometres from Hobart. It has stunning Georgian architecture, with many convict-built sandstone buildings still standing. It's a very small town, with a population of only about 500 people.

It's a curious place to choose to take two young children, as surely Billy would have found it easier to find work in Hobart or Launceston. Susie thinks it's possible her father was hiding them. 'We lived in a little stone cottage,' says Susie. 'Adam and I shared a room. I don't know how long we were there; I know I had a birthday while we were there, I think my fourth.'

The children played on the shores of Lake Dulverton and enjoyed the snow of their first southern winter. 'One day we were in the lounge room, playing Lego, which Adam loved. I flicked a piece into the heater. Adam told me get it out, quick, so I tried to get it out and it flicked onto my wrist and burned me. I still have the scar, and it's actually my pride and joy because it reminds me so much of my dad. He was so angry at my brother for telling me to get the Lego out. I was crying, and Dad sat me up on the kitchen bench and tended to my wrist. I got ice cream and Adam didn't,' Susie says with a laugh. Susie can't remember how long they were in Tasmania, but thinks it was no longer than six months. One day, unexpectedly, her mother arrived in Oatlands. For a short time, all four of them lived in the little stone cottage together.

Perhaps with the promise of a fresh start for them all, Billy, his wife and the two children returned to Brisbane. Susanne was living in Townsville, and Billy asked her if she could look after the children for a while. 'Billy rang me and said he just needed a break from the children for a few weeks,' says Susanne. 'I said that was great, they could come to Townsville for a holiday with me. Adam was in grade 2 so he would have been six or seven, and Susie was four.' Susanne enrolled Adam in the local school, and they stayed with her for about a month. However, the children were desperate to go home to be with both their parents. 'As most children do, they wanted their mother,' says Raye. The children returned to Brisbane.

Billy and his wife were unable to reconcile, and they made arrangements to share custody of the children. 'I lived with Mum and Adam lived with Dad,' says Susie. 'Then we'd both spend one weekend with Dad and the next with Mum. Dad was living with Grandma and Adam. Dad would feed us watermelon and make faces out of the skin. He loved playing chess and had a computer chessboard. He'd play against the computer, and he was really good, and when he'd be winning the computer would chuck a fit and make all the pieces jump off the board,' she says with a laugh. 'Adam and Dad played chess together a lot, which I always thought was boring until the computerised chessboard would upheave the chess pieces. I found that so amusing! I would purposely try to get the board to do it!'

Raye also remembers her brother's love of chess. 'He loved playing chess against the computer. He was always up for any gambling or a laugh. Once he went to a party, and someone at the party had dared him to dye his hair blond. I nearly died when he came home and I saw his hair. None of my sisters believed me that he'd done it. He was a larrikin.' Dianne remembers this event too. 'Mum was minding the kids while Billy went out. He came home, went to sleep and next morning little Susie crawled into bed with him. She started calling out for us – there was this man with white hair and eyebrows in the bed, and she didn't know who it was!'

It was around this time, as he tried to deal with the break-up of his marriage and his desperate need to be with his children, that

Bill started drinking heavily. 'The emotional pain was so bad, he'd have done anything to alleviate that,' says Dianne. 'It was so dysfunctional, I don't know how they lived through it,' says Susanne. 'It was awful, dealing with all that grief and biliousness. Bill finally said, "Look, I can't do this anymore." He said it was devastating for him, and for the children it was just wicked. They were getting really messed up. It wasn't harmonious. There was always anger and bitterness and strife. Billy said for the sake of the children, their mother should look after them. Billy said, "I just need to go away somewhere, just to allow them to get on with it." So, he moved to Adelaide and got a job on a building site.'

Billy lived in Adelaide, South Australia for a short time, but he was becoming more and more mentally unwell. 'The next I heard, he'd been put into hospital,' says Susanne. 'I presume that was for his mental health. I contacted the people at the flats where he'd been living and found out he'd been quite depressed.'

Billy discharged himself from hospital and disappeared, leaving his family to retrieve his meagre belongings from the flat. They had no idea where he'd gone. He was 32.

This was the first time the family had seen real indications of a mental illness in Billy, but their mother had been suffering from bipolar disorder for several years. 'Bill never showed any signs of mental illness at home,' says Raye. 'But he went to this Eastern mystic, and he used to sit and meditate, and I used to think it was just so odd. That was the only thing I thought was a bit odd. But I believe that Billy had the same illness as Mum. He once told Mum he understood now. He'd started to hear the voices.'

The family discovered that after he left the Adelaide hospital, on 4 June 1985, Billy returned to Tasmania and went to see some friends who lived on a coastal property near Saltwater River, in south-east Tasmania. 'From what we heard later, he just set himself up in a tent on a beach,' says Susanne. 'This is in winter, in Tasmania. I think his body was running hot, so there was something wrong.'

'Mum had been propping him up financially all the time,' says Susanne. 'When Billy phoned Mum from Tasmania, on 13 June, he asked her for some money so he could come back to the mainland. Mum said no, she'd had enough, that was it. She said she couldn't do it anymore.' According to police reports, Billy sounded 'dazed and confused' during this phone call.

Four days later, on 17 June 1985, Billy destroyed all his property on the beach and told his friend he was going to the doctor in Hobart, then he was going to travel to see his sister Susanne in Townsville. He was seen attending a medical appointment in Elizabeth Street, North Hobart. This is the last known sighting of Billy Steffen.

Billy's sister Dianne did send him some money, care of the post office in Hobart. Susanne also sent some money and a gift for Billy's upcoming birthday: a woollen jumper to help battle the Tasmanian winter. However, in September 1985, the parcel was returned to Susanne, as it had never been collected. Susanne rang the Hobart post office and asked if the money she and her sister had sent in June had ever been collected. She was told Dianne's money had been collected, but Susanne's had not. 'At the time, in June, I never actually knew whether or not the money had been collected, but I understand now that it was,' says Dianne.

Susanne believes Billy knew to expect the delivery from Dianne but not from her, even though the deliveries should have been there on the same day or the next, and thinks this is perhaps why her parcel and money were not collected by Billy.

Raye also sent money, but it was not collected.

'That was when we listed him as a missing person,' says Susanne. 'Raye did all of that.'

Raye reported Billy as missing to Brisbane Police and the Salvation Army. It proved not to be an easy task. 'My mother had a history of mental illness, and I'd had to go three times to the court to get an order putting her into psychiatric care. So, I was used to going to the police and reporting things, and having people not take me seriously. The last time I did it the clerk of the court looked at me and said, "You know these things don't go anywhere?" and I thought, you don't know what I'm dealing with.'

Because of her own mental illness, Billy's mother didn't have the strength to cope with Billy's disappearance, so it was down to her daughters. 'All my sisters, and Susie when she was old enough, took on the responsibility to look for Billy,' says Susanne. 'Mum never really did. It was mainly Raye. She had the strongest bond with him, as she was living in Brisbane.'

Dianne's first thought when Susanne's parcel was returned and they realised Billy was missing was why he hadn't turned up to their sister Susanne's place.

I thought, where is he? He had a good relationship with Susanne, she was probably the closest to him of all the children and I know he would have attempted to make his way up to her. What's happened?

We contacted the police immediately to find out whether he'd left Tasmania. We were told yes, he had, but not in those words. The police told me they were confident that he was no longer in Tasmania. But they gave me no more information than that. How do they know he didn't go up Mount Wellington and throw himself over the side? So, they've obviously got evidence that he's left Tasmania, but we always wondered how they knew. They haven't told us how they know.

I received a phone call from Tasmania about six or seven years ago when I was making some enquiries, and the police down there said, 'We've got no bodies that are unaccounted for down here, so we think he's on the mainland. So, I don't know if they know he's left Tasmania.

It is unclear whether police ever checked the passenger records for the ship to the mainland. These days photo ID is required to board, but in 1985 the shipping companies in Tasmania were in the middle of great change. The TT Line ship *Abel Tasman* started operating on 1 July 1985, just a couple of weeks after Billy was last seen. Before this date, the ship would have been the *Empress of Australia*.

The sisters tried other avenues to trace Billy. 'The Salvation Army were really good – they went through everything, but nothing ever came back to us, they couldn't find him,' says Raye. 'We were contacted by a TV show and they were going to do a story on Billy, but I think I got scammed, because I paid $100 and I never saw him on the show. But you're just so desperate, you'd do anything to help find him.'

That just breaks my heart; you can't get much lower than scamming the family of a missing person.

'We went through all the agencies that you go through,' says Susanne. 'It's been a bit of a dilemma since; initially there were ads, in magazines – "Have you seen this man?", but we heard nothing back. He'd had a good nine months or so to make his way up to me, but he never arrived. Mum was still in the house at Mount Gravatt, so people were around in places where they could be found.'

Adam and Susie continued to live with their mother. When he left Brisbane, Billy had made a promise to Adam, which his sisters are certain he would have kept if he could. 'Billy had written a letter to Adam,' says Susanne, 'and he said that when he turned 13, Billy would come and get him, and they would trek across the Nullarbor together. That was a really big thing. Adam would have been seven or eight when Billy went missing. That was the next junction in our lives, when that date came up, when Adam turned 13, and Billy didn't appear. We knew then for sure that something was desperately wrong. He would have followed through.'

The photo of Billy on my website, and on the NMPCC website, shows Billy in bow tie and tuxedo, taken at Raye's wedding about a year before he went missing. Susanne tells me he looks gaunt in this photo, not at all his usual self, and it was taken when Billy was in the middle of his traumatic divorce and custody issues.

Susanne says:

For the first five or six years, if you'd go anywhere new, you'd look at all the faces. If you saw someone who vaguely looked like him, across a crowded shopping centre, you'd chase the person to see if it was him. I don't do that as often now, but you do still scan crowds. He looked like Mum's brothers, so I think that's what he'd look like now. There may have been a sighting at some stage, but we think it actually was Mum's brother, who also took off by himself one day and ended up near Darwin. Must be something in the genes. A wanderlust.

Raye says: 'Billy used to use different names when he gambled. He would use Stephen, or Billy Stephens. Adaptations of his own name.' Bill's profile on the Australian Federal Police website includes the alias Stephen Steffen.

The sisters have been frustrated in their attempts to discover what happened to Billy, as there has been no information about him: no leads and, until very recently, no inquest. Susie was called in to Browns Plains Police Station in Brisbane, and they took some DNA from her in case they were able to match it with any Queensland bodies. When they changed the computer system over, Billy was missed in the transfer. It was only very recently that he was added as a missing person in the national system. So, when they took her DNA, Susie asked them to please make sure it was kept on file.

'It traumatises each of us every time this comes up,' says Susanne. 'Susie feels like she hasn't followed through with it, because you just get on with life. So, I found you, and you put Billy's notice up for us, and I thought, I'll do another check online. Then I came across the official Australian Federal Police register, and I went through that, and he STILL wasn't there! I got in touch with them and they told me it has to be the state where he's listed as missing (who puts in the request to have it listed with the AFP).

'So, really, the whole confusion has been between Tasmania and Queensland. He actually went missing in Tasmania but they seem to have handed it over to someone, or no-one, and it's just been dropped. There's never been an inquest, there's been nothing. Susie tried to get that enacted quite a few years ago. I'd given her all the paper and documents I had. I told Susie she should ring the Federal Police, and she did. They were then going to contact Tasmania and try to get the information put on there.' (Billy's profile has since been added to the National Missing Persons Co-ordination Centre's website and an inquest was finally held in 2021).

'I'm just surprised that they have so little information about him,' says Susanne. 'If he hasn't got himself back into social security or used his Medicare, I'm surprised that they don't have any of that information. But any bit of information I get, I spread it around, I tell everyone.'

Raye says that everything she collected about Billy over the years she gave to Susie so she could follow up on it, and so has Dianne.

Susie has struggled with the idea that her father may have chosen to not contact her or his family again.

I learned from police that apparently men have this switch that they can just flick off and it's like it never happened; they just make a decision and it's like they never had children and they decide not to live that life anymore. I couldn't believe that was possible. They decide to relocate and not acknowledge the kids. It's easier for them to switch off. Women have that maternal feeling and we can't do it. Sometimes I think about that and think okay, if that's what he had to do to cope ... but then again, I think that's no excuse.

Billy's mother was heartbroken over the disappearance of her son, but kept her emotions hidden. Her daughters knew, however, that she was in pain.

'Mum was alive at that time, and it really affected her,' says Dianne. 'It affected all of us. We'd had a difficult time with Bill. I was never as close to him; right from the beginning we had a different value system. He spent time with my girls and they loved him, but we were not what you'd call close. So, I was concerned about him, but when no further information came and we assumed the police had done what they could, then we could do nothing.'

I prayed about it, and I had to work it through in my head ... well, where is he? I don't know, and I can't do anything about it. I spoke to Mum about it, but she was a bit cold and distant. She'd resolved it in her head. So, it wasn't like we sat around together and discussed what to do. Sue was in North Queensland, I was busy with a young family, Mum was disinterested. In hindsight, it should have been something that pulled us together; we should have sat down and said, where to from here? But it never happened. We just went on. It still affects us as a family, because it's always the elephant in the room.

Susanne says: 'I'm sorry that Bill didn't resurface before Mum died, because she died not knowing, at all. Mum never spoke about things anyway; she kept everything to herself.'

Several years later, Dianne and her two nephews, including Adam, flew to Tasmania to see where her brother had been living immediately before he went missing. 'I took Adam to Tasmania and we visited the man who owned the property Bill had camped on,' says Dianne. 'He said Bill just torched the tent he'd been in and walked away, and he never heard from him again.' She remembers driving up a sand dune, and the property was fenced with wire, then they drove on sand tracks to a house. There were orange trees, but Dianne says the people there seemed to be living a bare existence with very few possessions.

'We didn't go down to the beach, we didn't see where Bill had been,' says Dianne. 'Bill had left that property, gone in to Hobart, collected the money from the post office, and I don't think he would have gone back to that property, because he'd burned the tent.'

Susanne wasn't surprised that Bill had destroyed all his possessions, as he had always travelled light. She says: 'When Billy had his 21st birthday none of us knew what to give him, because he wasn't a person you could give anything to; we just gave him an overnight bag for his travels. He lived very light, he had no possessions.'

Dianne says: 'Bill, at the time, would have been on a tight string, having discharged himself from the hospital in Adelaide. I understand that he wasn't registered with Centrelink. He had no income. So, he was without any visible means of support.'

Dianne says Adam didn't cope well during the trip, with his reaction to be expected. 'He was concerned, and we consoled him. We talked about how Bill had left the property and we didn't know where he was. When Adam returned home after that trip, I know he went off the rails. He had great difficulty at school.'

Adam would never recover from the trauma of his father's disappearance. When his father failed to show up on his thirteenth birthday as promised, Adam became a very confused and angry young man. He went on to lead a troubled life in north Queensland. While in police custody in Townsville, in his early 20s, Adam took his own life. The tragedy devastated the Steffen family. Not only had they lost Billy but now his son as well. 'He tried to get his life together, but in the end, it was just too much,' says Dianne. 'That's the grief, for me. I loved Adam with a great love, and still do.' Raye and Susanne were also grief-stricken. 'I'm fortunate, in a very odd way, that both of the boys – Billy and Adam – felt they could find a home with me.' Susanne breaks down in tears as she continues. 'They both said they were coming to me.'

Susie is exceptionally close to all her aunts and carefully considers her actions in relation to the search for her father, with them in mind. 'Whenever I've wanted to do something regarding Dad, I've never done it unless I had all three of my aunts' permissions, because I don't want to make life any harder for them, and they have their own emotions. For me, it's the decent thing to do. Any information that I need, they hold it. I've tried to speak to them a couple of times about Dad, but I get the sense that it's still so raw for them all, even though they're all under the impression that he's passed away and hasn't been found. It's too difficult to talk about and I can respect that. I don't want to push to find my dad, to have that come between me and my aunts, because they're the only family I've got. I'm not willing to do anything unless I have their 100 per cent blessing. Even if just one of them said, "No, I don't want you to do that,"

I wouldn't do it.'

I asked Susanne how Billy's disappearance, and the subsequent tragedies in her family, have affected her. It's a question I have asked everyone I interviewed, but Susanne hesitates before answering, I sense not wanting this to be in any way about her. 'You don't like to say, do you?' she says, her voice catching. She struggles to go on, as I tell her that she has shouldered a huge amount of pain and responsibility for her family, that started when she took on the role of being more than just an aunt to Billy's children when they were small. When she answers, she deftly turns the focus away from herself, and back to Billy.

'I feel sad that his family didn't get the chance to live a normal, well-functioning life. I feel sad for the loss of the life, the life that we could have shared. If you've got a bit of a rascal for a brother, it adds a bit of flavour to your life,' she says with a chuckle. 'You get a lot of pain, but it's nice to know he's still there. I miss the fun Billy. And with Adam, that's just … just awful.'

I asked Susanne if she thought Adam might still be alive had Billy not gone missing. 'I think at least he would have had that opportunity. And Susie … she was just so young, she really didn't know her father at all. She just wants to know about him now. As much as you can say to her, "He really loved you," she says, "But he left me." But he left because he thought he was doing the right thing. He didn't want that disaster of a situation to continue. He also didn't have the opportunity to get out of Mum's place. It was difficult for him.'

'When people ask me how many brothers and sisters I have, I just say the two sisters,' says Raye. 'Because if I say a brother, I've got to go into all the details. People are going to feel sorry for you and I don't want them to. It still hurts. It's the elephant in the room,' she says, using the exact same expression her sister used to describe Billy's disappearance. 'I don't share it with people. My daughter is in her 30s now, and Billy doesn't even know I've got daughters. When Adam died, it raised a lot more pain, and my sister said I was probably still also upset about Billy. She's probably right. It was, like, here we go again.

'So, everything that's happened, that's just the way life is, and it's never going to be the way you think you want it. I'm not embarrassed about my brother, but I just don't want to relive it, because people ask, "Oh, where's your brother, what's he doing?" and I have to say I don't know, I haven't seen him in over 30 years. They look at you odd. They say why don't you do something? I HAVE done everything possible. I wish I could check if he's collecting the dole. I wish someone could tell me what name he's collecting it under. It does occupy your mind, but like anything painful, you push it to one side. It's in the bottom compartment; it comes out every so often. If I knew he was dead, I could grieve. When Adam died, I grieved then, because it was like a little part of Billy had died.'

'Bill's disappearance has changed me,' says Dianne.

I've grieved. I continue to grieve. You don't grieve, then get over it. It's something that hits you at times. And I grieve for Mum, and the lost relationship they had, that pain of close relationships where people hurt themselves and don't realise they're hurting others. Mum was hurt in many ways.

'Bill lived at home, and he'd go to the pub, and he rarely worked. There was a time when he got a taxi licence, and I remember visiting Mum's place one day and the taxi was outside. I went inside and asked Bill why the taxi was there. He said, "Oh, I don't feel like driving today." I said, "Shouldn't you tell the owner, so he can get another driver?" Bill just said, "Whatever." And, of course, that was the end of that job.

'There was this attitude of, I'll do whatever I want to do, it doesn't matter what other people want. Maybe that was a coping mechanism, maybe it was part of the depression. But lots of things Bill did affected Mum. I feel sad about that, because Mum did her best. In the end, she just had to protect herself. When people ask me about my family I say I had a brother, he's no longer alive, but I don't know where he is. It's like a hole that never fills. There's no end point to the grief. It has caused me to live incomplete. Because with Adam's death – and I continue to grieve over that – I know, I saw him, I know what happened. I'm not happy about it, but I know what happened and I know I'll see him again. But Bill, I don't know, and because of that spiritualism he was into, I don't know into eternity either, because I believe that the spirit lives forever. So, the only way I deal with it is prayer. I release it, because when it comes, it can overwhelm you. I don't get into the space where I allow it to overwhelm me. Prayer brings me comfort, absolutely.'

Dianne was also concerned about the Eastern religion Billy practised. 'He was into a spiritualism that I believe is deceptive – Zen Buddhism. He started that as a teenager, or in his early 20s. I used to discuss spiritual issues with him, and that was part of the discord that we had; we didn't connect on many levels at all. He went to meetings in Brisbane, and the fellow that Bill stayed with in Tasmania was into the same spiritualism, and that's how they met and connected. Bill was involved in it while he was in Tasmania with the children. It was his spiritual connectedness, his preferred worship. His understanding of life, a constant thread.'

The Coroner's finding includes a statement from Robert Walter, the Zen Buddhist practitioner, who Billy went to stay with in Hobart. Walter, who is now deceased, stated in 2009 'that he received several letters from Mr Steffen seeking advice about the spiritual consequences, if any, of suicide'.

'The very last contact I had from Dad was a get well card,' says Susie. 'It's the only thing I have from Dad beside my scar. He sent it when I was first diagnosed with asthma and had pneumonia in Maleny hospital. I was given Dad's stuff. He had a small life insurance policy, and when I contacted them to claim it they needed documents like the Coroner's report and death certificate, so for me to get those things I needed to contact the police. When I did, I was told there had been a sighting of my father in the Northern Territory in about 1995 or 1996. So, because of that sighting, I couldn't go any further.'

I was alarmed when Susie told me this. The alleged sighting is actually thought to have been Bill's uncle, who he strongly resembled, who was known to be in the Northern Territory at the time of this sighting. For an unconfirmed sighting, that was very likely not Billy Steffen, to be used as an excuse not to proceed with a missing person investigation, or a coronial inquest, is unacceptable. Susie was unaware, until our phone interview in 2016, that this sighting was thought to have been her great uncle. She still believed it was her father. She had no idea, until I told her, that her great uncle was in NT at that time.

Susie was very young when Billy went missing, and has had to fill in many blanks herself. 'When you just have the figment of a person, who is apparently a man that loved you beyond measure, but you have nothing to connect you to that person other than a few memories and the reiteration from your aunts that he loved you, it all feels surreal. There's nothing to comfort me that, yes I am his, I am connected, we do share common ground and of course DNA.'

Susanne has a strong faith and credits her church family for supporting her through the many difficult years. 'The spiritual side of things has definitely been a strength for me. The fellowship I belong to has been very supportive. I don't really pray about Bill, I just let things run. I don't want to pray that he's found, then they find a body. You have those romantic ideas, like maybe if I go to that meeting over there, he'll be in that church assembly. But then I think that's unreal, because if he was, he'd be back with his family. Occasionally, you do see people who look like the people you know. When you look closely, you can always see the differences. I have a blended image in my head of him and Mum's brothers, as they aged. I do think it would be very difficult to recognise him if I saw him today.'

Raye also says her church was a great support and comfort to her when her brother went missing.

I asked Susanne if having a missing person in her life has changed her, and she surprised me by saying it's made her a better person. 'Having a missing brother has made me far more compassionate. It's really sad that we haven't had an answer, that we don't know, but there's still that vestige of hope, if you haven't heard anything. But it's a painful bit of luggage to carry around with you.' Susanne remembers happy times with Billy playing with her daughter, when she was about six months old. 'He loved children, and he was a wonderful uncle as well as a wonderful dad. He was very loving. He was a good brother.'

The sisters don't discuss their theories about what happened to their brother with each other, so reading this may be a revelation to them all about what the others think. Susanne is in two minds about where she thinks Billy is today. 'It's really difficult to picture him alive, anywhere. I don't see him dead, though. But I can't see him living a life with a new family, separately. I wonder if he's been hospitalised somewhere and doesn't know where he is. I just don't know. But I don't see a dead body, and not with a new family. So, you learn to live with a gaping hole in your life. Odd, isn't it? It's difficult to realise the attachment that we have with people. The threads that run there. There's no reason that those threads should be there. There's emotional threads that have no function, it's not a physical thing. You've got this thing that you carry around, and when it surfaces it causes you a vast amount of emotional pain.

'Everyone makes choices in their life, and you have to live with that. We were thinking, well, did he jump on the ship to the mainland, then jump off it and no-one knew he was gone? I don't see him as having taken his own life, because he said he was coming to me in Townsville. He'd asked for money to come across to the mainland, so he had the thought that he was going to make his way up to my place. Bill would have come to family or a friend. When he was in SA and Tasmania he kept in touch, so it was unlike him to disappear, though mental illness can influence the way we react to life's circumstances.'

Raye believes her brother may have been murdered, but also thinks anything is possible.

He might have ended up in South Australia. Or he might have got a really nasty psychosis because of drugs and is in a vegetative state somewhere. I don't believe he could just walk away and not have anything to do with his family; that just wasn't him. He always knew he had family to fall back on. So, maybe he's been murdered, or died somehow and the authorities just never told us. It would be a real shock if he was still walking around, enjoying life.

Until I discussed it with her, Raye hadn't ever thought about whether Billy could have taken his own life. 'Now that you mention it … yes, maybe. I never thought of that. When he rang Mum and told her about hearing the voices, he was being treated in Adelaide, at the hospital. But he can't have been too unwell if he discharged himself.'

Dianne believes her brother took his own life. 'The only way I can cope with Bill's disappearance is to think that he's dead,' she says. 'I don't see any possibility of him being alive. I think he would have made contact with Sue and with his children. Without question. That was the turning point for Adam, when Bill didn't come back for him when he turned 13. He would have made some contact. That's why I think he was in a bad place in his head, and took action that was fatal.'

Dianne doesn't speak very much about her brother, but she's more than happy for her niece to carry on the search. 'I'll speak about it when Susie raises it. I think Susie values us; I think she's glad she can share her life with people who love her. I think she needs to know what happened to her father; you'd hate to get to the end of your life and say I could've, I should've. But I'm resolved. I think Sue finds it hard; I hear her sometimes, she cries and grieves openly. I don't do that, because I have no need. In my brain, I think, he's not there. I've dealt with my grief. Susie hasn't. Neither has Susanne, because he was coming to her in Townsville. That hope that she has is good, but it hurts her.

'There's nothing you can do with a love for somebody who's passed. I'm happy to help Susie, but I can't give her any hope that he's alive. I don't have a need to know what happened to him. It wouldn't bring me any comfort. I see Bill as an adult, making choices in his life, and whatever the outcome for his life, that was his responsibility. I wasn't close enough to him to speak to him about those issues. If it was an unresolved issue about Adam and Susie, then absolutely, I wouldn't rest until I knew what happened, why it happened, where it happened, how it happened, but for Bill – no. I don't. That sounds a bit cold. But at some point, in all our lives we have to say, "I'm accountable." I know Bill was disturbed. He was a gambler and a risk taker, and I've seen his behaviour when he was intoxicated; anything could have happened, if he was in a state of despair.

'Always in my mind, I thought if he bought his passage on the boat back to the mainland, maybe he did just jump. That would be part of his behaviour, his despair at not being with his children, and I believe he was still distressed about the break-up of his marriage. Perhaps he felt like a failure. He had the money I sent; it wasn't a lot of money, only about $150, which at that time would have gotten him back to the mainland. The casino was in Hobart and there's every possibility in my mind that he would have gone to the casino, done his dough, then done himself in. I do think that.'

Susie does not believe her father killed himself. She very carefully considers my question of whether she believes he is alive and well and just living his life somewhere. 'I really don't know. I think sometimes I want to say yes, because I want to live in hope, because it's just too hard to live otherwise.' Susie breaks down in tears, and struggles to continue through her sobs.

'I used to say when Adam died, he was with Dad, but as time goes on, I just don't know. I don't think he is dead. I'm different to my aunts, I wasn't brought up with religion, but I respect that's the way they were brought up, as I love my aunts dearly, and I don't talk about my beliefs to them. There have been times when I've said whoever did my life plan really sucked, and they've come back saying that God has His own plan.

'I dreamed a couple of times about Dad; one of them I was about 16, so Adam was still alive, and the dream was based on graves. We were all there – me, Mum, Dad, Adam. None of the graves had been covered over except my family members who had actually passed away, but I could read inscriptions. Adam's had his date of death. Dad's wasn't covered over but had been dug out and his headstone had his date of birth, but nothing for his date of death. Adam's hadn't been dug yet, but it had just a headstone. In the dream I was asking Dad what it meant, what he was trying to tell me. I think that was when I first started to want to know about Dad.

'I've never really looked closely into his case or had anything to do with it, except when I gave DNA, and I learned a bit then. As much as I want to dig, as much as I want to research further, I know my limitations. I know I can't get to breaking point, as I have two children, and it hurts way, way too much. I'm someone who needs answers. But some things in life just can't be explained, like what happened to Dad. Sometimes you're best not knowing the full extent of it. I've seen psychics and card readers. One said they could see him in the Northern Territory wearing stubbies, a blue singlet and thongs, driving a truck. Two of them said he's overseas – one of them said he's in New Zealand. That one said he thinks about me every day, but he knows there's no coming back, even if he wants to. It's too hard when he thinks about what he's got to face when he comes back.'

Susanne is aware her niece doesn't believe Billy is dead. 'I know that this is her underlying belief, and yet her logical mind negates it too. It is a really hard basket of whys and wheres. I know how much he loved his children; it hurts me to think of his anguish. As much as we tell Susie how Billy loved both of them, she cannot really comprehend it. If I was Susie, I would be clutching to life too. I hope that she is right; I am now praying for an answer.'

In May 2021 the Tasmanian Coroner handed down his Record of Investigation Into Death (Without Inquest). It is just 12 points long and contains inaccuracies, such as the statement that Billy was not reported missing until 1989, four years after he was last seen. It is sparse in conclusions, simply stating there was no evidence Billy ever left Tasmania and that the Coroner believes Billy is deceased. The cause of death and location of his body is unknown. Susie is bitterly disappointed. However, she is feeling more accepting about her father's loss, and has come to believe in recent months that he may have taken his own life back in 1985.

Susanne, Dianne and Raye continue the search for their brother, along with Billy's daughter Susie. When I ask Susie what she'd say to her dad if he's out there reading these words right now, she's almost overwhelmed. 'I often think about that, and it varies on different days.'

I once had a dream that I saw him driving back and forth past me and I was really excited, but it was mixed emotions. I'd be excited but also angry. I'd hit him, give him a really good sock on his chest. Sometimes I would like nothing more than for Dad to knock on my door today. But would I really want that? Because I have all that supressed emotion that comes up. At the end of the day, it would be wonderful, it would be amazing, and that's why I live in the hope that he's alive, because that's all I've got left. It would never be too late. I know years have turned into multiple decades but if you love someone that much, it's never too late to fight for them.

If he's out there and he reads this, it's never too late, Dad. If he walked back into his old life today, he still has his three amazing sisters, he's got great nephews, three amazing granddaughters, and grandson, and he's just become a great-grandfather. There's so much more for him to walk back into than there ever was before. Obviously, we'd have a million questions, and I think that's something that stops a lot of people who are missing persons from taking that step – they might sit there every day wondering where are they, how are they, what are they doing but that fear of rejection and the fear of someone being angry with them, of coming back but no-one being positive about it, I think that's what stops a lot of people from making contact.

I totally get that everyone needs a break but sometimes that couple of months turns into years, and then turns into decades. How do you turn that around? Fear is what stops a lot of the human race from doing a lot of things. But, Dad, if you're out there, don't be scared. Yes, I might be angry, and I'm going to punch you hard, but COME BACK. You have so much more in your life now.

If you have any information about the disappearance of William 'Billy' Steffen please call Crime Stoppers on 1800 333 000.

CHAPTER NINE

Richard Leape

Richard Leape was last seen by his family in inner city Sydney
in April 1993. He was 37. There were unconfirmed sightings
of him around Sydney after this time.

Richard Leape seemed to have the perfect life. He was well educated, a very high achiever, had a great job as a teacher which he enjoyed, had a beautiful wife and daughter whom he adored. But very gradually, Richard began to change.

Richard was 37 when he went missing in April 1993. He was last seen in the inner city area of Sydney. I had Richard on my website for many years before I met his wonderful sister Annette, and I remembered his case particularly because of his vivid blue eyes in his missing person photo. Annette has been searching for him for decades.

There were four children in the family: Richard had a younger brother, Tony, and a much younger sister, Mandy, who was 13 years younger than Richard. Annette is the oldest sibling. Richard had been a happy child, the sort of kid everyone liked. 'He and I were very close as children; we were close in age and Mum said I always mothered him. I always got the blame for the things he did.' says Annette with a chuckle. 'He was a dear little boy. He was fairly quiet, but as he got older he became very sociable. He was always saying positive things to everyone around him. When I was freaking out, he'd always have something to say that would calm me down. He was a real character. He just had this way about him, and he was so interested in people from all walks of life, especially when he got into his late teenage years. He'd talk to anybody, he was very friendly.' Richard made lots of friends at boarding school and at university in Armidale, where he studied to become a teacher.

At first his family thought Richard was just a bit eccentric. He was a very intelligent man, if a little naïve, and he had more of an academic mind than a practical one. Sometimes his clothes wouldn't quite match, and his family started to buy him ties that would go with his clothes that were more appropriate for his position teaching English, History and Science at private schools. Richard really got a kick out of that.

His mental health seemed to decline after the birth of his daughter, but years later a close university friend of Richard's told Annette of a curious conversation they had had when Richard was in his early 20s and had just started teaching. 'He told me that Richard had said his grandfather had schizophrenia and he said, "Maybe I'm heading down that way too."' The strange thing was, Richard's grandfather had not suffered from schizophrenia. Why did Richard say that he did?

Richard's family in northern NSW were unaware anything was wrong until Richard had become quite unwell. His wife loved him very much and accepted most of his behaviour as just Richard being 'a character'. When they were both teaching and working full time, life became busy, and it was easy to miss the signs. Annette thinks it was hard for the people who loved him, including his mum, to accept that he was becoming ill. She wishes she'd realised the extent of Richard's mental illness earlier. At the time that his mental health started to decline she lived on the Gold Coast in Queensland and Richard's mother lived in Murwillumbah, in northern NSW.

When you're not seeing someone on a regular basis, you're only having phone contact, you can miss a lot. But I couldn't get my head around it. How did I not know these things? How did I not see what was happening to him?

Gradually, Richard's eccentricities and erratic behaviour increased and one day, after his daughter was born, he announced he wanted to give up teaching and become an actor. This was his dream, he told his family. He wanted to be the best, and he started attending acting classes in Sydney, taking trips away from his home in the Illawarra district of NSW. When Richard started making the regular trips to Sydney for the acting classes, his marriage started to suffer, as he would often be away for days at a time. Eventually Richard moved, on his own, to Sydney permanently.

He would stay with friends he'd met in the theatre world, and it was around this time that he became involved in a spiritual organisation, Kenja. Annette had concerns about Richard being in the group, as she felt he was very vulnerable. She feels his mental health problems significantly worsened around this time.

Richard had been attending 'support sessions' in an attempt to deal with abuse traumas he'd experienced as a child. He ended up practically destitute, as he did not have regular work. Richard's wife decided to move to Sydney in an attempt to reconcile with Richard; Richard desperately missed his little girl. He was still trying to become an actor and had roles in live theatre projects. He had some success with his acting career, appearing in TV advertisements such as for Steggles chicken, and had minor roles in *A Country Practice*, *Home and Away* and *Neighbours*. 'It was his dream,' says Annette. 'He wanted to be an actor.'

Around this time, Richard was attacked on the street and violently assaulted. He'd been on his way home from theatre rehearsals and saw a group of men nearby as he left the train station. One of the men called out to Richard, so he stopped to ask them what they'd said. The men started taunting Richard, who was trying to work out what was going on. Before he realised it, they'd bundled him into a car. The men, heavily intoxicated, took Richard into the bush, stripped him naked, and belted him black and blue. He had a broken jaw and a broken nose, and was in a bad way. Richard later said he thought they were going to kill him. He heard them say they were going to put him in the boot of the car and take him to another location, and at that point Richard managed to escape. He made it back to a main road and found some houses. He jumped a fence and took some clothes from a washing line, and managed to get himself home, but refused to call the police.

His wife said he was terrified, but Richard didn't want his daughter to see him in that state so he waited until the next morning before agreeing to go to hospital, as he was by then in a great deal of pain from his injuries. He needed immediate surgery on his broken jaw.

Richard eventually went to police and made a report about his assault, and also lodged a claim for victim's compensation but later dropped the claim. I asked Annette if she thought Richard may have been sexually assaulted during the attack and after a long pause she said she thought he may have been, but that Richard had never talked about that. 'It's crossed my mind. Why was he stripped naked? But the police said he didn't put that in his report. I believe that assault, on top of everything else, is what pushed him over the edge.'

Richard's mental health had already started to deteriorate, and such a horrifying assault would have undoubtedly done great damage to him mentally. It was clear that Richard's childhood abuse also contributed significantly to his mental illness. Richard and his wife were unable to reconcile, and his marriage once again fell apart, this time for good.

Around this time Richard wrote an emotional and angry letter to his parents telling them he was severing all ties with them. 'It was very abusive; quite deranged actually,' says Annette. Their mother was very concerned about Richard and asked Annette what they could do to help him. Annette decided to go to Sydney to try to speak to Richard. She found him, penniless, living in a boarding house in Paddington. 'It was quite obvious he was under a lot of stress,' says Annette. 'He had no job and no money. I asked him if he wanted to get out of Sydney for a while and come and stay with me on the Gold Coast, but he said Sydney was where his acting opportunities were and he wanted to stay there. I asked him how long it had been since he had seen his daughter; he told me it was only two weeks but I knew that wasn't true, it had been months.'

Over the coming months Richard occasionally phoned his mother but the conversations were bizarre and brief. He said he was selling flowers, which his family thought was very strange as he knew nothing about flowers, and in return he received accommodation. There was a lengthy period where Richard did not communicate with his family at all. Then, his mother received another letter, this time written in red pen. Annette remembers reading this letter with alarm. She said to her mother, 'He's got a mental health problem. This is not Richard; this is

somebody else talking in his head. I think he has schizophrenia.'
Her mother dismissed the idea. Annette tried to tell her mother
that Richard would have never said those words to his mother
in person, that it was the illness talking, and she took the letters
from her mother. She has never given them back. Annette still
has these letters; she didn't want her mother to keep reading them
and becoming distressed, so she's kept them. She's not sure why,
as they're horrible to read, but she feels she should keep them in
case Richard is one day found and they are needed as evidence of
his handwriting and also his state of mind.

Annette contacted Richard's ex-wife to ask if Richard had seen
their daughter. His wife said that she had organised a visit with
him in a local park, but when Richard turned up he was filthy
and clearly unwell. He was mumbling to himself and his wife
was so alarmed at his behaviour she didn't feel safe to allow him
to take their daughter on the visit.

Richard didn't see his daughter again, and had no further
contact with his ex-wife, but strangely he telephoned his ex-
wife's new partner and asked him to look after his little girl, a
move that shocked Annette, as she knew how much Richard
doted on his daughter. 'Richard said he needed four years to
get himself together and do all the things he needed to do, and
he asked his ex-wife's partner to look after his daughter, telling
him that he knew he would. That's the part we found so hard
to accept, because he just adored that child. When she was
born he rang me and it was like she was the first child to ever
be born on the planet; he was overwhelmed. Every week I'd get
these phone calls and he'd talk for hours and hours about her.'
Annette says it would have been such a huge thing to do, to ask

someone else to look after his child, and he must have realised at this point his mental health was very fragile.

Richard ended up one day at Katoomba, in the Blue Mountains, and was found pacing up and down outside a boarding house. A local resident called the local mental health services, and Richard was taken to Nepean Hospital. Richard was in hospital for three days before he finally told staff his real name. The hospital contacted Richard's mother but he refused to speak to her. Two days later the hospital phoned Mrs Leape again to tell her that Richard had absconded during the night, telling staff he knew how to get out of the hospital 'because I built the place'. Annette says with a laugh, 'Richard couldn't operate a dustpan and brush, let alone build anything! He did not have those skills.' Annette contacted the police but the police informed her that because Richard had not been medically certified they were unable to force him to stay in hospital.

Richard then turned up at Hornsby Hospital requesting medication, but this was refused. Annette made enquiries to try to get guardianship of Richard, feeling that may have helped her to have him hospitalised, but she was unable to.

I don't believe someone like Richard would have chosen to live on the streets like that, going through the garbage for food, exposed to the cold, no means to feed himself or get accommodation; you can't tell me that's not putting yourself at risk of harm. My idea was to get him hospitalised, even for a week or two, get him onto medication, then maybe he'd have a chance of being a productive person again, and be able to see his daughter.

However, the guardianship board rejected Annette's application, as they needed to speak to Richard, and at that time he could not be located. Annette and her mother tried to pursue other legal means to try to help Richard in the event of him being located and needing medical assistance, but they were turned down at every level.

After about three months of not hearing from Richard, Annette and her younger brother Tony went to Sydney to look for him, but could not find him. 'It was hard in those days. We didn't have mobile phones, so we had to wait for Richard to contact us from a public phone box,' says Annette. On Boxing Day of that year there was a phone call from Richard to the family home in Murwillumbah. Richard was in Newcastle and sounded distressed. Annette's younger sister answered the phone and told Richard that Annette was on her way, and would come to Newcastle to collect him, but Richard declined, saying he was 'all right now' and was going to stay with friends in Sydney. At this point Annette was not even sure Richard was telling the truth about where he was. She made numerous phone calls to his friends and associates asking if they'd seen Richard; they said they had not. However, shortly afterwards his associates contacted Richard's ex-wife saying they were concerned for Richard as they had seen him pacing up and down Commonwealth Street in Surry Hills, in inner city Sydney.

Annette and her brother immediately caught the train to Sydney to search for Richard, and had an experience that is quite extraordinary. Neither Annette nor her brother knew Sydney very well, being from the northern part of the state, but they felt they had to try to find Richard. They had no idea where to start looking in the vast city. They got off the train at busy Central Station, stowed their luggage in a locker, and looked around them. 'Out that door,' said Annette and they headed out to the street and walked up a short hill. Tony looked at her and said, 'Now what?' Annette says, 'I didn't know which way to go, but told Tony to turn left; we turned left and I said, "There he is!" and there was Richard, literally standing there in front of us, on the corner of the street. I reckon I was just guided by "somebody".

'We ran up to the corner as he started walking away and when he first saw Tony, he said, "What are you doing here?" Richard then looked at me and said to Tony, "Don't let her come any closer, because I'm wired and I'll get blown up." Tony looked at me said, "He's bloody mad!" I told him it was all right, just let me get a bit closer to him, but every time I got closer to Richard he'd cross the street to get away from me. Richard then seemed like he was looking for cigarette butts in the gutter.'

Annette feels she should have warned Tony about Richard's deteriorated mental state, as Tony was really unprepared for what he saw. He and Richard had always been good mates, but Tony was shocked by Richard's behaviour. Annette was able to get a little closer to Richard, but he again said, 'I don't want you to get harmed. They're going to blow you up if you're seen with me. I'm scum and they're after me!' She says, 'I wasn't scared of him or his behaviour, I knew it was the illness talking, but poor Tony was in total shock.' Annette felt utterly helpless. He truly believed he was wired; he was terrified.

In the midst of his ranting and raving, Richard told Annette he'd been pushed down a flight of stairs. He said, 'Annette, they [the unknown people Richard was paranoid about] even got to my friends, they pushed me down the stairs,' and pointed to the stairs. He told Annette he'd been told to sever all ties with his family and friends 'for the good of all concerned', and told her 'The Master' had told him this. Richard also said he needed to go to Drummoyne for a while. He didn't want Tony and Annette to go with him. He got on an empty bus, with only the driver aboard, walked through the bus and straight out the rear side exit. He said it was full of Nazis who wanted to kill him.

Annette says, 'I ran to a phone box and called triple 0. I told the police I needed help, I wanted to get my brother to hospital. They asked me if he was trying to hurt me, I said, "No, no, he would never, ever hurt me, or my brother," but they said unless he tried to hurt me or himself then there was nothing they could do to help me. I said, "You've got to be kidding!" I went back and told Tony what they said and told Tony to try to provoke Richard, get him to take a swing at us. I just wanted to get Richard taken to hospital so we could help him. Tony called him every name under the sun, but Richard just wouldn't react. So, I made a decision, and I told a lie. I called the police back and said, "He's trying to strangle my brother." They said they'd be right there. The police turned up in their paddy wagon and said to Richard, "Hop in, mate," and he got in the police wagon, just like a little boy.'

The police took Richard to St Vincent's Hospital, where he was assessed by the medical staff. The doctor told Annette that Richard had definite mental health issues, and he'd give him some medication to calm him down. Richard was not agitated or violent, but he was talking to himself and mumbling, and clearly terrified. He kept repeating that someone would blow him up, blow Annette up, blow the hospital up. His paranoia had become extreme. But despite his obvious illness, moments of the old Richard that Annette remembered were still evident. 'After Richard was given medication at the hospital, and while we were waiting to speak with the doctor, an elderly lady who was wandering up the corridor said she was lost, so Richard linked arms with her and slowly walked her up the corridor until he found her room! This really brings me to tears recalling this. There he was, barefoot, filthy, long, matted hair, tracksuit pants inside out, helping a little frail old lady. That was truly Richard's character,' Annette recalls fondly.

Staff wanted to keep him in hospital, but Richard refused, saying he would be all right. He said he had somewhere to stay, but could not tell anyone where that was. The police explained, as they had before, that they could not force him to stay at the hospital. Annette and Tony asked him to come out and have something to eat and have a talk about things, and Richard seemed happy to go with them. They went to a cafe but Richard refused to go inside, saying the food was poisoned. Annette said they could go somewhere else but Richard said, 'No, they know me now, I can't.' He still seemed to believe Annette and Tony were in danger simply by being seen with him. He seemed to know every side street, back alley, every nook and cranny of the city, and he led his brother and sister to another cafe. He began pacing back and forth in front of it but again, would not go inside. Tony and Annette said they'd wait for him in a park nearby so the cafe owners would not know they were together and in Richard's mind, that kept them safe. Richard agreed to this but still could not bring himself to go into the cafe. He returned to the park.

Annette decided to try to convince him to come home with her. She asked him to return to Nerang with her and stay for a while. Richard said he didn't want to go to his parents' home, and Annette said that was fine, he could stay at her place for as long as he liked, and nobody would know he was there. Richard seemed to agree to go along with this plan. He looked at Tony and said, 'Do you promise you won't tell anyone I'm there, especially the other relatives?' Tony promised to not say a word, he'd do whatever Richard wanted, and told him he'd be fine with Annette. Richard agreed to go with them, so they hailed a taxi and were going to find him some clothes; Richard had no shoes on, his pants were inside out, and he was putrid. Annette told Richard that Tony would return home by train, and that she and Richard would be flying up to Queensland, but they needed to get him cleaned up first.

Annette and Richard got in the taxi and as they drove along, Annette looked at him and was struck by how sad he looked. She broke down in tears telling me this part of her story. 'I put my hand on his leg, and when the taxi pulled up at traffic lights he suddenly jumped out of the car and took off.' Tony ran after him, and he and Richard soon disappeared out of sight as Annette tried to deal with the taxi in the middle of the road. After about 45 minutes, Tony finally found Annette again, only to tell her that he'd been unable to find Richard – they'd lost him, again.

The hospital had given Richard an appointment with a Community Health clinic. After the day's events none of them expected him to turn up, but Annette and Tony stayed the night in Sydney and went to the hospital early the next morning in the hope that he would. And he did. He had what looked like straw in his hair and mismatched thongs. Annette asked him where he got the thongs from and he replied, 'Oh, I have my means.' Annette was worried that he'd stolen them from a homeless person. She had no idea how he'd managed to turn up on time for the appointment when he didn't have a watch, but she was just very glad to see him. Richard attended his appointment and afterwards the doctor spoke to Tony and Annette, advising them she'd diagnosed Richard with paranoid schizophrenia. Richard told the doctor he needed to use her phone to make some important calls about parking fines that he was worried about. Annette told the doctor Richard had not had a car for about nine months, as it had been stolen.

Annette spoke to Richard after his appointment and again tried to convince him to let her look after him. Richard said he didn't want to go with her just yet, that he wanted to sort some things out, and then he'd make his own way up to Nerang. Annette said okay and gave him her contact details, but then Richard changed his mind, and said he'd meet them at the hospital the following morning and 'see how it goes'. Annette agreed, and asked him if he wanted something to eat. Richard refused, then almost ran out of the hospital. Annette and Tony followed him but as he had before, he disappeared into the nooks and crannies of inner city Sydney. 'He must have known every rabbit hole in Sydney,' says Annette. 'He didn't want us to follow him and kept turning around to see if we still were.' Richard once again vanished.

Annette bought a backpack and filled it with clothes and shoes and a small amount of money. She was haunted by seeing him searching the gutters for discarded cigarette butts so she bought him a packet of cigarettes and lighter and put these in too. She had been advised by the Community Health staff not to put a lot of money in there, because he may be assaulted and robbed by the people on the streets if they thought he had any cash. She put in enough for some train fares and food. The following morning, they went back to meet Richard at the clinic, as he'd agreed, but he didn't turn up. Annette left the backpack for him, asking the staff to please give it to Richard if he came at a later date. She and Tony spent the rest of the day searching the alleys and back lanes of the city, but they didn't find him.

They asked about him at a hostel and staff members thought they'd seen Richard, but under a different name. He'd been asked to leave the previous week for causing a disturbance that required police to attend. Annette and Tony spent the next few days searching wherever they could think of – deserted train tunnels, homeless shelters, soup kitchens, through Kings Cross at night, in all the parks – but there was no sign of Richard. 'Someone up there was definitely protecting us, as we went to some pretty dangerous places, Tony and I, and we didn't know anything about Sydney, but we were on a mission to find Richard. We were rolling over homeless people who were sleeping; they could have easily pulled a knife on us, but we were never harmed. Someone was watching out for us,' says Annette.

Then Annette got a phone call from the clinic to say Richard had been in, and had collected Annette's backpack. The staff told her they'd tried to give him some information about support groups for people with schizophrenia but Richard said, 'No, I'll be right.' He never went back.

'He's always had the idea he could fix whatever was wrong with him,' says Annette. 'He injured his back as a young man, playing football, and they told him he'd need surgery but he said, "No way in the wide world" and decided to fix it himself. I remember him hanging upside down by his legs on a tree branch trying to stretch his back, like a monkey. I think that's how he felt about his mental illness, that he could fix it himself.' Richard leaned towards alternative medicine and the power of the mind, and didn't like the thought that everything had to be fixed with doctors and surgery.

Three months later Annette listed Richard as a missing person with police. Three months after that she and Tony went back to Sydney and despite another extensive search on foot, they could not find him. Their sister Mandy was away teaching and could not go with her siblings to look for Richard, although she was just as concerned as they were. About another three months later they went to Sydney again and were searching around the Darling Harbour area where many homeless people had previously lived. The area was being developed and the security guards had instructions to move the homeless people on. One guard recognised Richard from Annette's photo. He told Annette he'd seen Richard in the area, pacing up and down, talking to himself. He was positive it was Richard. She asked the guard if Richard had a green backpack with him but he said no, he hadn't had anything with him. Annette asked the guard to please call police if he saw Richard again, but he was not seen again in the Darling Harbour area.

The Leape family have certainly had their ups and downs with the police handling Richard's case over the years. The year after he went missing Richard's photo was featured on a badge for National Missing Persons Week (held in July/August each year). A constable from the NSW Missing Persons Unit rang Richard's mother after Missing Persons Week to let her know that a reporter who had received one of the badges returned home to the Albury-Wodonga area and believes she saw a man there who looked very much like Richard, pacing up and down in front of a supermarket. The constable asked Mrs Leape whether she felt the man could be Richard. Mrs Leape did not see how Richard, who was destitute and ill, could have possibly gotten himself to Albury-Wodonga and said no, she thought it was a waste of time to check. She rang Annette and told her about the phone call and Annette felt that anything was possible, and the man may have been Richard. Annette phoned Albury-Wodonga police and asked them to check whether the man could be Richard, but her enquiry was never properly followed up.

Over the next few years Annette and Tony still searched when they could, but their young families restricted the time they were able to spend away. No trace of Richard was found, and there were no records of him having attended any more medical appointments (under his own name).

One incident leaves Annette seething with anger. 'Out of the blue, a constable rang me. He said there was a police officer who Richard had taught at school, and Richard also taught his brother, so he knew him personally. This officer said he had seen Richard in central Sydney. This would have been about 18 months after I had last seen Richard and reported him missing. He said when he saw him, Richard could not even hold a conversation, and had no memory of ever being a teacher, but he said he was okay. I asked the constable how long ago the officer had seen Richard and he said it was the previous November! I asked why he was only coming forward now. He said because there had been a bit of publicity about Richard and he'd seen Richard's photo in the paper. He'd been unaware Richard was a missing person.'

Annette asked to speak to the constable herself but the police officer said there was no need. Annette insisted and tracked the officer down. 'He said to me, "I didn't know he was a missing person, otherwise I would have let the unit know."'

When he told me that Richard couldn't even hold a conversation, that was just the living end of me; I was just so upset to think that someone had seen him back there in central Sydney, someone who knew him personally before he became ill, and knew how productive and talented he was, how he was before, and they didn't think that warranted following up. I was devastated.

To make matters worse, because this officer had spoken to Richard they decided he wasn't a missing person anymore, so they removed the report! That was in the January and it wasn't until April, when I phoned them again about Richard, that they told me about this officer having seen him. They said, 'But your brother isn't missing anymore.' I said, 'He IS missing. We weren't told that anyone had seen him. He is still a missing person. If he's not missing, then you tell me where he is!' It took a lot of pleading and talking, and eventually they told me I'd have to make another statement and another missing person report.'

Annette rang the Australian Federal Police and spoke with an 'incredible' police officer who listened to all her concerns, and made sure Richard was listed immediately on the AFP missing persons list, and his face was then used for Missing Persons Week.

There was another sighting of Richard, at a cafe in George Street, in the city, that he had previously frequented. After Richard was reported missing, Annette asked the cafe owner to put up a missing poster of him. A short time later the cafe owner saw a man pacing up and down outside the cafe, behaviour that was typical of Richard. She went out to speak with the man and asked him if he was Richard, and if it was his face on the poster. The man said, "Yes, it is." The cafe owner said, "Your family are looking for you; do you think you should call them?" Richard replied, "Yeah, I suppose I should." But he walked away, and never returned to the cafe. That was in May 1994, and Annette is horrified to think that at this time he still knew his name was Richard, but by November 1994, when the police officer saw him, he didn't even know he'd been a teacher.

After some publicity on television about Richard, a priest in South Australia contacted Annette and said he was fairly positive that a man he used to see quite regularly walking up and down the Rundle Mall in Adelaide was Richard. The priest was able to obtain a photograph of the man and sent it to Annette. 'We were convinced it was Richard; even Mum thought it was him,' says Annette, who then flew to Adelaide to see for herself. But it turned out not to be him. Another dead end. 'It's amazing how many fair-haired, possibly-used-to-be-redheaded men you can think look like the person you're looking for, because you're so desperate to find them,' she says.

Skeletal remains of a man were found in Thornton, near Maitland in Newcastle in 1996, and police commissioned a forensic anatomist to reconstruct the skull and create a face to find out what the person may have looked like. The resulting sculpture was pictured in local newspapers. Annette says: 'That sent everyone into a frenzy; several friends of Richard's who saw that photo in the paper believed it was him.' Richard's dental records were requested to compare them to the remains. This is the source of more frustration for Annette, as she later discovered the records were never collected by police, then they were left in Newcastle. Police started calling Annette to ask her where the dental records were. She discovered they had been misplaced after being sent for comparison with the Newcastle remains.

Annette's original statement and diary entries were also misplaced by police, requiring her to redo them all. They also lost the original missing person report made by Annette, requiring her to lodge another one five years later, only for that one ALSO to be lost! Annette has learned to make copies of everything, and her notes are detailed and organised; she can tell you every date and every event.

She was also frustrated in her attempts to convince police that the dental records they were using for comparison would not be accurate because after Richard's jaw was broken in the assault he'd had teeth removed, been fitted with false teeth on a plate, a wire inserted and bridging work done, and his entire jaw would have been quite different in an X-ray to the originals they had. Police applied to Canterbury Hospital for his medical records but were told they'd been destroyed after five years. However, during the inquest it was noted the records from Canterbury *Dental* Hospital were destroyed, not those from Canterbury Hospital. Richard's surgery was performed in the hospital, not the dental clinic, and the hospital should still have had his records. Annette thought that having Richard's death certificate, issued after the inquest, may assist her in applying for Richard's medical records, but she has still been denied access to the information.

The family were told the bones discovered in Newcastle had to be sent to Victoria for forensic analysis, which led to a lengthy wait for results. Says Annette:

> *We've been lied to and fobbed off so many times over those skeletal remains. My mother, to this day, insists that's Richard.*

NSW Police, three years later, informed the family the remains were not those of Richard, after they had been sent to New Orleans in the USA for mitochondrial DNA testing (which was not available in Australia). 'But when you see the results of the Coroner's inquest – which, by the way, we weren't notified about at all until it was over – although we were told Mum's DNA was tested against those bones, it seems the bones may have not even sent to the USA at all. They were not sent for another 12 months after the inquest, and even then there is still some confusion about whether they're even the same set of remains that we're talking about,' says Annette in disgust.

Annette wants another inquest for her brother, as she feels her family were not informed, consulted or asked to give evidence, and she's very angry that the detective handling Richard's case got 'a pat on the back' in court for the work he'd done on the case, when Annette says he was merely reading out word for word Annette's own diary entries that she had sent to him. 'We can prove we've been lied to. I have telephone records, even when I have made a call to a commanding officer's personal mobile phone; she gave me the results of the forensic testing of the remains found over the phone, but clearly, as it came out in the Coroner's Court, there wasn't even a result back at that time. How else would I have her personal mobile number unless she gave it to me? It seems very convenient that that phone call happened on her last day in that department and I've never been able to speak to her again. It breaks my heart to think maybe something could have been done, but red tape has got in the way.'

Police said they'd been unable to contact her to inform her Richard's inquest would be held, only informing her after it was over. She is very angry about this, saying that she's had the same email address since she first got a computer, and the same mobile number for 14 years, and if they didn't have her phone number, how were they able to phone her after it was over? Her mother's phone number has also been unchanged for years. Annette is especially distressed that the Coroner twice asked police had the family been notified about the inquest and if there were any family members present in court, and was told yes, they'd been notified and no, there was no family present.

She felt like they thought no-one cared about Richard, when nothing could be further from the truth. 'That really, really hurt,' says Annette, the distress evident in her voice. 'That just destroyed Mum, and me.'

In January 2009, a neighbour of Annette's family's from Murwillumbah who knew Richard well growing up told the family that she had been visiting Sydney and was in a park near Central Station. She saw a man in the park who she felt strongly resembled Richard, and commented on it to her husband, and later phoned Mrs Leape to tell her about her sighting. Annette called the Missing Persons Unit to pass on the information.

The officer she spoke to said to Annette, 'So, what would you like me to do?' Annette said, 'Well, can you go and have a look??' She felt the information was very valid, as the sighting came from a woman who knew Richard personally. The officer replied, 'We don't have the resources to do that.' Annette said, 'Well, should I come down and look myself?' He said, 'No, no, no need for you to do that, I'll ring the local boys and ask them to have a look while they're doing their patrols.' Annette says, 'I was flabbergasted. I was so upset. I could not believe it. What is the Missing Persons Unit for?'

Annette rang Tony to ask him if he could come with her to Sydney for another search, but he was unable to make the trip, so Annette decided to travel alone, despite being quite unwell. It was about four weeks before Annette was able to get to Sydney, and when she checked the park she could not see anyone resembling Richard. Again, she was frustrated by the lack of help she was getting. 'It was like, who else cares?'

Annette's frustration was building with every dead end she encountered, and she found it very difficult at times dealing with the various government departments.

> *I don't like being fobbed off, and I will just keep ringing until someone speaks to me. Don't keep telling me that I need counselling, that my mother needs counselling – I want to know why they keep telling us the funding's there to identify all those bodies they have in Glebe morgue, that they're doing the cross-matching, but here we are years later and we still have no results? We're still waiting. One minute they say they have funding, the next they don't. Apparently, the funding is only for new cases that come in, and not for families like us who have been waiting for decades.*

Annette feels they've been really let down by the police. 'I know they can do some incredible work but as far as we're concerned, there's been so many stuff-ups. It's worse if you're an adult male missing person, and even worse if you have a mental health issue.'

A newspaper article about a group of New Zealanders who were living on the streets in Woolloomooloo caught Annette's attention when she looked closely at the photograph accompanying the article, and thought one of the faces, of a man who stayed in the homeless shelters nearby, looked a lot like Richard. 'There was something about the way he was sitting. He looked maybe too tall, and it wasn't a close up-photo, but I really thought it could be Richard.' Annette tracked down the journalist who wrote the article and learned the journalist had since returned to New Zealand and the photographer was freelance. Annette was given the photographer's name and asked the paper to forward her contact details to him. The photo had been taken two months prior, but that was all she could find out.

Annette got on well with one Bondi detective who did try hard to locate Richard. He had been on leave at the time of Richard's inquest, but was the one who phoned Annette afterwards to tell her it had already been held. The detective had told Annette that despite the Coroner ruling that Richard was likely to be deceased, his file would always be open, and if there was any further information police would investigate it. So, when Annette found the photograph she called and asked him to go to Woolloomooloo and look for the man in the photo. She sent the detective some other photos of Richard showing him with longer hair and a beard, which more closely resembled the man in the Woolloomooloo photo. The detective told Annette he would be unable to get over there for about a week as he was in court and asked had she called the Missing Persons Unit to ask them to look into it. Before Annette had a chance to reply he corrected himself and said, 'What a stupid question to ask you. I know you wouldn't call them.' (knowing Annette's previous frustrating encounter with them). He asked Annette if she wanted him to ask the local patrol car to check and she said no, she wanted him to do what he'd promised her and go and check it out himself. She said waiting a week was better than nothing.

During that week Annette contacted some of the homeless shelters around Woolloomooloo and spoke to a man who agreed to ask his volunteers if they recognised any of the people in the photo. The man in the photo had a grey beard and fading red/grey curling hair; it was clear he'd once had red hair – like Richard. The man's hands also reminded Annette of Richard but she acknowledges that when you want so desperately for that person to be the one you've been searching for you can convince yourself that it's him. She showed the photo to Tony and their mother, who agreed the man could be Richard. Tony wanted to drive to Sydney to check.

In the meantime, Annette received an e mail from the homeless shelter. They said they had identified the man in Annette's photo as someone they knew, who was only in his mid-30s. I have seen this photo and strongly feel the man is much older than this: his hair and beard are grey and even the toll homelessness takes on the appearance could not account for this man being that young.

Annette asked them were they certain that this man in the photo was the one the staff had identified and they said yes. 'That guy looked exactly the age that my brother would be,' says Annette. 'I'd been so excited thinking finally, yep, that's him.' She phoned Tony and discussed what had happened. They came to the conclusion that if the man was indeed Richard, at least he looked well cared for. He was dressed warmly and was receiving help, and they felt they'd be grateful if that was the case but still needed to know for sure. Tony decided to make the trip to Sydney to check it out. The day he arrived in Woolloomooloo it was pouring rain, and there were no homeless people anywhere on the streets. He went back the next day and managed to find a few people, but no-one who resembled Richard or the man in the photograph. Tony found it difficult getting any information from the homeless people he did see; no-one wanted to talk to him or give out any information at all, as they were wary of strangers.

A few days later the Bondi detective called Annette and said he hadn't yet had a chance to go to the park. Annette told him Tony had been to the park but hadn't found the man in the photo. The detective asked if he needed to go as well, then. Annette wasn't letting him off the hook, though, and insisted that he go and take a look. He agreed and a few days later came the dreaded but by now expected dead end – the detective had not found anyone in the park in Woolloomooloo who resembled Richard.

The search for Richard has taken a heavy toll on Annette, not only during the time she has spent actively looking, but also because of what she believes have been failures on the part of police and the coronial inquest process. She ended up on antidepressants and says she became 'absolutely obsessed' with looking for Richard.

I still go through periods of being obsessed. Every time there's a body found, the first thing I need to know is, is it male or female? Then, is it Caucasian? Then, there's the waiting to see when they identify it, is it Richard? It just goes on, and on, and on. Dad passed away a few years ago, but he had suffered a terrible stroke, which took away his speech and left him unable to drive. If he'd been able to, he wouldn't have come home from Sydney until he'd found Richard, he would never have stopped searching.

Annette has become a coffee addict and at one point probably drank a little too much wine, she says with a laugh, and has visited places, especially around inner city Sydney, that she didn't know existed. The search for Richard has caused the family financial hardship, especially because he disappeared interstate, meaning each search involved paying for expensive air and train travel and accommodation, as well as countless long distance phone calls.

I was a single mum when Richard went missing and it affected everything about my life, my children, my relationships. People you meet just don't get it, they don't understand how I can just drop everything and look for Richard if there's a new lead, or why I'm on the computer in the middle of the night looking up unidentified bodies. My children are grown up now but at the time, they saw a tired and distressed mum. I had to go away a lot and look for Richard and stay wherever I could. Having a missing person in your life has an impact on more areas than anyone ever realises.

She's been waiting for years for the DNA cross-matching to be implemented nationally. Her mother has become an expert on schizophrenia; before learning about Richard she might have seen someone in the street behaving erratically and crossed the road in fear. Now, she has a much greater understanding of the condition that afflicts so many. Mrs Leape has even been into a park in Murwillumbah at night and searched through the homeless people there in the hope that Richard might have returned to his hometown.

The family feels there's every chance Richard has changed his name, due to his extreme paranoia and having learned about the way the system works. They think he may even be living and receiving assistance with supported accommodation and benefits under an assumed name. They also fear it's possible Richard's body might have been discovered and buried without ever having been identified.

Annette does not believe Richard would have taken his own life, despite the Coroner's report indicating this was a possibility. 'I don't care what anyone says about schizophrenia and living out there on the streets, I know my brother well enough to know that he would not suicide, no matter how mentally ill he became. He did have that tough life, he did stay at the hostels and he would have gone to the soup kitchens, he would have done whatever it took to just keep going physically. If he'd started drinking again then he may have become violent. But suicide to him – that's just not fixing it. From what I've read about schizophrenia, the voices in your head tell you to hurt somebody else, not yourself.'

Former homeless man Ken, of the Homeless Persons' Legal Service, said in a YouTube interview:

> We don't normally hear about homeless people committing suicide … happens all the time. The ones who are found dead might get a mention in the paper. Nine times out of ten, it doesn't.

Annette reflects on her long search.

> It's been quite a journey, and I would do it all again, in a heartbeat, but if I knew then what I know now I would do it very differently. I will just keep going, until such a time as I know what happened to my brother. If Richard had gone missing today, we would have found him. It was so much harder years ago.
>
> I am a big believer that things don't happen until they're meant to, but I have to remind myself of that sometimes.

To me, this is the cruellest thing that could ever happen to a person, watching my mother, in particular, go through it. I can't begin to imagine how I'd feel if any of my own children went missing. This has just about killed my mum.

Mrs Leape has lived every parents' nightmare, with a missing son, but Annette thinks in the beginning she chose not to believe Richard was so ill. Annette and Tony took on the search for their brother while their mum remained somewhat in denial about the true situation. 'Richard was so talented and such a high achiever, winning academic scholarships to boarding school, and Mum shares that intelligence. But when it comes to things like mental illness, she didn't think it was possible with someone so talented. It was easier to think he was okay, and she also had Dad to look after when he had the stroke. She was a country girl and quite naive, and she had no idea that illnesses like Richard's could be so devastating. She didn't want to believe it.' It wasn't until after she received Richard's letters containing their wild and irrational statements, much of which she did not understand, that Mrs Leape finally realised just how unwell he had become.

'Nobody really talks to Mum about it. Tony, my brother is very quiet; he has a very different personality to Richard. He will talk to me about Richard if I bring it up but what he'll say to me is, "Where are we going and what do you need me to do? Where do you want me to take you?" Tony would never just go looking for Richard on his own. I am the one who always decides when we should search again. When Tony travels around and goes to different places, I know he looks, everywhere he goes, but I'm the instigator. Whenever I ask Tony to come with me, he always says yes,' says Annette.

Youngest sister Mandy would get very upset in the early days of Richard being missing, particularly when she saw how upset her parents were.

Annette tells me about a dream her mum had. Richard was there, on the bank of a river and he was dressed all in white. Annette sounds sceptical about this: 'Richard being Richard, there's just no way you'd entertain the idea of that man wearing white. He'd end up spilling something on himself before he'd even left the house, he was so clumsy.' Nonetheless, that's what he was wearing in his mum's dream, and the water in the river was thick and dirty. Richard was wearing a black hat. He threw the hat into the river, then he vanished. This dream makes Annette think of a body that was found in the Manning River in December 2011 that has never been identified and she still wonders ... could it be?

Annette said she had been close to her grandfather and her father and she would have thought one of them would have given her a 'sign' if Richard had died. 'But they've let me down. I told both of them while they were dying, let me know!'

Like many families of the missing, Annette has consulted many clairvoyants in a desperate attempt to find answers about Richard's disappearance but has decided not to spend any more money on them. One clairvoyant asked Annette if Richard had ever been involved with Aboriginal people and Annette told her Richard had always been fascinated by people from all walks of life and had actually told her some years before that he wanted to spend a day with the Aboriginal community in Sydney. The clairvoyant went on to tell Annette she felt that Richard had become involved with some people and 'something went wrong' during an argument over alcohol, in a park, and Richard had been killed by being struck over the head. The clairvoyant said the body had been found but never identified. Annette said this made her feel sick to the stomach.

She then saw a different clairvoyant who asked her if she believed Richard was deceased. She said sometimes she does, and then sometimes she thinks, no, he's still out there alive somewhere. 'My gut feeling confuses me sometimes, with regards to Richard. I'm usually spot on with things, but when it comes to Richard there's too much emotion there and I'm very confused.' Then the second clairvoyant astounded Annette by asking her whether Richard had anything to do with Aboriginal people. She told Annette she felt Richard had had a relationship with an Aboriginal or part-Aboriginal woman and they'd had a son together. Annette did feel sceptical about this, but kept listening. The clairvoyant told her Richard had schizophrenia and she felt he'd had issues with alcohol.

Annette says Richard had not touched alcohol for many years, because he didn't like the way it made him feel. She does think it's possible Richard started drinking after living on the streets, as it may have been a substitute for the medication he needed but was not taking. The clairvoyant went on to tell Annette she felt Richard had a severe Schizophrenic episode, and two people connected to the woman he was involved with had assaulted him, and he'd died of head injuries. She said this happened in the Redfern area. This was a remarkably similar story to the one told by the first clairvoyant. Annette tried to pass the information to police but nothing ever came of it. She doesn't think someone who looked like Richard – fair, red hair, blue eyes – would be able to mingle with the close knit Aboriginal community in Sydney without coming to the attention of local police.

'I honestly don't know how to approach finding Richard anymore, other than every unidentified body that turns up, I'm onto it,' says Annette firmly.

Her determination astounds me; she's kept up this fight for decades, and her drive is still as strong today as it was when her brother first went missing. I find her truly amazing.

We just have to hope and pray that he turns up, or hope and pray that they find his remains.

Annette says telling his story has brought up a lot of emotions and it's been hard, but she's also enjoyed remembering the good times. Richard had a great sense of humour and Annette loves recalling his antics.

After the inquest, when her mother received Richard's official death certificate, Annette thought her mother may have gone to her grave, it affected her so deeply, but she found an inner strength and has had a memorial plaque made for Richard which is next to his father's grave. Her faith is what keeps her going.

Richard's daughter is still in touch with her father's family, and has the teddy bear Richard gave her, and lots of photos. She finds it hard to talk about him, being only seven when her father went missing. Annette keeps her up to date with any news about Richard, as she doesn't want her to read anything unexpectedly about her dad on Facebook. Annette dearly wishes Richard was here to see his first grandchild.

I asked Annette if she's angry with Richard.

I'm not angry, but I'm peeved off with him. We had such a close relationship, and I was so upset that he didn't feel he could talk to me before it got to the point of him ending up homeless and in that position. I always looked after him, at school, if he was crying, it was always me he came to. I'm more upset than angry.

Annette says finding my Facebook page, which her children taught her how to use, made her feel like she was no longer alone, and that other people really did care and want to help. 'I felt like I wasn't crazy, even though sometimes I think that I must be.' It helps her to hear other people's stories of their own searches.

She has told me she thinks I am an angel who has been placed in her life. I feel very honoured that Annette has allowed me to tell her story and allowed me to share her journey; it's been a privilege for me to get to know this extraordinary family. She tells me her devoutly Catholic mum prays for me every Sunday, and especially on All Souls Day in November when prayers are said for those who have passed away and for those who have had a positive impact on a person's life, and that means the world to me.

I hope that telling Richard's story here will help to bring him home to them.

If you have any information about Richard Leape please call Crime Stoppers on 1800 333 000.

CHAPTER TEN
Mark Leicester

Mark Leicester went missing from his home in Tecoma, Victoria on Wednesday December 19th, 2012. His body was found January 12th, 2013, not far from his home. He was 52 years old.

Mark Leicester's story doesn't have a happy ending. Unlike all of the other stories in this book, Mark is no longer a missing person. His story is sad but important, as it gives a great insight not only into the journey he travelled towards the day he went missing, but also the impact his disappearance had on his family.

The Leicester family lived in the Dandenong Ranges region of Victoria. There were five kids altogether, two girls and three boys – Bronwen, Alison, Gary, Mark and Craig. The family lost a three-month-old baby before eldest daughter Bronwen was born, a son who was born in between Mark and older son Gary. When Mark was born his parents were extremely protective of him and were attentive to his every need. They were terrified of losing another child. Alison remembers her mother saying to the other children, referring to Mark, 'He doesn't realise how much I wanted him.'

Mark was a rebel even at the age of three or four. Gary recalls, 'If he didn't want to wear something he'd just walk around with no clothes on. He was very strong willed but also very focused.' Mark and Bronwen were very similar in personality, both loud and outspoken, and also Craig to a lesser degree, whereas Gary and Alison were more laidback and calm, preferring to watch the dramas rather than take part. They all remember it as a fantastic Aussie childhood.

'Growing up in Belgrave South we had a great house and a big block; we had our own cricket pitch and little soccer field and putting green,' says Bron.

Mark did fairly well at school, but he was younger than most of the other children. He was upset at having to repeat Grade 6 at the insistence of his mother, and that was something he kept bringing up in family arguments, even into adulthood. When Mark would sink into his dark moods he would blame his repeating for his later problems. Brothers Craig and Mark were very close, but Mark was very competitive with Craig. Bronwen doesn't mince her words. 'As an older brother, he was mean. Mark was a bit of a bully. You'd watch him play tennis and if he lost an easy point he actually dropped his daks. One time he made me play tennis, I didn't even win the match, all I did was win a game off him and he made me walk home, about 15 kilometres.'

'Mark was best friends with Paul Hester, who lived across the road from us.' Gary says, 'They were as thick as thieves, those two. They were always up to no good, up to mischief.' Paul Hester was the drummer with popular bands Split Enz and Crowded House. Bron remembers the boys' friendship well. 'One memorable time was when Mark and Paul Hester were being chased by a group of teenage boys who Mark had rubbed up the wrong way. The boys were 15 but Mark, at age 11 and much smaller, had taken them on. The boys hid behind Gary, who went out to deal with the teenagers.' When I ask Gary about what he remembers best about his brother, the first thing he says is 'Loyalty'. Mark was fiercely loyal to his family and despite his crankiness when it came to losing at sport, he would also defend his family to the nth degree when needed.

Craig says, 'If I was playing football and some bloke would be about to clobber me, next thing I know Mark would be off the bench, running over to grab the guy. No-one would ever touch me. He had no fear, no matter how big the guy was.'

Mark suffered from severe teenage acne and Bronwen thinks the embarrassment of this condition led to him having a difficult time in his teen years. 'He became troublesome,' she says. 'He was put on an acne medication, and they now know it causes depression.'

'I think he was a bit jealous of me,' says Craig. He thinks Mark's social difficulties began during his high school days. 'He had a terrible time,' says Craig. 'He was badly acne-scarred and at a private school, they can be cruel. I think that's what made him always angry and defensive. Even when he went to the 20-year reunion he wanted to take half of them outside and take them on! He really made a scene; it was pretty full-on.'

Mark never had a girlfriend. Bronwen is sure this is due to Mark's paranoia about his acne-scarred skin, but she felt Mark was very awkward around girls and just didn't know how to behave. He had a great personality and seemed to be confident but inside was deeply insecure.

Mark broke down in front of his mum not long before he disappeared and told her he didn't know what it was like to be loved, as he had never been loved by a woman.

'It was probably about this time that he started smoking hooch,' says Bronwen. 'My bedroom was next to his and I could smell it, he'd smoke it in his room. I'd go to parties with him, where he'd smoke it. At those parties there'd be magic mushrooms too, and speed. The drugs affected Mark's moods very badly. He failed his driving test the first time and he blamed Mum and Dad for that. I remember that day, we were a bit scared of him. He got Mum very upset. We found out much later that Mum was bipolar. We knew something was different with Mum, but as a kid you sort of think, Oh, well, that's just Mum. She was always cleaning, but it wasn't until much later in her life that she was finally diagnosed. So, it all made sense. And then we started to wonder whether Mark could be suffering from that too, but he didn't have the extremes of moods like Mum had.'

I asked Bronwen if she thought Mark's extreme mood swings and aggressive behaviour were something inherent in him, or caused by a combination of the drugs he was taking, including the prescription drug for his acne, and she thinks it was simply the way Mark was born. 'But I think drugs did have an influence, especially with the findings they've made with marijuana use, and magic mushrooms, and the speed would have caused some of his aggression, when he was coming down. He hadn't tried heroin at all back then. And when Mark would go out, he wouldn't just have a couple of drinks; Mark would go out to get pissed. I think it was the only way he could have fun.'

His moods were increasingly dark and he'd blame everyone around him for the things that had gone wrong. Even into his 30s and 40s Mark would tell anyone who would listen that his parents never loved him, and that they favoured the other children. Bronwen knows this isn't true; her parents loved them all equally and no-one had any different treatment than another. Alison remembers Mark saying that no-one had ever told him they loved him, and her mother replying, 'Well, *I* love you.' She says that was a big deal for her mother as she and their father were not used to expressing their feelings out loud.

Alison recalls that instead of studying for his HSC, Mark went surfing. He passed, but he didn't get a high enough grade to get into university. He did clerical work for a time, and seemed reasonably happy in his life. Craig and Mark moved into a flat together, then Mark moved in with Bronwen for about six months. Mark then moved back in with Craig. This cycle of living on and off with his siblings would continue for many years. Craig and Mark moved to Perth, and Craig thinks Mark was envious of his close group of friends and the relationships he was able to easily form there, but at the same time he was proud of Craig's achievements.

I think I was the closest one to Mark. He was very protective and he loved a fight. He was volatile and outspoken and very left wing... I wish he'd put more energy into his own life than he did into other people's and other causes. That's what sort of guy he was. He'd go up to the Daintree forest and tie himself to a tree.

Mark was still taking party drugs – ecstasy was now widely available, but he had not yet started to use heroin. He did drink heavily during his time in Perth, which caused some issues. 'He was a bad drunk,' says Craig. However, he had a job, good friends, and seemed happy. Mark returned to Melbourne in 1994 after he and Craig had a falling out. This deeply affected Mark and it would be years before the brothers regained the closeness they'd once shared. Mark moved in with an old friend in Melbourne and again was working and happy. He was still taking drugs, but Bronwen describes him as a 'functioning addict'. She says, 'He used to do bike rides and 10 kilometres runs; he was still playing soccer. He was binge drinking and taking party drugs on the weekends, and probably smoking dope during the week.'

In the late 1990s, Mark started to show more signs of depression, and around 2000 he first tried heroin. He was 40 years old. 'I didn't know he'd started taking it,' says Bronwen. 'I didn't know what a person on heroin looked like, but Craig told me he'd started using it. Mark's words to me were, "It's under control." I always thought that once you started using heroin you had to have it every day, but Mark was still functioning, still playing sport.'

Craig became a born-again Christian around this time, something that annoyed Mark. Mark had ambivalent feelings about religion and he didn't appreciate Craig 'preaching' to him, as he saw it. 'I went from Buddhism to Christianity,' Craig says with a laugh. 'I was always on a journey to find something. Mark did have a slight belief. He hated the judgemental side (of organised religion) but he'd pray. Things like the devil and *The Exorcist*, those things scared him, so he must have believed in something; he wasn't an atheist.'

In 2001 Bronwen received a phone call from her parents that stopped her in her tracks. Mark was in St Vincent's Hospital in Melbourne: he had tried to kill himself. He remembered the church camps they'd gone to as children, near Mount Wombat, and this was the location he chose for his suicide attempt. The camp no longer exists, but Mark tried to find the spot where it had once been. He drank a lot of alcohol and took pills – so many the doctors told his family he should not have survived. He lay down beside a waterfall and passed out. He regained consciousness some hours later, on dusk, and ran through the bush, scratching himself badly in the process. He found his way back to his car but had lost his keys, so he smashed the window of his car. He then attempted to attach a hose to the car exhaust for a second suicide attempt. Luckily a park ranger found him and Mark was winched out of the park by helicopter and flown to hospital.

Bronwen remembers looking at Mark in hospital and thinking, 'What are you doing?' She vividly remembers Mark's eyes being very red and bloodshot. 'He seemed really out of it, but he said, "Bronwen, you've got to go to my flat." I did, and it was all packed up. There was a suitcase on his bed with all his clothes packed and three envelopes. One of them was for me; it was about how he still wanted his World Vision sponsor child to be paid for, which music he wanted played at his funeral, who he wanted to speak at his funeral – it was all done. There was a note for the real estate agent and instructions for me to hand the key to his flat back, and if there was any leftover bond money I was to donate it to charity.'

It was a shocking experience for Bronwen. She had felt that throughout his life Mark had tended to be a bit of an attention seeker, as evidenced by his frequent outbursts to his parents accusing them of not paying him enough attention, but Mark was serious about his suicide efforts. He had quit his job and cashed out his superannuation. After this suicide attempt, life settled down a little. Mark was living with his parents, and this provided him with security and safety. Bronwen lived close by, seeing her brother whenever she could. Craig and Mark were still not on speaking terms, and Alison and Gary didn't really take the suicide attempt seriously; Bronwen thinks they felt it was just Mark's regular attention-seeking behaviour. It was the shock of the suicide attempt that finally reconciled Craig and Mark, as Craig was very upset by what happened.

However, Craig was still living in Perth, so the onus was on

Bronwen to try to help her brother out of his very dark place. Bronwen realised Mark's drug use was the likely cause of his suicide attempt and she urged him to join Narcotics Anonymous. Mark refused point-blank, saying he believed the organisation was run by born-again Christians, like Craig, and he wanted nothing to do with them. He kept saying he didn't want to turn into Craig. Bronwen then tried to get him interested in Buddhist drug rehabilitation but his response was, 'No, it's cool, I've blown all my money so I can't afford it.'

Gary would see Mark just about every weekend when he'd visit his parents. They'd talk for a few hours each time, mainly about soccer and politics, and Gary can't recall ever arguing with his brother. 'Mark would take a particular point, like where the government was going wrong, and he'd wear away at it,' says Gary. Bronwen thinks she probably wasn't the best person to help her brother, as she suffers from depression herself. 'I'd say to Mark, "Can't you wait until Mum and Dad pass away? Or get back into your sports?" I tried to suggest anything I could think of to help him through it.'

About a year later Bronwen received a phone call from Mark's flatmate telling her Mark had once again tried to take his life. Mark had booked a hotel room and he took an overdose. When he didn't check out of the hotel room at the appointed time the hotel staff tried to rouse him. Mark answered the door in a dishevelled state, very groggy and incoherent. Despite his obviously unwell state the hotel staff told him to leave instead of calling for medical assistance. Mark got into his car and tried to drive away but sideswiped several cars and the police were called. Mark lost his driver's licence over that incident and never attempted to regain it. Bronwen went to see him after this latest attempt. 'I've stuffed my life up,' said Mark. This time his friends had seen Mark's suicidal behaviour first hand, so they rallied around him with support. They urged him to seek help, but instead of trying to stop his downward spiral, Mark starting using heroin even more heavily.

In the early 2000s Bronwen went on a trip to Queensland and gave her keys to Mark so he could keep an eye on her house. While he was there he trashed her front door and broke the flyscreen door, and claimed a burglar had tried to break in. But there was spray paint on the door and also on her fridge, which made Bronwen doubt a burglar had done it. Mark had no recollection of damaging the house himself, but Bronwen's neighbours had heard Mark's rampage. 'That's when we knew he had to have been on something. I've seen Mark on all types of drugs but for him not to remember … I thought that was really strange,' says Bronwen.

After another Queensland trip Bronwen received a phone call from her mum, who told her Mark had once again tried to kill himself. 'She said, "He's tried to gas himself." I just lost it. I said, "I'm not going to him." I said to Mum, "If he wanted to do it, then why did he call you? If he was serious, he would have just done it." He was found by a police officer friend of the family and they brought him home to Mum and Dad's.' Bronwen wasn't happy about her parents deciding to once again have Mark live with them. 'I told Mum she needed to give him tough love. I asked them why they wanted him back there when he caused them so much stress. Mum said, 'Because he's our son, and we love him.'

Mark's childhood mate Paul Hester had huge success with the band Crowded House, and he did keep in touch with Mark and his brothers, who would go to visit him if they were in the same town. Mark and his family still played footy with Paul when he came home. Paul took his own life in March 2005. Fellow band member Nick Seymour told biographer Chris Bourke that he felt Paul had 'a major chemical imbalance. He's always at extremes'. Did Mark see that in Paul, and also in himself? When Paul took his own life, did Mark see the same thing in his future? Paul had been in therapy for many years, and the depression still took over. Maybe Mark could not see beyond that darkness. If Paul could not keep going, a world famous rock star, what hope was there for Mark? Gary said Paul's death affected them all.

'We played football together. Paul was really good. We were quite close. Even as a kid we could see Paul was a manic depressive, he was always really up or really down, mainly up, though. He was very energetic and always joking around. Mark was a bit the same. You never saw the down side, as a kid, because it wasn't talked about.' Gary thinks Mark and Paul understood each other well, and that's why they were so close all through their childhood and into their teenage years. Mark would go backstage to see Paul after his concerts. Bronwen recalls that Paul always seemed happy, with no signs of depression, but quieter than he'd been as a child. Paul's death came after Mark's first serious suicide attempt, where he was located in the national park. When Paul took his own life in 2005, Mark learned about it on the news. He was very upset and shocked, but Bronwen remembers a strange reaction. Mark seemed intrigued as to *how* Paul had taken his life. He was fascinated that Paul had done it in at Elsternwick Park in Brighton, Melbourne. Mark said: 'What a way to go!'

Bronwen realised Mark's heroin addiction was getting worse. She remembers Mark having a jerking movement in his legs, where he would kick out occasionally. She now knows this is a side effect of heavy heroin use.

Craig was worried about him. 'That drug got hold of him,' he says firmly. 'He wasn't himself. I took some photos of him in July 2012 and he just looks as if he's staring off into space. He looked troubled.'

Bronwen could see Mark's pupils were constricted all the time, another sign of opiate use. She told him he was not welcome in her home if he was under the influence of drugs. 'I told him he could come if he was clean and he did, he was clean when he came over. I could tell by the clearing of his throat and the jerking of his arms and legs whether he was on something, and I told him I didn't want that crap around my kids. I said, "I don't care if you come stoned, but you're not coming like that." He was always sick,' recalls Bronwen. 'He'd tell me he had the flu, and he'd had it for months, it just wouldn't go away. But it wasn't, it was him on heroin.'

Mark denied to Bronwen that he was using heroin during his working week; he told her it was only on weekends, but Bronwen is sure it was all the time. Their parents started noticing Mark's increasing mood swings. Bronwen would call in for a visit and look at Mark and think, 'You're bloody on it!'

'I was looking at Mum and Dad thinking, can't you tell there's something different about him? He knew I knew. I ended up telling Mum and Dad he was on heroin. They asked me how I knew. I said it was the croaky voice and the clearing of his throat, and the super-loud talking. I remember asking him why he'd ever touched it, why he was taking it and he said, "It's my drug of choice, Bronwen, and there's nothing you can do about it." Mum and Dad didn't think it was as bad as it was, but Craig and I knew it was really bad.' Bronwen thinks Mark started 'doctor shopping' and gathering prescriptions for sleeping tablets and Panadeine Forte, telling the doctors he suffered from headaches. Not one of the doctors he visited picked up on Mark's serious heroin addiction.

Shortly before his disappearance Mark was diagnosed with depression by a doctor. Two years before he died Bronwen managed to get Mark to agree to see a psychologist; she organised the mental health visits under the Medicare scheme and made the appointment, but Mark failed to attend it. His reason for not going? 'I couldn't be bothered getting out of bed.'

One Saturday Mark rang Bronwen and said he needed to talk to her, and asked her to pick him up. She did, but was overwhelmed when he got into her car. 'He stunk. I felt like I was going to throw up. It's a smell heroin addicts get, I think because they sweat a lot, but it was like a homeless smell. Mark used to be so proud of his hygiene, so when I told him he stank he said, "*Really??*" He had no idea. I remember going to the movies with him and it was so bad I made my son sit next to him. I was horrified that he was catching the train to work every day and people had to sit next to him. I think he had a shower every day but heroin just makes you perspire with a disgusting smell.'

Bronwen drove Mark back to her place and they talked. He told her he wanted to give up the drugs. 'I thought, FINALLY!'

says Bronwen. 'So, we went on the internet and looked up some rehab places, but a lot of them are private and cost $5000, $10,000, and Mark didn't have private health insurance anymore, so I just didn't know how we were going to do this. I sent off a couple of emails and then we found this beautiful place in Thailand, but it was about $12,000 and you had to go away for about three months. He said, "Oh, I'd love to go there!" I thought that would be great, as he'd be away from everyone and he does like the Buddhist philosophy. Looking back, I really wish I'd borrowed the $12,000 to send him there,' she says sadly.

It was in September 2012 that Mark told Bronwen he wanted to get clean. Bronwen called Mark numerous times following their talk, asking him if he'd done anything about getting into rehab and he kept saying he'd call them the following day. It never happened.

On one visit home she recalls Mark asking their father for a belt and she realised just how much weight Mark had lost. 'I watched him for half an hour – that's how long it took him to put that belt on. It was like he forgot how to put it on; he couldn't work out how to put it through the loops in his pants. He saw me watching him and laughed but I asked him what on earth he was doing. I ended up getting Mum and Dad's attention and pointed at Mark and said, "Watch. You don't reckon there's something going on here?" That's when I found out Mark had hepatitis C. That's why he'd lost all the weight. He'd never shared a needle, so I don't know how he got it, but he re-used his own needles and I think you can get it that way. That's why he'd come to me and said he wanted to make a change, because getting hep C gave him a fright. He wrote on Facebook: "Something eye-opening today. Time to make a change." His friends all wrote really supportive comments so I thought, "Oh, this is good!'"

That night Mark broke down in front of his parents and told them everything. He told them he was a junkie and was out of control and didn't want to do it anymore. He confessed to them about other suicide attempts that he and Bronwen had kept from their parents. He once again told them he felt no-one had ever loved him and he'd blown all the good things in his life like his jobs and money. He said drugs were controlling his life and he needed help. He broke down in tears, something Mark never did. His parents promised to help him in whatever way they could and told him they'd support him even if he was unemployed.

Mark decided to start the methadone program. He had to travel an hour on the train each morning to have his daily dose before work, and the same trip on weekends, so he tried to convince the pharmacist to give him the weekend doses on Friday, but was not successful. He said he intended to start taking antidepressants and was scheduled to attend Maroondah Hospital in Ringwood East regarding his hepatitis C treatment, but failed to keep the appointment. He never did have any treatment for the illness. He kept making excuses that he was unable to get there. Mark knew he could always ask Bronwen for a lift when he needed one, so she feels he was deliberately avoiding doing anything about the virus.

The family celebrated their mother's 80th birthday at the local RSL club, but they planned to have a big party for her a couple of weeks later. It was 16 December 2012. Mark's latest work contract had wound up the week before and he was worried about not having any money coming in, so he quickly accepted another job, taking a dramatic drop in pay. He told Bronwen he was worried about paying his bills. She wondered what bills he could have, as he was still living with his parents and not paying any board to them. She was unaware that Mark had more than just the one credit card he'd told her about, and had actually racked up a substantial debt with other credit cards. He said he really hoped he would like the new job that he was due to start the following Monday, as he wanted some job security.

Bronwen knows depression can be a side effect of methadone use, and she believes antidepressants should be given to methadone patients, or at the very least mandatory psychological counselling. On the Monday morning (17 December 2012) Mark started his new job. When he came home his mother asked him how he'd liked it and he said, 'It was the worst day of my working life.' He ate dinner and went to bed. The following morning Mark got up and pretended to go to work. He caught the train to the city and picked up his dose of methadone. He withdrew $200 from an ATM and stayed in the city until his usual finishing time for work, then caught his regular train home.

Craig rang him on his mobile, but Mark told him he'd speak to him after he got off the train. Craig tried to phone him half an hour later, but the phone was switched off, something Mark did when he didn't feel like speaking to anyone. His mother said he came in the door and they asked him how his second day at work had been. He replied, 'Today was a better day.' He ate dinner and went to his room. He stayed in his room until about 10 o'clock, when he came out briefly – this was the last time his parents saw Mark.

On the Wednesday morning Mark's mother got up and went to put something on Mark's bed. She noticed that his bed was not made, which was very unlike him. His pyjamas were thrown on the floor and she thought he must have been running late for work. It wasn't until he didn't come home from work that evening that his family became concerned.

'We were always taught, growing up, that we leave notes,' says Bronwen. 'If we needed to say, "I'm crashing at so-and-so's house", or "Don't make dinner for me", always a note. Mark didn't come home, so Mum rang my sister Alison and asked if Mark was over there with her.'

'When Mum rang me, my first thought was that he'd gone to the cricket do [on Wednesday night],' says Alison, and suggested he might have stayed over with a friend in the city after the party. But none of his friends had seen him. Alison says, 'I thought that was weird. Where could he be staying? He doesn't have any money. And he didn't have a licence. Then Mum rang again and said his backpack was still in his bedroom. She said it had his reading glasses and his book in it. Mark wouldn't go *anywhere* without his reading glasses, and his book; Mark loves to read, especially on the train. I said to Mum, "If he doesn't come home tonight, ring me straightaway; we'll give him one more night." He didn't come home and on the Friday morning [21 December 2012] Mum rang me and said he's definitely not there. I told her to report him as a missing person and I would ring all the hospitals.'

Bronwen started making phone calls. She contacted the organisers of the methadone program Mark was on and they confirmed that Mark had not collected his methadone on the Wednesday, Thursday or Friday; that the last dose he had was on the Tuesday. Bronwen found Mark's Myki card in his room and swiped it at the local train station, which showed the card had been used on Tuesday morning and evening at Mark's usual commuting times, but had not been used since. Bronwen rang Craig in Perth on the Friday morning to tell him Mark was missing. Craig recalls that, strangely, despite an excellent driving record, he'd had a car accident around the exact time Mark went missing. She told him she'd called all the hospitals and police stations and Craig immediately said, 'He's done it.' He felt straightaway that Mark had taken his own life. He and Bronwen both thought Mark had gone somewhere and taken an overdose.

Gary's first thought, when he was told Mark was missing, was that his brother had gone interstate. 'He was always saying he wanted to go back to Perth, so I thought he'd just done a runner,' says Gary.

I didn't think he'd be running away from his debts, as they weren't that bad. I just thought he was a bit aimless. I thought he'd just gone away for a couple of weeks. When we saw him for Mum's birthday he was fine; it didn't look to me like anything was going to happen.

It wasn't until Mark didn't turn up for Christmas that Gary thought something sinister may have happened.

When Bronwen spoke to the police she told them she was sure Mark was still in the Tecoma area, because he hadn't used his card to travel anywhere else after he came home on Tuesday evening. She thought Mark had disappeared sometime between midnight, when his parents went to bed, and the time his mother got up the next morning. The police didn't treat Mark's case as a high priority missing person. He was an adult male with a history of drug abuse, so Bronwen thinks they believed he was probably just 'on a bender' and he'd come home soon. Bronwen still feels guilty that she told the police about Mark's drug use, as she thinks it may have influenced them to not look for him as soon as they may have for another missing person.

> I told them he was on the methadone program and that I thought he might have used the $200 he took out of the ATM to buy a last hit, and he would have gone out without pain. I told them they needed to look for him on one of the walking tracks or a picnic area. I told them he would have tried to OD, but he wouldn't have done it in a spot where children would find him.

That night, a police officer friend of Bronwen's drove around the local area and the places Bronwen had indicated Mark may have gone, but didn't find him. Bronwen and her family spent the whole weekend searching.

On 22 December 2012, Bronwen contacted me for the first time via my Facebook page. She asked me to post Mark's photo on the page and help find him. This is the original appeal that I wrote for Mark:

> Mark Leicester, aged 52, was last seen at home on Rutherford Rd in Tecoma Victoria around 9pm on December 18 2012.

*He was thought to be in the Dandenong Ranges National
Park or the area near the 1000 steps on Ferny Creek Rd in
Belgrave.*

I posted a couple of photos of Mark: a smiling, curly-haired man
who looked perfectly normal and perfectly happy. At that stage,
I was very hopeful of finding him safely, quickly, as about 99 per
cent of missing persons return home safely within a few days of
going missing.

Bronwen and I exchanged Facebook messages after her friend
Nikki asked me to speak with the family:

Conversation started 22 December 2012

AMPR: Hi Bronwen, I'm Nicole. Nikki has told me about
Mark and I just posted his photo and details. Has he ever
gone missing before?

Bronwen: No ... he did try to kill himself in early 2000s
in Mansfield but was found by a park ranger and that was
just overnight ... he is a creature of habit and always comes
home.

AMPR: Is it unusual for his phone to be off?

Bronwen: Yep, and not to take his reading glasses or even
his headphones ... he does not have a licence anymore, so
walks and catches the train ... his train card (myki) is still
in his top pocket of the shirt he wore Tuesday, so we know
he is around the hills locally. He always bush walks.

AMPR: Have the SES started a search?

Bronwen: No. A friend who knows the chief ranger has
just sent him an email. My friend who is in the police was

on shift last night searched the BBQ shelters, start of the walking tracks etc.

AMPR: If you are able to tomorrow, ask the police to request an SES search, they are the only ones who can.

Bronwen: OK … will do.

AMPR: Very best wishes for his safe return. x

Bronwen: OK, thanks for all your support.

AMPR: You're welcome, let me know whatever you need. I have some people near there also getting the other rangers on the search.

Bronwen: Thanks.

Bronwen found dealing with police very difficult. She felt she had to push and insist every day that they take Mark's disappearance seriously. For the first two weeks the police didn't keep Mark's parents informed about the investigation.

We put the missing person report in on 21 December, but they didn't come to Mum's house until Christmas Eve, to look around Mark's room. That's when we found his mobile phone in his room, so he didn't take that with him.

The family made up their own missing person posters and flyers. They'd contacted me to ask me to make social media appeals for Mark and had searched exhaustively on foot all around their local area but had come up with nothing. They were organising interviews with the local newspaper and giving as much information to police as possible. Bronwen insisted to police that Mark would not have left without his reading glasses, his phone and his iPod, as he listened to music wherever he was. All he took was a house key. Bronwen isn't sure why he took the key with him, but the Coroner later suggested Mark may have thought he might change his mind and return to the house.

Bronwen called her brother Gary and asked him to help look for his brother. They all felt the police were not doing anything to look for Mark. The focus became Christmas; they felt that if Mark had been staying with a friend he'd definitely walk back into the house on Christmas Day. He didn't. Christmas came and went with no sign of him.

25 December 2012

AMPR: Hoping with everything I have for you Bronwen xx

Bronwen: Thank you; no surprise visitor today at Christmas lunch.

AMPR: I'm sorry ☹

Bronwen: Ah well; he is probably at more peace now. My other brother and sister are doing a walk of the area we grew up in which had tracks that tourists don't know about tomorrow.

There's a certain helplessness I feel when I talk to the families when they're playing this painful waiting game. It was clear to me that Bronwen felt Mark had taken his own life and in that situation it's almost offensive of me to say, 'I'm sure he'll be home soon.' She knew her brother; I didn't. If she felt he'd ended his life, then there's a fair chance that's exactly what had happened. To give false hope to a family only makes the feeling worse if they are located deceased, so I try not to do it. I work out what they think has happened, then give as much support as I can.

I was posting Mark's photo on my Facebook page daily, and as Bronwen sent me new photos I'd post those too, in case someone recognised him looking different in other photos. I had people all around the area looking for him; any reported sightings would go to police, and I'd also let Bronwen know.

Around this time, on 28 December 2012, a man's body was located at Mt Buffalo in Victoria, and Bronwen was immediately concerned it may be Mark. Due to the distance from Tecoma I felt it was unlikely. As soon as the man's identity was confirmed I let Bronwen know, as I knew she'd have been waiting by the phone for any news. It was not Mark. Bronwen's agonising wait continued, while for another family the wait was over, and I think that affected her deeply.

On the same day a woman contacted me and said she had seen a man on McNicol Road in Tecoma, heading down the hill towards a park called Birdsland. The man was dishevelled and was carrying a gingham doona, like he'd been sleeping rough. Bronwen and I looked at photos of gingham doonas, trying to find one that resembled what the woman saw in the hope that Mark had something similar. Bronwen was really hopeful about this possible sighting, as the road where the man was seen was a direct route from Mark's home to the park. However, the man was never located and we now know it was not Mark.

29 December 2012

Bronwen: Can you also add these extra 2 photos? Thanks, Nicole.

AMPR: Sure.

Bronwen: Thanks. Going to organise some posters and post them up locally and also contact local papers.

Bronwen: Have posted this up: Latest photos of Mark for those that did not know him ... missing 11 days. Has not touched bank accounts since 17 Dec. All his 'necessary' items still at home (except wallet and we are now not sure whether he had his phone on him). As mentioned earlier – nice day for walking the dog, bush walk or bike ride. Please take one of the tracks that range around Kallista/Belg/Lysterfield/Birds Paddock/Courtneys Road area/Mt Morton/Sherbrooke. If you are up in the area on a pleasant Sunday in Melb ... just have that special look (with your eyes not your body as I don't want you to get lost) beyond the tracks for anything out of the ordinary. Thanks on behalf of the Leicester family. Remember call 000.

Shortly before New Year's Eve, in desperation, Bronwen begged that Mark's case be escalated by police. A friend of Bronwen's who worked with Victoria's emergency services contacted police to ask them to ramp up the search. Bronwen's family had even offered to pay for search dogs to be used. 'When you get the dogs out there, they can smell a corpse,' says Bronwen grimly. From this time, police were much more helpful and Bronwen found things much easier. The process of dealing with the police, especially when there was no news at all of Mark, became distressing for their mother, so Bronwen asked police to make her the family point of contact and to deal with only her from that time on.

Bronwen and Alison dealt with a female police officer who was very kind and helpful. 'She even came in one day when she was meant to be off sick,' says Alison.

29 December 2012

Bronwen: Hi Nicole, spoke to a great police officer at Belgrave who has been very helpful and will be the contact for the next 2 weeks whilst the other police officer is on leave. Can you stress on your page that people are to call 000 (as you already have before) if they have a sighting as they could attend the location much quicker than I or family ... The one in Birds paddock, by the time I read it, was hours later; however, the police could have driven down that road (2 mins from police station) and seen the guy to rule him out. They are going to print off posters for me to do tomorrow, make me the official contact (not the folks), and she will speak to the station boss when he is back on Tues re SES. Thanks so much for your support, your website is a gift xoxo

Bronwen asked her new police contact if they could organise an SES search, as I had been urging her to do. My main concern at this point was that I didn't want Bronwen or her family to find Mark's body; I wanted him to be found by police or SES who are trained in body recovery searches. She was told that a search had to be authorised by a senior sergeant who was on leave until 2 January, so the search could not take place. Bronwen continued to organise friends and family to do walking searches and I asked anyone in the local area, via my Facebook page, if they could go down and help search.

2 January 2013

AMPR: Hi love, no news?

Bronwen: Hi Nicole. No. Police rang today and the station sergeant said they cannot call SES as we don't have a definitive place as it could be many areas where he went for a walk; however, they did contact chief ranger, who is distributing the photo and comms to all staff (rangers) to be on the lookout as part of their daily jobs.

AMPR: I'm sorry. Will keep asking people to share.

Bronwen: Thanks Nicole x

On 7 January Bronwen did some newspaper interviews for the local papers. She asked me for some advice regarding Mark's financial affairs. It's a very common problem for the families of missing persons – what happens when someone disappears? How long do you wait before you clean out their flat? Do you re-register their car? Who keeps paying the car payments? How do you access their bank account? What about rent and mortgage? When do you tell their employer you don't think they're coming back to their job?

Bronwen started to experience some of these problems when mail started to arrive for Mark. Bronwen was trying to deal with the banks, as she'd just discovered Mark's extensive credit card debt problem. She found he'd also taken out a personal loan at the same time as he'd obtained the credit card in September. He had borrowed $12,000, but the family has no idea where the money went. I asked Bronwen if she thought Mark had intended to pay for the Thailand drug rehabilitation, as this was the exact amount of the treatment. She doesn't know – it's possible he thought about spending the money on that but changed his mind. She thinks it's possible Mark owed money to drug dealers. He may have used the loan money to pay off another credit card that the family was not aware of but his income from the new job would not have been enough to cover all his repayments.

Bronwen says Mark knew his family was always there to help him out if he needed them and he'd borrowed money from Craig in the past. New laws which took effect in Victoria in October 2010 allow families to apply to the Victorian Civil and Administrative Tribunal (VCAT) for an order appointing them (or someone else they trust) to manage the missing person's affairs. These laws were introduced with tremendous assistance from the family of another missing Victorian man, Daniel Rosewall, whose parents, David and Julie Rosewall, came across all the same issues Bronwen had to deal with.

The Leicester family had been arranging a big 80th birthday party for their mum, but they had postponed it because of Mark's disappearance. It had been moved to 11 January 2013, but as this date approached, Mark had still not been found. Bronwen says, 'I told Mum she should still have her party. I said I thought Mark would have wanted her to have it. Craig was meant to come over from Perth but he'd cancelled, so I called him and told him to come anyway, that Mum would be having her party.'

Bronwen was still constantly searching the bush tracks for her brother, and had searched his room over and over to see if he'd left a note or some clue. When he'd made his first suicide attempt he'd left three notes and detailed instructions, but this was very different – he hadn't even made his bed. The family tried to think of anywhere Mark may have chosen to go to, anywhere they'd loved visiting as children, that was within walking distance of the house. 'It was somewhere he'd gone to just lie down for the rest of his life,' says Bronwen.

Craig arrived from Perth and after picking him up from the airport, he quickly said hello to his parents then headed out with Bronwen to search the bush. He knew of some bush tracks he and Mark had walked through together in previous years. The local paper met them on the track and took some photos in the hope that someone reading the paper may have seen Mark. They also wanted to highlight that the family had had to conduct all the walks and searches on their own and that my Facebook page had been the only help they felt they'd had.

Then on 12 January 2013, the message I had been dreading.

12 January 2013

Bronwen: Hi Nicole, Mark has been found deceased. Thanks for all you have done. Take care.

AMPR: Oh, Bronwen, I am so sorry … I wish I was there to give you a hug. I am so, so sorry. Nic x

Bronwen: Thanks Nic.

AMPR: I know you were walking with your brother today. Did you find him? I'm not going to say anything on the Facebook page until you're ready for me to do so. I'm sure you have a lot of people you need to tell. Just take your time. Mark was the luckiest bloke in the world to have a sister like you who never gave up and loved him so much xx

Bronwen: A person walking on a train track found him. He would never have been found from a search, spot cannot get to except from bridge above.

AMPR: Sometimes I am amazed when people are found, I think that they would never have been found unless that person was doing something else in that exact spot which makes me think they were certainly meant to be found. I hope that makes sense. I think some missing persons are meant to be found and Mark was one of them.

Unfortunately, 'I'm so sorry for your loss' are words I have to say to families constantly, often several times a week. Despite this regularity, I am deeply moved every time I have to say them, and that day I shed a tear for Mark Leicester.

Bronwen still thinks if she'd initially worded things differently to police they would have looked for him sooner, but I pointed out to her that by the time they reported him missing to police he was already gone. She has no need to feel any guilt, but survivor guilt is something that has been experienced by every family member I spoke to for this book; it's a natural reaction to a situation they have no control over. I told Bronwen that by the time anyone knew he'd even left the house, it would have already been too late. She agrees with me and thinks Mark probably took his life at about 3 am the night he went missing. 'It was about 38–40 degrees during those two weeks, it was so hot, and I said even if he has gone for a walk and fallen and broken his leg, he wouldn't have survived the extremes of the heat up in the hills.'

Bronwen and Craig had spent the Friday evening with their parents then all headed home, exhausted. Craig was staying with Alison. After Bronwen arrived home, late at night, there was a knock at her door. It was the policewoman she'd been dealing with, who had been so helpful to her. Bronwen looked at the

officer and her partner and said, 'You've found him, haven't you?'
The policewoman said yes. Mark had his Medicare card on him,
which enabled police to quickly work out who he was. 'I had to
ring my sister, as my brother was staying there. I told them to
come over as the police had found Mark's body,' Bronwen says
sombrely.

She had asked the police to tell her before they informed her
parents, so they could have the whole family around them when
they received the tragic news. The police officers came inside
and Bronwen recalls asking them a million questions, like where
they had found Mark, and when they told her she said: 'Really??
There??' It was on a shortcut from the train station to their
parents' house, so it was a walk Mark knew well. Bronwen asked
the police what Mark looked like. The female officer looked at
her partner and said, 'Should we tell her?' He replied yes, so they
described Mark's body to Bronwen.

They told Bronwen that Mark had jumped from a height,
and her immediate response was to say no, he would not have
jumped.

Jumping was never an option, it was always either hanging or
another way, but the police said they could tell he'd jumped.
They said the whole back of his skull was missing.

Alison is upset that the police described Mark's injuries to
Bronwen so graphically, thinking they should have seen what
state of mind she was in, and known she could not handle such
distressing information at that time. Bronwen kept saying to
Alison: 'I have in my head a picture of a body with a skull sitting
on it.' The weather had been very hot during the time Mark had

been missing, and his body was badly decomposed. Alison says the police described the remains to Bronwen in detail. Whether she'd asked them to or not, it was probably not a good idea at that stage.

After this shocking revelation Bronwen managed to gather herself together enough to ask police not to contact her parents until she'd had a chance to speak to them first. She told them it was her mother's 80th birthday party the next day, and she wanted her mum to enjoy her party before learning the terrible news. Bronwen decided to tell her brothers and sister, but didn't want to spoil her mother's happy evening – she figured one more day would not hurt. There was no longer any urgency. The police agreed to abide by her wishes, and said they would pass on the request to the other officers at the station who were coming onto day shift.

Bronwen phoned Alison to tell her what had happened, and Alison woke Craig to tell him. He accidentally hit her as she broke the news to him. 'I shook him, but he wouldn't wake up. I said, "Craig, they've found Mark and it's not good." And he threw out his arm, yelling, No! And his arm hit me. He probably doesn't remember that.'

Bronwen was extremely distraught and wanted Craig and Alison to come to her place, but they had not yet been able to reach their other brother, Gary. They decided they needed to tell him in person, so all three siblings met up. Alison remembers Bronwen being very angry, and when she tried to hug her Bronwen would scream, 'Don't touch me!' She didn't want anyone to touch her, and even at the funeral refused to let anyone hug her. The three of them drove to Gary's together.

They woke him and told him the news. Gary says when he saw all three of his siblings arrive at his home together, in the middle of the night, he knew immediately that they'd found Mark. Gary went to hug Bronwen and again she screamed at him not to touch her.

There was a disagreement between the siblings about whether or not to tell their parents, as Gary felt they should be told. Bronwen, Craig and Alison wanted their mum to enjoy her night. 'Mum had never had a party, it had always been Dad. Mum had never had anything for herself. I said, let her have this 80th – what's another day?' says Bronwen. Gary felt like they were cheating their mother by not telling her right away, but he finally agreed not to tell them, agreeing with Bronwen that it was the best thing to do.

Bronwen went home and tried to sleep, but her phone kept ringing. One of the calls was from the Coroner, asking for Mark's medical and dental information. She realised it was because they needed to formally identify Mark's body. The Coroner told her the body was badly decomposed and would need to be DNA tested in order to identify it as Mark. Bronwen explained about her mother's party that evening and asked if the identification could be completed the following day, Sunday. The Coroner said that was fine and said he would tell the police that the identification was to take place on the Sunday.

Bronwen then received a phone call from police, who asked her for the same information the Coroner had just asked for. She told them she'd already given it all to the Coroner and was about to hang up when she thought she better check on something. 'I said to them, "Now, you definitely haven't spoken to my parents, have you?" They said, "What do you mean?" I said, "There were full instructions that you DON'T go to my parents' house." They said, "No, no, we haven't done that." So I hung up. I checked a message that had come through to my landline answering machine; it was from Mum, asking me to ring her. This was at 11.45. Then the Coroner rang again. He said, "Bronwen, I've got bad news for you. The police have already been to your parents' place and taken a DNA sample from them."

Bronwen was horrified. She asked if the Coroner had instructed the police to take the sample – as the police are supposed to wait for the Coroner's direction before proceeding with identifications and they said no, they had not instructed police at all. Bronwen phoned police again and spoke with the same officer who had just phoned her. 'I said, "You just lied to me. You just told me you hadn't been to my parents' house." And he said, "Oh, am I meant to know what the other day shift does?" I said, "There's only four of you on day shift for the whole station! Haven't you got the file in front of you?" and he said no, he didn't have the file. So, I said, "Then why did you ring me to ask me for the dentist and all that information? What were you going to write on if you didn't have the file in front of you?" He said, "Well, I'm not meant to know!" and I said, "YOU'RE LYING! I can't believe this has happened, you're the Keystone Cops, it's bloody ridiculous, it's been ridiculous from day one."

'I just went off. A few F-words came out! Then I rang my brother and sister and said, "Get around to Mum and Dad's NOW. They know." Alison and Craig bolted around there.' When they got to their parents' home it dawned on Alison and Craig that their mum had no idea what was going on, and hadn't actually been told about Mark being found. They asked her if she knew why the police had taken the DNA sample from her, and she said she didn't know. 'Alison and Craig just looked at each other, and Mum said to them, "You know something, don't you?" So, they had to tell her,' says Bronwen.

'When I got there, I just lost the plot. I went in and looked at Mum and Dad and I didn't know what to say. I said, "Mum, we didn't want to tell you, we wanted you to have the party tonight."' Alison went outside to phone her brother Gary to tell him what was happening at their parents' home, and Bronwen saw her on the phone. Bronwen started to get hysterical again. She says: 'I was actually screaming at my sister, "How did this happen?"' Alison remembers saying to her, 'Calm down!' She says, 'I don't know how, but me saying that just switched her and she came and apologised.'

Bronwen to AMPR: It was one of my daughter's friends walking home … and saw Mark's legs … very decomposed due to extreme heat so have to do DNA identification. Bloody police turned up to do DNA without us having a chance to tell Mum/Dad even though night shift was instructed not to tell them … apparently as I didn't answer the 'unknown' caller this morning … they decided to rock up to parents.

Alison says:

From the date he disappeared to the date he was found was three weeks. Every day that went by, I knew it wasn't going to be good news.

'Mum tried to cancel her party but we said no,' says Bronwen. 'But it was the worst, longest night of my life, that party.'

Bronwen's friend, who worked for the Parks service, told her they had not been asked by police to search the hills for a missing person, but police later gave her copies of email correspondence showing they had requested assistance from the Parks department. With this correspondence the police also included, possibly inadvertently, a copy of their log book, including all calls regarding Mark. The log book indicated the family had been contacted every 48 hours while Mark was missing even if there had been no update – this was not true. There were large gaps in the running sheet where no search or investigation had been continued. 'The disappointing part was, where they found him is a common suicide spot,' says Bronwen.

Alison had a distressing experience when she attended the police station to get the copies of Mark's death certificate signed. 'I said to the officer that we thought Mark had slipped. He said straight out, "He didn't. He jumped." I was at the counter and there was someone behind me, so he said this in front of everyone. He said, "It's a notorious place for jumpers." I'm thinking, if it's a notorious place and you knew he was a suicide risk, why didn't you check there? And he'd said it so loudly, in front of these other people, and it was the *way* he said it,' says Alison, clearly still upset. Bronwen says, 'He said to Alison, "Oh, that's where they found him? We didn't think, we should have looked there first." Alison just looked at him. She doesn't like confrontation so she didn't say anything, but I said it was lucky it wasn't me he said it to.' Bronwen and Alison were so upset by this they made a complaint about the officer.

Once Mark had been found, it became necessary to inform all his financial institutions. Bronwen had to deal with Mark's bank and the various loans and credit card debt that he had. She discovered he'd included an insurance policy with the $12,000 loan and that meant they didn't have to pay that back. The family were, however, responsible for around $8000 worth of credit card bills Mark had racked up. He only had $50 left in his account when he died. One company Bronwen dealt with were very helpful and over the phone agreed to freeze the debt until the finances had been sorted out, with hopefully a little of Mark's superannuation money (that he'd built up after cashing it all in the first time he attempted suicide) able to be used. But one of the major banks still sent the family 'Dear Mr Leicester' letters asking for the payments, and this was very distressing for Mark's parents. The bank refused to accept the family telling them Mark was dead, insisting on speaking with police and lawyers. Bronwen spoke to police who told her they'd never before been asked to speak with a bank regarding a deceased bank customer. It's not part of the police's duty to inform a bank that a person has died.

Bronwen contacted another bank, which told her their policy was to require only a certified copy of the death certificate, and that's all the other bank should have needed to freeze the account. They made an already distressing time much worse. Craig also tried to speak with them on the phone but got nowhere. The bank then reworded their letters 'To the family of Leicester', but were still demanding the payment. They also continued to charge interest on Mark's debts a full eight months after he died.

Craig eventually managed to get all Mark's debts paid off and sorted out but it took the better part of the next year after he died. They then had to sort out what was left of Mark's superannuation and his tax returns. They ran into increased difficulties because Mark did not leave a will. 'When I went through his bank statements, that's when I really started to feel sad,' says Craig. 'He got the loans and then there'd be $200 withdrawn at the train station ATM, another $200, then another. Three withdrawals within four hours. He'd just get out the money, get his hit, go to a toilet somewhere and shoot up. Pretty sad.'

Sadness is the overwhelming emotion the Leicesters feel when it comes to Mark. 'I wish he'd come to one of us and asked for help,' says Alison.

Bronwen thinks that while Mark planned the end of his life, it was not as planned as his first attempt. She thinks he thought about it while he was walking around the city after pretending to go to day two of the new job that he hated. She wonders what he did that day, whether he went to the cinema, as he loved movies. She's glad he didn't spend his final day on drugs; she will always be grateful for that. He made his decision with a clear head.

I think he lay in bed that night, had trouble sleeping and simply thought, 'Stuff it, I'm going.' I think he walked straight to that bridge, as it was less than a kilometre from home. If he was high as a kite he would have said, 'Yeah, I'm free!' and jumped, but maybe he sat there for a while thinking about it, hesitating, then thought, 'Bugger it, I'm going.' That's why I have the guilt now, for thinking he was high that last day, because the Coroner found there was nothing in his system.

Mark was a very charitable person, he always gave stuff to the homeless in the city and we reckon he gave the $200 to a homeless person. He didn't spend it on drugs. He didn't fall off the wagon, he had that $200 and could have gone out and bought a big hit of heroin.

Before he was found his close friends asked me what I thought happened, and I said I thought Mark had taken a big hit and shot up in the hills and died, that's what I was saying about him while he was dead, and it was never true.

Bronwen's ongoing guilt over Mark's death is evident and heartbreaking. 'When we packed up his room we found little hooks where we think he'd attempted to hang himself. Mum found them, just looked at me and I grabbed them and threw them in the bin. It would have been awful, if he'd done that – it would have been Mum who found him. That's why I'd say he jumped instead of doing something in bed, at home. I even asked the cops if they found any syringes near his body or up at the track and they said no, and when we searched his room we found spoons [that had been used for heroin] but we didn't find any syringes or anything like that.

Bronwen thought that reading the Coroner's report would answer her questions about Mark's death, but it hasn't. 'We can't know, even, whether he got hit by a train, as it was very narrow [on the bridge]. Was he sitting there thinking, "Will I, won't I?" It's only a one-train bridge. I don't have enough physics knowledge to go to the spot and say, "There's the drop, how the hell did he land here?" That's actually how he was found, someone moved out of the way of a train and looked down and saw legs.'

'It was a horrible way to die,' says Craig grimly. 'I think he would have crawled for a minute or so after he hit the ground. It wasn't instant.'

The funeral home gave Bronwen Mark's house key that had been on his body when he died. It smelled horrific, and she was very upset. She threw the key away. The key keeps running through her mind. Why did he take the key, if he was not planning to come home? 'Knowing Mark, and knowing where the spot is now, he might have walked there a few times in the past. This time I think he just saw an endless circle with these jobs. He might have thought, "I don't want to let people down again" as Mark had quit a few jobs before. He probably thought, what sort of quality of life would he have with hepatitis C? I've let Mum and Dad down, I still live at home, I'm 52 years old… And he hated his job. Maybe he just thought, "This is not ending. It's going on and on and on."'

5 February 2013

Bronwen: Hi Nic, I got a call from police tonight (gave me a heart attack, thought something had happened to someone else in my family) and they want Mum to go in and make a statement and for me to go in as support. They said the questions may be distressing and having her give info etc etc… They said they have not been requested to take a statement off me yet. Apparently the Coroners have requested this. I said Mum needs time as it was Mark's birthday on Sunday and things are affecting her now, so we are doing it Sunday week. I have yet to tell her due to time of night. My doctor said as it was a big fall they cannot say suicide as he may have fell as there is a walking track along the top. So do you think that maybe it is inconclusive and they are asking us his frame of mind and then say suicide … can they assume that?

6 February 2013

AMPR: Hi love, I'll bet it did scare you. The coroner's job is to determine how and why someone died, so during the inquest they gather as much information as they can from as many people as possible – from the family to police to SES who searched to the person who found him. As Mark didn't leave a suicide note then it becomes difficult, or impossible to know what his intentions were that day. And no-one saw it happen, so I would think the only option available to the Coroner would be to rule his death as misadventure. It wouldn't benefit anyone at all to rule it as suicide as Mark didn't leave a note and didn't say to anyone before he left 'I am going out to kill myself', which is him making his intentions clear. Mark walked in that area all the time, and you said to me he liked to go there when he was feeling down as it cheered him up? So that would give a strong indication that although he was depressed, he was trying to make himself feel better. I don't think we'll ever know what happened that day and the Coroner doesn't know either so I think he'll rule misadventure. The police would be interviewing you asking if he was suicidal – had he ever tried to take his life before? They will probably ask that. I'll double check if that's the correct finding he's likely to give. Nic x

Bronwen: Thanks Nic. We don't reckon Mark would have jumped hence why we were looking in the bush to see whether he fell off the wagon and lay down to die. When over the years we have discussed this, I know morbid but we both suffer depression, jumping was never an option.

AMPR: I think it's really healthy to discuss it. There's another missing guy who discussed suicide with his mum before he went missing and had really strong views that he never would or could kill himself and that's what the family is clinging to despite him being missing for so long. If there was no guard rail or anything on the bridge then hopefully the Coroner will recommend some safety upgrades?

Bronwen: It There is a track at the end of a road that leads to the Belgrave line and many people walk that ... that is why my optimistic copper friend who knew Mark asked, Why do you think he jumped? He could have fallen there ... too many clues ... too many red herrings. He took his house keys with him – why? But then, why not turn up to your 2nd day on the job and then go to bed in your PJs and then take off sometime after Mum/Dad go to bed? All surreal and not logical...

AMPR: Did he have the backpack on when he fell? As in, did he leave anything on the track above – shoes or backpack etc. – or was everything found with him?

Bronwen: The death certificate arrived today, says cause is multiple injuries from a fall. He only had house keys and wallet on him. Backpack and phone at home. So, if Coroner has issued certificate then why do police need statement?

AMPR: Not sure how they will work it. Usually with any unexplained death, i.e. one that was not witnessed so the exact means can't be determined, I would have thought they'd go to an inquest. Maybe they will still do that and that's why the police need the statement, but the death certificate would be needed for you to arrange his affairs etc.

14 February 2013

Bronwen: Today a copper friend is taking my sister and I to the spot where Mark 'fell' or 'jumped' so we can see in our mind if there is a possibility that he fell; our copper friend thinks he did. My psychologist suggested my sister go with Mum to the police on Sunday as I am at a breaking point and I may lose my cool…

At Mark's funeral, both Alison and Gary recall people telling wonderful, funny stories about their brother. Although sad, it was a celebration of his life. Gary remembers people telling stories of Mark he'd never heard before. Craig delivered Mark's eulogy and found it very difficult:

I was in shock. I didn't have my breakdown about Mark until a couple of years ago. It hit me. The first six months were a bit of a daze, there would be times I'd pick up the phone and start to ring him; I'd be watching our favourite shows, we used to pick up the phone to call other and have a laugh about Seinfeld and I'd go to do that and then realise oh, he's not alive. He's no longer here.

Alison misses Mark's laugh, his wicked sense of humour and their frequent chats about the footy. His death notice in the

Herald Sun reads: "A big hearted, loyal man with a very strong personality. Passionate about sports and a loyal club man. Very involved with the community and supportive of many concerns. A Man for the People"

As time went on, Bronwen started to accept that Mark's death was a suicide. When I asked her how she was feeling now, whether she was angry with Mark, or relieved that the decades of pain and suffering were over, or just sadness and grief, she surprised me with her answer. 'I would have preferred him to have had heroin in his system. A lot of people reckon that's the wrong way to think, but that would have meant he'd have had no pain, and that he would have gone to that bridge – which was really, really high, it was a trestle bridge it would have been dark and he couldn't see where he was jumping and he would have gone out like that. Whereas this, not on anything, he would have sat on the pole for a while thinking, "Will I?" and he would have felt that fear. I don't know about pain, with it being instant...' Her voice trails off. It's a distressing thought for her, imagining how her brother would be feeling in those final moments of his life.

Alison had difficulty coping with Mark's death because her natural instinct is to withdraw and keep her emotions in check. Bronwen's grief was much more apparent but Alison's was no less painful, just more hidden. Alison felt like she had to be strong for her older sister and help Bronwen cope. 'I broke down a few months later,' says Alison.

'We weren't prepared for it,' says Craig. 'It was the first person we'd ever lost; we always thought Mum and Dad would go first, not Mark.'

6 October 2013

Bronwen: Hi Nic, just an ongoing rollercoaster; got the Coroner letter the Friday before last, there will be no investigation. He didn't have any alcohol or illicit drugs in him (only methadone from the program and antihistamine). So, that has sent me on a different spiral … as he was lucid when he jumped, and knowing Mark he would have been there a while before deciding to do it (he took his house keys/wallet only) and would have been scared etc. On drugs, he would have just walked there and just jumped and felt no fear. So, it is a lose lose situation. Also read the nitty gritty of autopsy and broken bones to maggots etc. The superannuation stuff is still going on, just taking forever until that can be closed off. The other thing I struggle with is the guilt that if I didn't say to police he was probably high and went to OD somewhere, would they have made an effort instead of having days before reviewing the report (they accidently gave me their log of the time of report to time found)? If we just said he was missing and depressed, would they have looked where he was found as it is a known suicide spot? Thanks for asking about me and caring and you are still doing a fantastic job. You are a great soul Nic xo

Mark's mum finds she misses Mark's intelligent conversation in the evenings. After her husband's strokes he was unable to communicate very well, so it was Mark who she used to talk to. Before Mark died Bronwen tried, at one point, to talk her parents into moving into a retirement village, as that would give her mother the assistance she needed and would also force Mark to move out on his own, which she thought would have been good for him. Their mother refused, saying she liked Mark living with them, as she loved their conversations about politics and world events. Their mum says she 'has nothing now. No-one to talk to.' The day Mark's remains were located was also the date of the death of the baby they lost before Mark was born, a double blow.

'I try not to use my house key when I go to Mum and Dad's, because they think it's Mark,' says Bronwen. 'I always try to knock.'

Gary misses talking with Mark about 'bloke stuff: 'There's only so much you can talk to the girls about,' he chuckles.

Craig will miss the happy times they had over a couple of drinks, the phone calls, the laughs. When Mark first seriously attempted suicide he left Bronwen detailed instructions about how he wanted his funeral to be held, including what music he wanted played. The whole family are remarkably candid about their own mortality, and they have all now planned their own funeral music. 'Whenever Mark, Alison and I were together for a drink we would look at our list and then change a song here and there. So, she has my list and I have hers,' says Bronwen.

Bronwen continues to struggle with the trauma over her brother's death.

I have to stop thinking about it. The images in my head from the Coroner's report, and from what the cops described, wanting to go to the spot where he was, wanting to lay down in that spot ... a couple of times even feeling suicidal myself.

Wanting to just join him. But then I think, I don't want to put my family through what Mark has, the grief.

I asked Bronwen if she was happy to talk about her depression and suicidal thoughts in this book and she was adamant that she wanted it included. It's vital we talk about these feelings and thoughts with the people closest to us, and Bronwen wants people to understand the devastation suicide causes in families. Bronwen was struggling with her own depression before Mark went missing, and had even talked with him about committing suicide together, at Mark's suggestion. She bravely tells me this story, and says she made a pact with Mark that maybe they would do it after their parents passed away. Mark told her he had the perfect place picked out. 'That's why I didn't think he'd jumped, as his place was totally the opposite.'

I'm Facebook friends with Bron and Ali, and they have become actual friends, not just a family I have helped. I really enjoy seeing all their posts; their mum is still going strong and approaching her 90th birthday; she still has a cheeky grin for the camera, and the family spends a lot of time with her. What really strikes me about these siblings is how much they do together. An outing to the zoo for Ali and Gary. There's Bron and Ali, watching the footy together. They go on holidays together, out to the pub, to movies and concerts with their siblings and each other's kids. And every so often, they'll pop up a photo of Mark. They have bonded together as a family even more strongly, and Mark is still with them.

11 January 2014

Twelve months today the police found you, Mark, after

347

us searching relentlessly for over three weeks. The knock on my door and the two police officers standing there is forever imprinted in my brain. To be alone on the couch with them hearing the details is a moment I will never forget.

Bronwyn went on to quote some words, from a grief support group, that brought her comfort.

'The 'grief expiration date' myth must come from people who have never experienced a close death – otherwise they would know the truth. The one-year mark looms like some golden carrot over the heads of those who are grieving. It is a symbol of hope that if they make it to the one year mark they will be in a much happier and pain free place. The reality is they won't be over it, nor should they be. If someone spent years loving another person, the pain of that person's death simply will not be removed due to a date on the calendar.

The opposite actually might happen – people who are grieving may feel even more pain in year two because the initial numbness, which often serves as a protective barrier at the onset of loss, has worn off and they begin experiencing the full intensity of their feelings and grief. This is accompanied by the realisation that life with loss is their 'new normal'.[7]

Lynne B Hughes, 2010, Solace Grief Support Group WA Inc. https://solacegriefsupportwa.org.au/11 February 2014

Momentary lapse of reason; grabbed the phone to tell you something and realised that I can't. The fact that I still

---

7 Hughes, L.,B. (2010)'

have your mobile phone and I send texts to it, like it never happened; but tonight I really was, gotta call Mark and tell him ... the first 12 months it seems like a dream, I don't like this next part as it is becoming real.

Ironically, Mark spent his whole life telling people no-one had ever loved him, but it's abundantly clear from talking with his family and friends that they most certainly did. Mark was the luckiest man in the world to have his amazing family members, who tried for such a long time to bring him out of the darkness. They did not fail.

Postscript: During the writing of this chapter, Mark's dad Jim sadly passed away. When Bronwen announced the news she said, 'May you hug Mark once you see him at those pearly gates and tell him the Kangas won and Abbott is out.'

Ali said, 'May he be having a scotch with Mark up in heaven.'

He's always on their minds.

A FINAL WORD FROM THE AUTHOR

Books are meant to come with happy endings, most of the time, right? Or at least answers. I'm sorry that I can't give you either. This is just a glimpse into ten of the thousands of missing persons still out there, waiting to be found. What can you do, as a member of the public, as someone interested enough in missing persons to have picked up this book? Helping to spread awareness of each case is something we can all do. Follow my Facebook page so you can see all the public appeals I make, and share those to your own Facebook page, where they might be then shared by your Facebook friends, and that might just reach a person who happens to be sitting opposite a missing teenager on the train. This actually happens all the time.

The families who have shared their stories with me, and with all of you, have bravely opened up their personal histories and relived very painful times. They have done this in the hope that this might be read by someone who does have that missing piece of the puzzle, that vital piece of information that leads to answers about what happened to their missing person. If that's you, please call Crimestoppers on 1800 333 000 with your information. It's never too late, even if it's been decades.

For the families in this book, their journey continues. They keep going, keep hoping, no matter how long it takes to get their answers. Parents pass the batons to their other children for what is often an endurance race. They also want to help others in their shoes, other families who have joined that club that no one wants to belong to, the families of missing persons. These other families maybe freshly into their nightmare journey, overwhelmed by all the processes, and helpless to know what they can do on a practical level to find their missing family member.

For the family members of missing persons, their role in the search for a loved one is a job they never applied for, yet it's one none of them would have refused. It's what you do. It's family. I have a friend whose brother had cancer and she raised almost $50,000 in the community to get him a new treatment. He sadly lost his battle. At his funeral, I hugged her and told her she was the greatest sister ever for what she'd done for him. She whispered in my ear, "He'd have done the same for me."

ACKNOWLEDGEMENTS

The biggest THANK YOU goes out to all the families who directly or indirectly spoke with me and shared their stories:

Kevin Docherty, Mavia Cavanagh, Vicki Cavanagh.

Carl, Kim and Steve Herdman.

Jess, Jodie, Emma, Rose and Eva Mazurek.

Pat, Ian, Ginette and Sharon Govan.

Sue Lawson and Murray Cooper.

Tracey Tieste.

Tony, Paul and Mark Ryan.

Susanne, Dianne and Raye Steffen and Susie Stoodley.

Annette, Tony, Mandy and Judith Leape.

Bronwen, Alison, Gary, Craig and Monica Leicester.

Also the many people involved with the cases who provided valuable insights and additional information – Jeff Dakers, Tracey Shelton, Michael McMahon, Tim Hammel, Debbie Malone, Steve Nalder, Darren Kelly and Cathy Flood, Tasmania Police Media and Missing Persons Units, Hobart Coroner's Office.

A huge thank you to Diane at Big Sky Publishing for taking a chance on an unknown author, and to all the Big Sky team who have been amazing as well as Jenny for stellar editing and the Simon and Schuster team.

Thanks to fellow authors and friends Kate Kyriacou, Justine Ford, Mandy Sayer, Melissa Pouliot, Esther McKay who have all inspired me so much. Retired police officers Paul Horton, Greg Callander, and the late Bob Walsh, who along with Esther was patron of Australian Missing Persons Register.

The wonderful Suzie Ratcliffe, who is a daily inspiration, and Mark and Faye Leveson for years of love and mutual admiration.

Jason Manewell of Great Lakes Online for covering my webhosting for many years and building the computers I work on, and Koriilee for her assistance with photos. To all the followers of Australian Missing Persons Register, who currently number about 175,000, who share all the missing person appeals that I post, reaching sometimes a million people – thank you on behalf of those who need you to help find them.

My dear friends Lianne and Jenny, both of whom have or had missing family members, for constant love and encouragement, Lyn for all your support, Lynda for reading the early drafts and making me believe people will want to read my stories.

My parents, Ken and Glenda, and my sister Michelle, who have been so encouraging and proud of all my efforts, all my life, and Michelle's family Justin, Kristopher and my aspiring writer nieces Lily and Poppy who also helped with cover design ideas.

The late Greg Joubert and his sister Kathleen, who inspired this book.

To my beautiful family – Steve, Scarlett and Rowan – you are everything and I love you. Thank you Steve for years of quiet constancy and unwavering acceptance of this obsession of mine. Scarlett for enduring hundreds of hours of harrowing phone interview transcribing and helping with cover design, Scarlett's partner Lachy for much enthusiastic support, and Rowan for taking my author photo, being dragged on early morning photo shoots for cover ideas, and for loving my early drafts. I hope I make you all proud.

ABOUT THE AUTHOR

Nicole is the Director of the Australian Missing Persons Register, which she started in 2005. In 2012 Nicole won the Queensland Pride of Australia award for Community Spirit, then in the same year went on to win the National gold medal. She has been nominated twice for Australian of the Year. She has appeared many times on radio and television and in newsprint. She is a voice for voiceless missing persons, tirelessly making appeals for them, and raising awareness. She has provided comfort and guidance to countless families and friends of missing persons as they undertake their journeys to find their lost loved ones. Her Facebook page is followed by hundreds of thousands of people and she has gained the respect of law enforcement and government agencies both in Australia and around the world.

If you have any information relating to any of these stories, or would like to connect with Nicole or the Australian Missing Persons Register contact details below:

Facebook: https://www.facebook.com/austmissingpersons
Website: http://www.australianmissingpersonsregister.com/ NicoleMorrisAuthor.htm
Twitter: https://twitter.com/AMPRegister
Instagram: https://www.instagram.com/nicole_morris_author
Pinterest: https://www.pinterest.com.au/glittercot0859/_saved
LinkedIn: https://www.linkedin.com/in/nicole-morris-93410575

If this book has raised concerns for you or someone you know please contact Lifeline on 13 11 14 or Beyond Blue 1300 22 4636 or Mensline 1300 789 978, or the National Alcohol and Other Drug Hotline on 1800 250 015 or Family Drug Support on 1300 368 186.